D0862018

BARCELONA

TOP SIGHTS, AUTHENTIC EXPERIENCES

THIS EDITION WRITTEN AND RESEARCHED BY

Andy Symington,
Josephine Quintero

Lonely Planet's

Barcelona

Plan Your Trip

Welcome to Barcelona

From sunrise over the Mediterranean to the last dance floor whirl of an action-packed night, Barcelona holds your attention 24 hours a day. Its combination of natural attractions, hedonism and serious cultural cachet make it one of the world's great cities.

Barcelona's architectural treasures span millennia. Temple columns, ancient city walls and subterranean stone corridors provide a window into the Roman era. Then skip a thousand years to the Middle Ages by taking a stroll through the Gothic quarter, all shadowy lanes, tranquil plazas and soaring churches. Later bloomed the sculptural masterpieces of Modernisme, a heady mix of ingenuity and whimsy created by Gaudí and contemporaries. The Sagrada Família, still under construction, is already one of the planet's most sublime buildings.

Barcelona has long inspired artists too, including Salvador Dalí, Pablo Picasso and Joan Miró, whose works are in bold display in the city's myriad museums.

Art of another sort adorns the groaning bartops and stylish plates of Barcelona's tapas bars and avant-garde restaurants. Catalan cooking blends a long tradition of using flavourful, market-fresh ingredients, garnished with a soupçon of French savoir faire then given a real twist with the molecular wizardry of modern Catalan gastronomy.

Add to this the lazy days on the beach, paddling or cruising the deep blue sea, strolling into classy boutiques and quaffing sessions in sociable *cava* (Catalan sparkling wine) bars and you have just a fraction of the intoxicating cornucopia that is Barcelona.

Barcelona holds your attention 24 hours a day.

Park Güell (p68)
S-F/SHUTTERSTOCK ©

★ BARCELONA ★

Park Güell

Camp Nou, Pedralbes & La Zona Alta
A medieval monastery, an intriguing museum and lofty Tibidabo – all capped by football thrills at Camp Nou.

◉ **Museu-Monestir de Pedralbes**

La Sagrada Família & L'Eixample
Modernisme rules in the city's 19th-century 'extension', replete with masterpieces by Gaudí and others. *(Map p254)*

◉ **Camp Nou**

Estació Sants ◉

MACBA (Contemporani de M

El Raval
A once-seedy area that's now home to cutting-edge museums and bohemian bars and eateries. *(Map p249)*

Museu Nacional d'Art de Catalunya (MNAC) ⊕

Montjuïc, Poble Se & Sant Antoni
Home to manicured parks, excellent museums and cinematic city views *(Maps p249 & p256*

IAKOV FILIMONOV/ SHUTTERSTOCK ©, MATTHEW DIXON/GETTY IMAGES ©, MICHAEL HEFFERNAN/LONELY PLANET ©, GALINA SAVINA/ SHUTTERSTOCK ©, ANGELA N PERRYMAN/SHUTTERSTOCK ©, FLYDIME/GETTY IMAGES ©, TKEMOT/ SHUTTERSTOCK ©, SPECTRAL-DESIGN/ SHUTTERSTOCK ©,

Plan Your Trip
This Year in Barcelona

2018

Barcelona

Barcelona is a place where there's always something happening. Traditional fiestas maintain their riotous blend of popular religion, devil-may-care revelry and time-honoured customs. Meanwhile, concerts, festivals and modern celebrations keep things ticking right through the year.

From left: Día de Sant Jordi (p9); A *castell* (human castle) at Festes de la Mercè (p14); Festa Major de Gràcia (p13)

2018

★ **Top Festivals & Events**

Festes de Santa Eulàlia February (p7)
Festival Pedralbes June (p11)
Festival del Grec July (p12)
Festa Major de Gràcia August (p13)
Festes de la Mercè September (p14)

KARSOL/ SHUTTERSTOCK ©

IAKOV FILIMONOV/ SHUTTERSTOCK ©

Plan Your Trip
This Year in Barcelona

January

Some barcelonins head to the Pyrenees for ski slope action, while others simply enjoy a bit of post-holiday downtime (school holidays go to 7 January).

✤ Cavalcada dels Reis Mags   5 Jan

On the day before Epifanía (Epiphany), children delight in the Cavalcada dels Reis Mags (Parade of the Three Kings), a colourful parade of floats and music, spreading bonhomie and boiled sweets in equal measure. Pictured above: Cavalcada dels Reis Mags.

☆ Daniel Barenboim   11 Jan

The turbulent, gloriously political, brilliant and evergreen maestro comes to play piano for the evening at the Palau de la Música Catalana (p197).

✤ Festes dels Tres Tombs   around 17 Jan

The festival dedicated to Sant Antoni features a parade of horse-drawn carts and music, after which locals bring their pets to be blessed by priests. The celebrations

◉ 1917. Picasso en Barcelona   until 28 January

This major exhibition at the Museu Picasso (p80) focuses on the centenary of this important year, the last extended period that the artist spent in Barcelona. During this period he was experimenting with more realist forms and moving away from cubism.

Museu Picasso

go for over a week in the neighbourhood of Sant Antoni, but the parade is held on the first Saturday after the saint's feast day.

2018

02

February

Often the coldest (and seemingly longest) month in Barcelona, February sees few visitors. Nonetheless, some of the first big festivals kick off, with abundant Catalan merriment amid the wintry gloom.

☆ Metallica 7 Feb
The legendary heavy metal kings play the Palau Sant Jordi (p202) as part of their World Wired tour. Horns up!

⚑ Carnestoltes (Carnaval) 8–14 Feb
Celebrated seven weeks before Easter, this festival involves several days of fancy-dress balls, parades, merrymaking and fireworks, ending on Ash Wednesday. Down in Sitges a wilder version takes place. Pictured above: Carnaval dancing in the Plaça Comercial.

⚑ Festes de Santa Eulàlia around 12 Feb
This big winter fest (santaeulalia.bcn.cat) celebrates Barcelona's first patron saint with a week of cultural events, including parades of *gegants* (papier mâché giants), art installations, theatre, *correfocs* (fire runs) and *castells* (human castles).

☆ A Night at the Opera
14, 17, 19, 22, 24, 27 Feb & 2, 4 Mar
Romance is guaranteed with a night out at the Gran Teatre del Liceu (p194) and even more so when the production is Charles Gounod's *Romeo & Juliet*. Exciting Albanian tenor Saimir Pirgu and Russian soprano Aida Garifullina sing the star-crossed lovers.

⊙ Adolf Loos Exhibition until 28 Feb
This exhibition at the Museu del Disseny (p40) focuses on the work of Austrian architect Adolf Loos. It evokes the cultural buzz of turn-of-the-20th-century Vienna.

Plan Your Trip
This Year in Barcelona

March

March brings longer, sunnier days, though the nights are light jacket weather. There are relatively few tourists and fair hotel prices for most of the month, though Easter week is a different story.

✥ Festa de Sant Medir
around 3 Mar

This characterful religious procession in Gràcia includes the throwing of sweets to the masses, who await with buckets and bags to catch the treats. Pictured above: Handing out sweets in the Festa de Sant Medir parade.

✦ Barcelona Marathon
11 Mar

Runners converge on Barcelona to participate in the city's spring marathon (www.zurichmaratobarcelona.com).

◉ William Morris Exhibition
22 Feb–20 May

At the MNAC (p54), this exhibition examines the Arts and Crafts design movement that began in Edwardian Great Britain. Morris pioneered the movement, which was an early reaction against mass production.

♟ Barcelona Beer Festival
mid-Mar

Come see the latest craft-beer tastemakers in action at this three-day beer and food fest (www.barcelonabeerfestival.com), with over 450 craft beers on hand. So many beers, so little time!

✥ Setmana Santa
25–30 Mar

On Palm Sunday people line up to have their palm branches blessed outside the cathedral, while on Good Friday you can follow the floats and hooded penitents in processions from the Església de Sant Agustí in El Raval.

✗ Brunch Electronik
Mar–Jul

On selected Sundays from March through July, you can enjoy a day of electronic music (barcelona.brunch-in.com), food and children's activities at an outdoor space on Montjuïc. It attracts a mix of young families and party people.

2018

04

April

Spring arrives with a flourish, complete with wildflowers blooming in the countryside, although April showers can dampen spirits.

🌸 Passejada amb Barret
8 Apr

Inspired by New York's Easter Parade, this 'Stroll with a Hat' welcomes the spring with a casual walk along Rambla de Catalunya. Make sure you wear your hat!

🍴 Alimentaria
16–19 Apr

Though it's a serious trade fair (www.alimentaria-bcn.com) rather than a gastro festival, this is well worth visiting for foodies. A highlight is the show cooking area, where top chefs demonstrate their skills.

🌸 Día de Sant Jordi
23 Apr

Catalonia honours its patron saint, Sant Jordi (St George), with couples traditionally exchanging roses and books – and La Rambla and Plaça de Sant Jaume fill with colourful stalls. Pictured above: Books and roses on a La Rambla street stall for Dia de Sant Jordi.

☆ Barcelona Open
23–29 Apr

The city's premier tennis tournament, an important fixture of the international clay-court season, sees some top names slug it out.

🌸 Feria de Abril de Catalunya
late Apr–early May

Andalucía comes to the Parc del Fòrum with this 10-day-long southern festival featuring flamenco, a funfair and plenty of food and drink stalls.

☆ D'A – Festival Internacional de Cinema d'Autor de Barcelona
late Apr–early May

This well-curated film festival (www.dafilmfestival.com) presents a selection of contemporary art-house cinematic work over a few days.

Plan Your Trip
This Year in Barcelona

May

With sunny pleasant days and clear skies, May can be one of the best times to visit Barcelona. The city slowly gears up for summer with the opening of the chiringuitos (beach bars).

☆ **Salón Internacional del Cómic de Barcelona**   early May
Spain's biggest comics event (www.ficomic.com) takes place over three days. It's generally in early May but has been held as early as late March, so keep an eye out.

🌿 **Festa de Sant Ponç**   11 May
To commemorate the patron saint of bee keepers and herbalists, locals fill Carrer de l'Hospital in El Raval with the chatter and bustle of a street market.

☆ **Spanish Grand Prix**   mid-May
One of the fixtures of the motor-racing calendar, the Spanish Grand Prix is held at the Circuit de Barcelona-Catalunya, northeast of the city.

☆ **Ciutat Flamenco**   mid-May
One of the best occasions to see great flamenco in Barcelona, this concentrated festival (ciutatflamenco.com) is held over four days in May at the Teatre Mercat De Les Flors.

☆ **Plácido Domingo**   20 May
The legendary tenor will raise the roof of the Gran Teatre del Liceu (p194) alongside the soprano Ana María Martínez. They'll sing a series of excerpts from their favourite *zarzuelas* (Spanish comic operettas).

🌿 **L'Ou com Balla**   31 May
On Corpus Christi, l'Ou com Balla (the Dancing Egg) bobs on top of flower-festooned fountains around the city. There's also an early evening procession from La Catedral and traditional Catalan folk dancing. Pictured above: An egg 'dancing' on a fountain.

☆ **LOOP Barcelona**   late May–early Jun
This multiday fest features video art and avant-garde films shown in museums, theatres and nontraditional spaces (like food markets) around the city. It usually runs in late May or early June.

2018

06

June

Tourist numbers are well on the rise as Barcelona plunges into summer. Live music festivals and open-air events give the month a festive air.

☆ **Primavera Sound**   early Jun
For one week the open-air Parc del Fòrum stages an all-star line-up of international bands and DJs (www.primaverasound. com). There are also associated concerts around town, including free open-air events.

☆ **Berlin Philharmonic**   8 Jun
This is vibrant British conductor Simon Rattle's last year in charge of the wonderful Berlin Philharmonic, so grab this opportunity to hear them in action at the Palau de la Música Catalana (p197).

☆ **Sónar**   mid-Jun
Sónar (www.sonar.es) is Barcelona's massive celebration of electronic music, with DJs, exhibitions, sound labs, record fairs and urban art. Pictured above: Confetti at Sónar.

☆ **La Revetlla de Sant Joan**   23 June
Locals hit the streets or hold parties at home to celebrate the Revetlla de Sant Joan (St John's Night), which involves drinking, dancing, bonfires and fireworks. In Spanish, it's called 'Verbenas de Sant Joan'.

☆ **Festival Pedralbes**   mid-Jun–early Jul
This summertime fest (www.festivalped ralbes.com) takes place in lovely gardens and stages big-name performers (Sting, Carla Bruni, the Beach Boys).

Plan Your Trip
This Year in Barcelona

July

Prices are high and it's peak tourist season, but it's a lively time to be in the city with sun-filled beach days, open-air dining and outdoor concerts.

☆ Pride Barcelona   27 Jun–8 Jul
The Barcelona Gay Pride festival (www.pridebarcelona.org) is over a week of celebrations with a crammed program of culture and parties, along with the traditional Gay Pride march on the final Saturday. Pictured above: Rainbow flags in front of the Palau Nacional during Pride Barcelona.

☆ Rock Fest Barcelona   early Jul
This three-day summer festival (www.rockfestbarcelona.com) pulls some very big names indeed from the hard rock and metal end of the spectrum.

☆ Crüilla   early Jul
This well-attended music festival (www.cruillabarcelona.com) runs over three days and features an eclectic line-up covering everything from rock to flamenco.

07

☆ Festival del Grec   throughout Jul
The major cultural event of the summer is a month-long fest (grec.bcn.cat) with dozens of theatre, dance and music performances held around town, including at the Teatre Grec amphitheatre on Montjuïc, from which the festival takes its name.

☆ Sala Montjuïc   Jul–early Aug
Picnic under the stars while watching a movie at this open-air cinema (salamontjuic.org), which also features concerts.

☆ Music in the Parks   Jun–Aug
A series of open-air concerts held in different parks and green spaces around the city. Over 40 different concerts feature classical, blues and jazz groups.

2018

August

The temperature soars. Barcelonins leave the city in droves for summer holidays as huge numbers of tourists arrive. It's a great time to hit the beach.

✿ Circuit Festival   mid-Aug
Running for about two weeks, this is a major gay fiesta (www.circuitfestival.net) with numerous party nights, including an epic final all-day all-night bash in a waterpark. There's a parallel lesbian event, GirlieCircuit (www.girliecircuit.net).

✿ Festes de Sant Roc   around 16 Aug
For four days in mid-August, the Barri Gòtic becomes the scene of parades, dances, a craft fair, street games, fireworks, traditional music and the *cucanya* (greasy-pole) of Plaça Nova.

✿ Festa Major de Sants   late Aug
The district of Sants hosts a five-day fest (www.festamajordesants.net) with con-

✿ Festa Major de Gràcia   around 15 Aug
Locals compete for the most elaborately decorated street in this popular week-long Gràcia festival (www.festamajordegracia.cat) held around 15 August. The fest also features free outdoor concerts, street fairs and other events. Pictured above: A decorated Gràcia street.

certs, outdoor dance parties, *correfocs* (fire runs) and elaborately decorated streets.

Plan Your Trip
This Year in Barcelona

September

After a month off, barcelonins return to work, although several major festivals provide ample amusement. Temperatures stay warm through September, making for fine beach days.

✣ Diada Nacional de Catalunya   11 Sep

Catalonia's national day curiously commemorates Barcelona's surrender on 11 September 1714 to the Bourbon monarchy of Spain, at the conclusion of the War of the Spanish Succession. Pictured above: In recent years, big independence rallies have been held on this day.

🍷 Mostra de Vins i Caves de Catalunya   mid–late Sep

At this wine and *cava* event, you can taste your way through some of the top wines of Catalunya. It's usually held on Passeig Lluís Campanys near the Arc de Triomf over four days towards the end of September.

✣ Festa Major de la Barceloneta   29 Sep

This big September celebration in Barceloneta honours the local patron saint, Sant

✣ Festes de la Mercè   around 24 Sep

Barcelona's co-patron saint is celebrated with fervour in this massive five-day fest (merce.bcn.cat). The city stages sporting events, free concerts, dance performances, human towers of *castellers*, parades of *gegants* (giants) and a fiery *correfoc* (fire run).

Miquel, on 29 September. It lasts about a week and involves plenty of dancing and drinking, especially on the beach.

2018

October

While northern Europe shivers, Barcelona enjoys mild October temperatures and sunny days. With the disappearance of the summer crowds and lower accommodation prices, this is an excellent month to visit.

🔒 Liber
early Oct

This major international book fair (www.liber.es) brings together authors, publishers and keen readers for a few days at the beginning of October.

☆ Symphony for the Senses
throughout Oct

With amazing acoustics in a modern building, seeing a show at L'Auditori (p198) is a must for music lovers. Visit www.auditori.cat to see the program and buy tickets.

✗ Mercat de Mercats
mid-Oct

The 'market of markets' is a celebration of Catalan cooking and those wonderful locally sourced ingredients that have made Barcelona such a foodie destination. Over one weekend in October, this food fair features great foods, wines and workshops. Held in front of La Catedral.

☆ Festival de Jazz de Barcelona
throughout Oct

With an excellent program of high-quality concerts throughout the month, this long-standing festival (www.jazz.barcelona) is a musical highlight.

Human Castles

One of the highlights of a traditional Catalan festival is the building of human *castells* (castles). Teams from across the region compete to build towers up to 10 'storeys' tall.

Plan Your Trip
This Year in Barcelona

November

Cooler days and nights arrive in Barcelona, along with occasional days of rain and overcast skies. For beating the crowds (and higher summer prices), though, it's an excellent month to visit.

✿ Día de Todos
los Santos   1 Nov
All Saint's Day is traditionally when locals visit the tombs of family members, then get together for the Castanyada, when roasted chestnuts and other winter foods are eaten.

☆ Camp Nou   throughout Nov
See a football match at Camp Nou (p72), hallowed ground for football fans across the globe. There are likely league, cup or Champions League games to choose from this month. Or take a self-guided tour of the stadium and learn about the sport's most famous players at FC Barcelona's museum.
Pictured above: Visitors at the FC Barcelona museum.

☆ L'Alternativa   12–18 Nov
Showcasing feature-length and short films, plus premieres by new directors, the Barcelona Independent Film Festival (www. alternativa.cccb.org) includes free and ticketed events.

✿ Fira de
Santa Llúcia   late Nov–late Dec
Held from late November to Christmas, this holiday market (firadesantallucia.cat) has hundreds of stalls selling all manner of Christmas decorations and gifts – including the infamous Catalan Nativity scene character, the *caganer* (the crapper) (pictured right).

✿ Festival
Mil·lenni   late Nov–May 2019
Running from November to May each year, this festival (www.festival-millenni.com) consists of a series of high-profile concerts in various venues around town.

2018

DANIELLOVE/SHUTTERSTOCK ©

December

12

As winter returns barcelonins gear up for Christmas, and the city is festooned with colourful decorations. Relatively few visitors arrive, at least until Christmas, when the city fills with holidaying out-of-towners.

☆ Barcelona
World Race   late Dec or early Jan
This non-stop round-the-world sailing race (www.barcelonaworldrace.com) starts and ends in Barcelona every two years or so. Two-person crews will kick off in either December 2018 or January 2019.

❄ Christmas   24 Dec–6 Jan
Christmas in Spain is a two-week affair, with the major family meals on the night of Christmas Eve, New Year's Eve and 6 January.

❄ New Year's Eve   31 Dec
On 31 December, the fountains of Montjuïc (Font Màgica) take centre stage for the biggest celebration in town. Crowds line up along Avinguda Reina Maria Cristina to watch a theatrical procession and audio-visual performance (plus *castells*), followed by fireworks at midnight.

NITO/SHUTTERSTOCK ©

Christmas Crappers
At Christmas some rather unusual Catalan characters appear. The *caganer* (crapper) is a chap with dropped pants who balances over his unsightly offering (a symbol of fertility for the coming year). There's also the *caga tío* (poop log), which on Christmas Day is supposed to *cagar* (crap) out gifts.

Pictured above: A *caganer*. Top: A pile of *caga tíos*.

Plan Your Trip

Need to Know

Daily Costs

**Budget:
Less than €70**

- Dorm bed: €17–30
- Set lunch: from €10
- Bicycle hire per hour: €5

**Midrange:
€70–200**

- Standard double room: €80–140
- Two-course dinner with wine for two: €70–80
- Walking and guided tours: €15–25

**Top End:
More than €200**

- Boutique and luxury hotels: €200 and up
- Multicourse meal at top restaurants per person: €80–160
- Concert tickets to Palau de la Música Catalana: around €50

Advance Planning

Three months before Book a hotel and reserve a table at a top restaurant.

One month before Check out reviews for theatre and live music, and book tickets.

One week before Browse the latest nightlife listings, art exhibitions and other events to attend while in town. Reserve spa visits and organised tours.

Useful Websites

Barcelona (www.bcn.cat) Town hall's official site with plenty of links.

Barcelona Turisme (www.barcelonaturisme.com) City's official tourism website.

Lonely Planet (www.lonelyplanet.com/spain/barcelona) Destination information, hotel bookings, traveller forum and more.

BCN Mes (www.bcnmes.com) Trilingual monthly mag of culture, food, art and more.

Spotted by Locals (www.spottedbylocals.com/barcelona) Insider tips.

Arriving in Barcelona

El Prat airport You can get there by Metro for €4.50. *Aerobuses* make the 35-minute run into town (€5.90) from 6am to 1am. Taxis cost around €25.

Estació Sants Long-distance trains arrive at this big station, which is linked by metro to other parts of the city.

Estació del Nord Barcelona's long-haul bus station is located in L'Eixample, about 1.5km northeast of Plaça de Catalunya, and is a short walk from several metro stations.

Girona-Costa Brava airport The 'Barcelona Bus' operated by Sagalés (one way/return €16/25, 90 minutes) is timed with Ryanair flights and goes direct to Barcelona's Estació del Nord.

Currency

Euro (€)

Language

Spanish, Catalan

Visas

Generally not required for stays of up to 90 days. Some nationalities need a Schengen visa.

Money

ATMs are widely available (La Rambla has many). Credit cards are accepted in most hotels, shops and restaurants, but few bars.

Mobile Phones

Local SIM cards can be used in unlocked phones. Other phones must be set to roaming. With an EU phone, you'll pay normal call costs.

Time

Central European Time (GMT/UTC plus one hour).

Tourist Information

Oficina d'Informació de Turisme de Barcelona (p238) provides maps, sights information, tours, concert and events tickets, and last-minute accommodation bookings.

When to Go

The sweltering summer (July and August) is peak tourist season. For pleasant weather, but without the ocean dips, come in late spring (May).

Barcelona

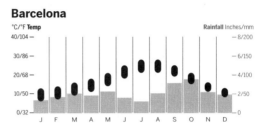

Reus Airport Buses operated by Hispano-Igualadina (one way/return €16/25, 90 minutes) are timed with Ryanair flights and go direct to Barcelona's Estació Sants.

Getting Around

Barcelona has abundant options for getting around town. The excellent metro can get you most places, with buses and trams filling in the gaps. Taxis are the best option late at night.

Metro The most convenient option. Runs 5am to midnight Sunday to Thursday, till 2am on Friday and 24 hours on Saturday. Targeta T-10 (10-ride passes; €9.95) is the best value; otherwise, it's €2.15 per ride.

Bus A hop-on, hop-off Bus Turístic, from Plaça de Catalunya, is handy for those wanting to see the city's highlights in one or two days.

Taxi You can hail taxis on the street (try La Rambla, Via Laietana, Plaça de Catalunya and Passeig de Gràcia) or at taxi stands.

On foot To explore the old city, all you need is a good pair of walking shoes.

Sleeping

Barcelona has a wide range of sleeping options, from inexpensive hostels hidden in the old quarter to luxury hotels overlooking the waterfront. Or you could choose one of the charming neighbourhoods packed with restaurants and nightlife. The small-scale B&B-style apartment rentals scattered around the city are a good-value choice.

Wherever you stay it's wise to book well ahead. If you plan to travel around holidays such as Christmas, New Year's Eve and Easter, or in summer, reserve a room three or four months ahead of time.

More information about accommodation can be found under Rest Your Head (p213).

Useful Accommodation Websites

Oh-Barcelona (www.oh-barcelona.com) Good-value selection of hotels, hostels and apartment rentals.

Booking.com The most comprehensive hotel-booking engine for Barcelona.

Airbnb (www.airbnb.com) Apartment and room rentals.

Lonely Planet (www.lonelyplanet.com/spain/barcelona/hotels) Huge range of hotels, hostels, guesthouses, B&Bs and apartments.

Top Days in Barcelona

MARK AVELLINO/GETTY IMAGES ©

Barcelona's Must-Sees

On your first day in Barcelona, visit the city's major highlights: stroll La Rambla, explore the atmospheric lanes of the Barri Gòtic and linger over the stunning artistry of La Sagrada Família. History, great architecture and a celebrated food market are all part of this sensory-rich experience.

❶ La Rambla (p44)

Start with La Rambla. Don't miss the human statues, the Miró mosaic and key buildings facing La Rambla, including the 18th-century Palau de la Virreina.

➲ La Rambla to Mercat de la Boqueria

🕏 Find the market's entrance on La Rambla's west side.

❷ Mercat de la Boqueria (p94)

Packed with culinary riches, this staggering food market is the favoured stomping ground for chefs and conjurers, weekend cooks and hungry-looking tourists. Don't leave without having a few snacks – perhaps from one of the delectable tapas bars in the back.

➲ Mercat de la Boqueria to Barri Gòtic

🕏 Head back down La Rambla, then turn left into Plaça Reial after passing Carrer de Ferran.

Day

01

❸ Barri Gòtic

Delve into Barcelona's old city. Cross picturesque Plaça Reial (p48) before wandering narrow lanes that date back to at least the Middle Ages. Make your way to the magnificent Catedral (p64), then visit the Temple Romà d'August (p67).

➲ Barri Gòtic to Cafè de l'Acadèmia

🚶 Cross Plaça de Sant Jaume, walk along Carrer de la Ciutat and take the first left.

❹ Lunch at Cafè de l'Acadèmia (p133)

Arrive early to get a seat at this small atmospheric restaurant serving excellent Catalan cuisine. The multicourse lunch special is fantastic value.

➲ Cafè de l'Acadèmia to La Sagrada Família

Ⓜ Take Line 4 north from Jaume I; transfer at Passeig de Gràcia for Line 2 to Sagrada Família.

❺ La Sagrada Família (p36)

Roll the drums, turn on the stage lights and get ready for Spain's most visited sight. This one-of-a-kind religious monument is as unique as the pyramids and as beautiful as the Taj Mahal.

➲ La Sagrada Família to Tapas 24

Ⓜ Take Line 2 back to Passeig de Gràcia. Walk southeast down the street of the same name, then take your second left.

❻ Evening Bites at Tapas 24 (p142)

This great basement spot does a smart line in innovative takes on traditional tapas. It's a top place for a light bite or a full meal.

From left: Tapas at the Mercat de la Boqueria; Dining in Plaça Reial, in the Barri Gòtic

Plan Your Trip

Top Days in Barcelona

LITTLEAOM/SHUTTERSTOCK ©

Mar i Muntanya (Sea & Mountain)

This itinerary takes you along the promenade that skirts the Mediterranean, then into the old fishing quarter of Barceloneta before whisking you up to the heights of Montjuïc for fine views, fragrant gardens and superb art galleries – including two of the city's top museums.

❶ Barceloneta Beach

Start the morning with a waterfront stroll; this scenic but once derelict area experienced a dramatic makeover around the 1992 Olympics. Look north and you'll see Frank Gehry's shimmering fish sculpture, while to the south rises the spinnaker-shaped tower of the W Hotel.

➲ Barceloneta Beach to Can Ros

✦ Look for Carrer de l'Almirall Aixada just north of the rectangular beach sculpture. Can Ros is about 350m back from the beach on this road.

❷ Lunch at Can Ros (p141)

Take your pick of the seaside restaurants if you want the view, but otherwise head back a few streets to this family-run gem, which has been dishing up excellent seafood for generations.

➲ Can Ros to Teleférico del Puerto

✦ Walk to the southern end of Barceloneta and you'll see the cable car to your right.

Day

02

ARKANTO/SHUTTERSTOCK ©

❸ Teleférico del Puerto (p61)

After lunch take a scenic ride on this aerial cable car for fantastic views over the port and the dazzling city beyond. At the top, you'll arrive in Montjuïc, a mini-mountain that's packed with gardens – both sculptural and floral – as well as hosting a few first-rate museums.

➡ Teleférico del Puerto to Fundació Joan Miró

🚡 Take the cable car up to Montjuïc, disembark and follow the main road 800m west.

❹ Fundació Joan Miró (p58)

See a full range of works by one of the giants of the art world. Paintings, sculptures and drawings by the prolific Catalan artist are displayed along with photos and other media. Outside is a peaceful sculpture garden with views over Poble Sec.

➡ Fundació Joan Miró to Museu Nacional d'Art de Catalunya

🚶 Follow the path through the sculpture gardens east, take the steps up to the main road and continue east to the museum.

❺ Museu Nacional d'Art de Catalunya (p54)

Not to be missed is the incomparable collection of artwork inside this enormous museum. The highlight is the impressive Romanesque collection – rescued from 900-year-old churches in the Pyrenees. Out front, you can take in the view over Plaça d'Espanya to the distant peak of Tibidabo.

➡ Museu Nacional d'Art de Catalunya to Tickets

🚶 Descend toward Plaça d'Espanya. Turn right before the fountain, left on Carrer de Lleida and right on Avinguda del Paral·lel.

❻ Dinner at Tickets (p145)

You'll need to book weeks in advance, but it's worth the effort if you can score a table. The celebrated restaurant is run by the Adrià brothers and showcases an ever-changing menu of molecular gastronomy.

From left: Barceloneta Beach; Teleférico del Puerto

Plan Your Trip
Top Days in Barcelona

PAOLO GALLO/SHUTTERSTOCK ©

La Ribera

Like adjacent Barri Gòtic, La Ribera has narrow cobblestone streets and medieval architecture galore. Yet it's also home to high-end shopping, a brilliant Modernista concert hall and a treasure trove of artwork by Picasso. Great restaurants and a fanciful green space complete the Ribera ramble.

❶ Museu Picasso (p80)

You can see Picasso's early masterpieces inside this inspiring museum, which contains some 3500 of his works. The galleries themselves are set in a series of merchant houses dating back to the 1300s.

➲ Museu Picasso to El Born

🏃 Stroll southeast along Carrer de Montcada.

❷ Window Shopping in El Born

The medieval streets of El Born hide an abundance of shopping intrigue, from magic shops to purveyors of fine wines, along with plenty of eye-catching fashion boutiques.

➲ El Born to Cal Pep

🏃 Walk across Plaça de les Olles.

❸ Lunch at Cal Pep (p139)

For lunch, sit at the bar at this bustling eatery for some of the city's tastiest seafood tapas.

➲ Cal Pep to Basílica de Santa Maria del Mar

🏃 Stroll northwest along Carrer de la Vidrieria and turn left on Carrer de Santa Maria.

Day
03

FTH:SHUTTERSTOCK ©

❹ Basílica de Santa Maria del Mar (p116)

A few blocks away, this captivating church is built in the style of Catalan Gothic. The 14th-century masterpiece soars above the medina-like streets surrounding it.

➲ Basílica de Santa Maria del Mar to Parc de la Ciutadella

🏃 Walk northeast on Carrer de Santa Maria and continue around the former Mercat del Born site to the park.

❺ Parc de la Ciutadella (p84)

After the compact streets of La Ribera, catch your breath and stroll through the open green expanse of this manicured park. You'll find sculptures, a small zoo, the Parlament de Catalunya, and the centrepiece, a dramatic if utterly artificial waterfall dating from the 19th century.

➲ Parc de la Ciutadella to Palau de la Música Catalana

🏃 Take Carrer de la Princesa back into El Born and turn right after 200m, making your way northwest.

❻ Palau de la Música Catalana (p102)

Designed by Domènech i Montaner in the early 1900s, this intimate concert hall is a Modernista masterpiece, with luminescent stained glass and elaborately sculpted details throughout. Come for a concert, but it's also worth returning by day for a guided tour.

➲ Palau de la Música Catalana to El Xampanyet

🏃 Make your way back (southeast) to Carrer de Montcada.

❼ El Xampanyet (p178)

Just up the road, El Xampanyet is a festive spot to end the night. You can sample mouth-watering bites and let your cup brim with ever-flowing *cava* (Catalan sparkling wine). It's usually crowded but friendly, just politely elbow your way in for a bit of refreshment.

From left: Inside Santa Maria del Mar; Parc de la Ciutadella

Top Days in Barcelona

Art & Architecture

This tour takes you up to the enchanting (if accidental) Gaudí-designed park that overlooks the city, down the elegant architectural show-piece avenue of Passeig de Gràcia and into El Raval. There you'll find the city's top contemporary art museum anchoring Barcelona's most bohemian neighbourhood.

Day 04

❶ Park Güell (p68)

Go early to Park Güell to beat the crowds and see the early morning rays over Barcelona and the Mediterranean beyond. Stroll the expanse of the park, ending your visit at Casa-Museu Gaudí (p71), where you can learn more about the life and work of the great Catalan architect.

➲ Park Güell to Gràcia

Ⓜ Take Line 3 from Vallcarca to Fontana.

❷ Gràcia

The village-like feel of Gràcia makes for some great exploring. Stroll from plaza to plaza along the narrow shop-lined lanes, stopping perhaps at open-air cafes along the way. Good streets for browsing include Carrer de Verdi, Travessera de Gràcia and Carrer de Torrijos.

➲ Gràcia to Botafumeiro

🚶 Walk southwest along Travessera de Gràcia and turn right on Carrer Gran de Gràcia.

TONIFLAP/SHUTTERSTOCK ©

❸ Lunch at Botafumeiro (p147)

One of Barcelona's best seafood restaurants. If the tables are full, you can usually get a spot at the bar.

⮕ Botafumeiro to Passeig de Gràcia

🚶 Amble southeast along Carrer Gran de Gràcia, which leads into Passeig de Gràcia after 400m.

❹ Passeig de Gràcia

Head to L'Eixample to see high-concept architecture. Passeig de Gràcia is a busy but elegant boulevard lined with exquisite Modernista buildings, including Gaudí's La Pedrera (p74) and Casa Batlló (p50).

⮕ Passeig de Gràcia to MACBA

🚶 Continue on Passeig de Gràcia, cross Plaça de Catalunya to La Rambla and turn right on Carrer del Bonsuccés.

❺ MACBA (p96)

A few streets away from Plaça d'Espanya you'll reach the city's top contemporary art gallery, MACBA. It houses an excellent range of Catalan and European works from WWII to the present.

⮕ MACBA to El Raval

🚶 Walk along Carrer dels Àngels and turn left on Carrer del Carme.

❻ El Raval

Spend the early evening strolling the lively multicultural street scene of El Raval. Stop for a breather in the pretty courtyard of the Antic Hospital de la Santa Creu (p95) and check out Gaudí's Palau Güell (p92).

⮕ El Raval to Koy Shunka

Ⓜ Take Line 3 from Paral·lel to Catalunya.

❼ Dinner at Koy Shunka (p134)

Top off your night with a feast at Koy Shunka, where the haute cuisine features a magnificent marriage of Catalan creativity with Japanese tradition.

From left: Passeig de Gràcia; MACBA

Plan Your Trip
Hotspots For...

GLITZ AND GLAMOUR

⛁ **Shopping in the Quadrat** (p124) Browse the boutiques in Barcelona's most fashion-conscious district.

💆 **Rituels d'Orient** (p210) Relax with a spa and massage session at this sumptuous North African fantasy.

✗ **Botafumeiro** (p147) Rub shoulders with Barcelona's VIPs at this upmarket temple of quality seafood.

☆ **Palau de la Música Catalana** (p197) Dress your best and catch a concert at this wonderful venue (pictured above).

🍸 **Dry Martini** (p181) Enjoy as-they-should-be cocktails with impeccable service in this classy bar.

SEA DOGS

👁 **Museu Marítim** (p88) Barcelona's seafaring history encapsulated under the mighty arches of the former royal shipyards.

🏖 **Beaches of Barcelona** (p122) Recline on the salty sands or lazily backstroke under the Mediterranean sun (pictured below).

✗ **Can Ros** (p141) Gorge yourself on traditional seafood dishes at this centenarian Barceloneta restaurant.

🚣 **Orsom** (p209) Head out to sea in style on these catamaran tours of the bay.

🚣 **Molokai SUP Center** (p210) Cut a cool figure around maritime Barcelona on a stand-up paddleboard.

GASTRONAUTS

🏠 **Mercat de la Boqueria** (p94) This legendary produce market is a cornucopia of sights and smells.

⊙ **La Ribera** (p104) Stroll this intriguing district and browse its gourmet shops.

✗ **Cinc Sentits** (p143) Delight in the superb tasting menu at this top-notch modern restaurant.

✗ **Disfrutar** (p143) Have the meal of your trip at this superbly inventive molecular gastronomy restaurant.

🍴 **Espai Boisà** (p211) Learn to whip up some classic tapas and Catalan dishes in this excellent cooking school.

ROMANTICS

⊙ **Park Güell** (p68) Stroll the gardens and admire the views among the Modernista fantasies of Gaudí (pictured above).

⊙ **Barri Gòtic** (p86) Amble around the historic centre and explore its hidden corners.

✗ **La Vinateria del Call** (p132) Intimate and exquisite, this little old-town eatery is perfect for cosy dining.

✗ **Caelum** (p135) Beautiful medieval cafe with a candlelit downstairs.

🍴 **Swing Maniacs** (p210) Learn swing dancing at a drop-in course, then hit the dance floor.

CULTURE VULTURES

⊙ **MACBA** (p96) The city's top destination for contemporary art, with top views to boot.

⊙ **Fundació Joan Miró** (p58) A comprehensive collection of this local's works, in a brilliant building.

✗ **Els Quatre Gats** (p134) Admire the Modernista decor in this historic restaurant (pictured above).

✗ **Tickets** (p145) If food can be art, then this is the most spectacular performance in town.

☆ **Gran Teatre del Liceu** (p194) Enjoy state-of-the-art acoustics in this atmospheric venue on La Rambla.

Plan Your Trip
What's New

Hipster Central

Sant Antoni continues to be where it's at for edgy creative trends, enlightening counterculture and state-of-the-art eating. Here, and in nearby Poble Sec, can be found some of the most talked-about restaurants in the city.

Opera Samfaina

This totally bizarre eating place (p133) inside the Gran Teatre del Liceu (p194) could come straight from a David Lynch movie but is actually a creation of the celebrated Roca brothers of El Celler de Can Roca fame. Aiming for a total sensory experience, they lay on weird audiovisuals, hallucinatory decor, weird curios and a variety of ambitious food and drink. Does it work? You be the judge.

Hotel Almanac

A notable newcomer in converted insurance headquarters on Gran Vía, this moderately sized five-star hotel opened its doors in the summer of 2017. The rooftop terrace with pool is a highlight and the restaurant is aiming high.

Tastes of Peru

Authentic pisco sours and excellent ceviche are just the beginning at Lascar 74 (p145), a wonderfully appealing spot for the fresh flavours of Peru. Asian influences are also present and it's a buzzy spot to just drop by for a drink.

Adrià's Culinary Kingdom

Famed chef Albert Adrià now runs six celebrated restaurants (www.elbarriadria. com), including Tickets (p145) and the most recently opened Enigma, which is said to be the successor to the lauded El Bulli. They are all within strolling distance of one another in Sant Antoni.

Above: One of Albert Adrià's artful dishes

Plan Your Trip
For Free

Free Barcelona

With planning, Barcelona can be a surprisingly affordable place to travel. Many museums offer free days and some of the best ways to experience the city don't cost a penny – hanging out on the beach, exploring fascinating neighbourhoods and parks, and drinking in the views from hilltop heights.

Festivals & Events

Barcelona has loads of free festivals and events, including the Festes de la Mercè (p14) and the Festes de Santa Eulàlia (p7). From June to August, the city hosts Música als Parcs (Music in the Parks) (p12), a series of open-air concerts held in different parks and green spaces around the city. Over 40 different concerts feature classical, blues and jazz groups.

Walking Tours

Numerous companies offer pay-what-you-wish walking tours. These typically take in the Barri Gòtic or the Modernista sites of L'Eixample.

Sights

Entry to some sights is free on occasion, most commonly on the first Sunday of the month, while quite a few attractions are free from 3pm to 8pm on Sundays. Others, including the Centre d'Art Santa Mònica (p49), Basílica de Santa Maria del Mar (p116), Palau del Lloctinent (p67), Temple Romà d'August (p67) and Antic Hospital de la Santa Creu (p95), are always free.

Picnics

It might not be for free, but you can eat very well on a budget if you stick to set menus at lunchtime. For even less, you can put together a picnic of fresh fruits, cheese, smoked meats and other goodies purchased at local markets such as Mercat de la Boqueria (p94), El Raval's Mercat de Sant Antoni (p164) or La Ribera's Mercat de Santa Caterina (p106).

Barceloneta and the other beaches are good places for a picnic. For more shade and seclusion – and pretty views – head up to Montjuïc.

Above: Spanish singer/songwriter Lopez performs at an outdoor festival

Plan Your Trip
Family Travel

Need to Know

o **Change facilities** Not as ubiquitous as in North America, but generally good and clean.

o **Cots** Usually available in hotels (ask for '*una cuna*'); reserve ahead.

o **Health** High health-care standards. Make sure you have your child's EHIC card (see p236) before you travel within the EU.

o **Highchairs** Many restaurants have at least one.

o **Infant supplies** Nappies, dummies (pacifiers), creams and formula can be found at any of the city's many pharmacies. Nappies are cheaper in supermarkets.

o **Strollers** Bring your own (preferably a fold-away).

o **Transport** Barcelona's metro is accessible and great for families with strollers. Just be mindful of your bags, as pickpockets often target distracted parents.

Catalan Style

Going out to eat or sipping a beer on a late summer evening at a *terraza* (terrace) needn't mean leaving children with minders. Locals take their kids out all the time and don't worry about keeping them up late. To make the most of your visit, try to adjust your child's sleeping habits to 'Spanish time' early on, or else you'll miss out on much of Barcelona. Also, be prepared to look for things 'outside the box': there's the childlike creativity of Picasso and Miró (give your children paper and crayons and take them around the museums), the Harry-Potter-meets-Tolkien fantasy of Park Güell and La Pedrera, and the wild costumes, human castle-building and street food at festivals.

Babysitting

Most of the midrange and top-end hotels in Barcelona can organise babysitting services. A company that many hotels use and that you can also contact directly is

VENIAMIN KRASKOV/SHUTTERSTOCK ©

Barcelona Babysitter (📞 622 511 675; www.bcnbabysitter.com), which offers multilingual babysitters (€20 per hour).

Eating with Kids

Barcelona – and Spain in general – is super-friendly when it comes to eating with children. Spanish kids tend to eat the Mediterranean offerings enjoyed by their parents, but some restaurants have children's menus that offer burgers, pizzas, tomato-sauce pasta and the like. Good local – and childproof – food commonly found on tapas menus are *tortillas de patatas* (potato omelettes) or *croquetas de jamón* (ham croquettes).

Family-Friendly Meals

Monvínic (📞 93 272 61 87; www.monvinic.com; Carrer de la Diputació 249; mains €24-38; ⊙1.30-3.30pm & 8-10.30pm; Ⓜ Passeig de Gracia) is a good choice for a quick meal while the kids entertain themselves drawing on the glass wall. At **Dos Trece** (📞 93 301 73 06; Carrer del

Top Five Experiences for Kids

CosmoCaixa (p101)
Papabubble (p156)
L'Aquàrium (p91)
Poble Espanyol (p57)
Museu de la Xocolata (p106)

Carme 40; mains €10-15; ⊙10am-midnight; 🛜📞; Ⓜ Liceu), you can enjoy quality food or a drink while the younger generation enjoys the playground. If you're after something sweet, **La Nena** (p146) is fantastic for chocolate and all manner of tasty things. There's also a play area and toys and books in a corner. And don't miss **La Granja** (p134). No kid will be left unimpressed – and without a buzz! – by the thick hot chocolate here.

From left: Park Güell (p68); Poble Espanyol (p57)

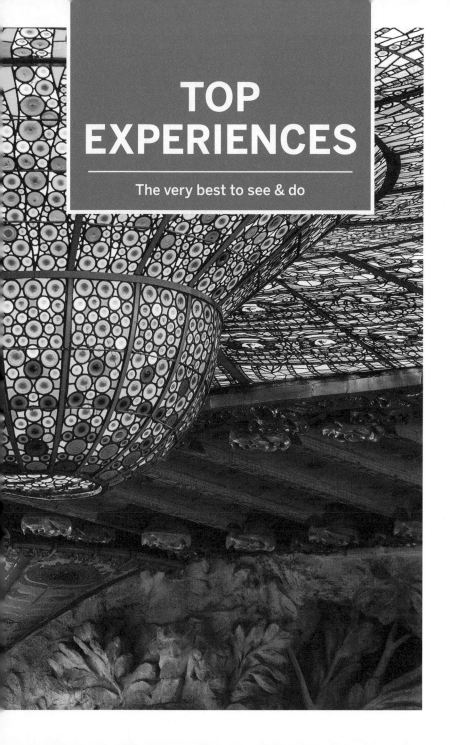

TOP
EXPERIENCES

The very best to see & do

La Sagrada Família

If you have time for only one sightseeing outing, this is it. The Sagrada Família inspires awe by its sheer verticality, remarkable use of light and Gaudí's offbeat design elements.

Great For...

☑ **Don't Miss**

The apse, the extraordinary pillars and the stained glass.

In the manner of the medieval cathedrals La Sagrada Família emulates, it's still under construction after more than 100 years. When completed, the highest tower will be more than half as high again as those that stand today.

A Holy Mission

The Temple Expiatori de la Sagrada Família (Expiatory Temple of the Holy Family) was Antoni Gaudí's all-consuming obsession. Given the commission by a conservative society that wished to build a temple as atonement for the city's sins, Gaudí saw its completion as his holy mission. As funds dried up, he contributed his own, and in the last years of his life he was not shy of pleading with anyone he thought a likely donor.

Gaudí devised a temple 95m long and 60m wide, able to seat 13,000 people,

❶ Need to Know

Map p254; ☏93 208 04 14; www.
sagradafamilia.cat; Carrer de Mallorca
401; adult/concession/under 11yr €15/13/
free; ⊙9am-8pm Apr-Sep, to 6pm Oct-Mar;
Ⓜ Sagrada Família

✕ Take a Break

Michael Collins (p183) across the
square is good for a beer.

★ Top Tip

Buying tickets online in advance is a
must to beat the frequently dispiriting
queues.

with a central tower 170m high above the
transept (representing Christ) and another
17 of 100m or more. The 12 along the three
facades represent the Apostles, whIle the
remaining five represent the Virgin Mary
and the four evangelists. With his characteristic dislike for straight lines (there
were none in nature, he said), Gaudí gave
his towers swelling outlines inspired by the
weird peaks of the holy mountain Montserrat outside Barcelona, and encrusted them
with a tangle of sculpture that seems an
outgrowth of the stone.

At Gaudí's death, only the crypt, the apse
walls, one portal and one tower had been
finished. Three more towers were added by
1930, completing the northeast (Nativity)
facade. In 1936 anarchists burned and
smashed the interior, including workshops,
plans and models. Work began again in

1952, but controversy has always clouded
progress. Opponents of the continuation
of the project claim that the computer
models based on what little of Gaudí's
plans survived the anarchists' ire have led
to the creation of a monster that has little
to do with Gaudí's plans and style. It is a
debate that appears to have little hope of
resolution. Like or hate what is being done,
the fascination it awakens is undeniable.

Guesses on when construction might
be complete range from the 2020s to the
2040s. Even before reaching that point,
some of the oldest parts of the church,
especially the apse, have required restora-
tion work.

The Interior & the Apse

Inside, work on roofing over the church
was completed in 2010. The roof is held up
by a forest of extraordinary angled pillars.
As the pillars soar toward the ceiling, they
sprout a web of supporting branches,
creating the effect of a forest canopy. The

tree image is in no way fortuitous – Gaudí envisaged such an effect. Everything was thought through, including the shape and placement of windows to create the mottled effect one would see with sunlight pouring through the branches of a thick forest. The pillars are of four different types of stone. They vary in colour and load-bearing strength, from the soft Montjuïc stone pillars along the lateral aisles through to granite, dark grey basalt and finally burgundy-tinged Iranian porphyry for the key columns at the intersection of the nave and transept. The stained glass, divided in shades of red, blue, green and ochre, creates a hypnotic, magical atmosphere when the sun hits the windows. Tribunes built high above the aisles can host two choirs: the main tribune up to 1300 people and the children's tribune up to 300.

Nativity Facade

The Nativity Facade is the artistic pinnacle of the building, mostly created under Gaudí's personal supervision. You can climb high up inside some of the four towers (at extra cost) by a combination of lifts and narrow spiral staircases – a vertiginous experience. Do not climb the stairs if you have cardiac or respiratory problems. The towers are destined to hold tubular bells capable of playing complex music at great volume. Their upper parts are decorated with mosaics spelling out '*Sanctus, Sanctus, Sanctus, Hosanna in Excelsis, Amen, Alleluia*'. Asked why he lavished so much care on the tops of the spires, which no one would see from close up, Gaudí answered: 'The angels will see them'.

Three sections of the portal represent, from left to right, Hope, Charity and Faith.

Detail from the Passion Facade

Among the forest of sculpture on the Charity portal you can see, low down, the manger surrounded by an ox, an ass, the shepherds, the kings and angel musicians. Some 30 different species of plant from around Catalonia are reproduced here, and the faces of the many figures are taken from plaster casts done of local people and the occasional one made from corpses in the local morgue.

Directly above the blue stained-glass window is the archangel Gabriel's Annunciation to Mary. At the top is a green cypress tree, a refuge in a storm for the white doves of peace dotted over it. The mosaic work at the pinnacle of the towers is made from Murano glass, from Venice.

> **ⓘ Did You Know?**
> La Sagrada Família attracts over 4 million visitors yearly and is the most visited monument in Spain.

NINETAILS/SHUTTERSTOCK ©

To the right of the facade is the curious Claustre del Roser, a Gothic-style mini-cloister tacked on to the outside of the church (rather than the classic square enclosure of the great Gothic church monasteries). Once inside, look back to the intricately decorated entrance. On the lower right-hand side you'll notice the sculpture of a reptilian devil handing a terrorist a bomb. Barcelona was regularly rocked by political violence, and bombings were frequent in the decades prior to the civil war. The sculpture is one of several on the 'temptations of men and women'.

Passion Facade

The southwest Passion Facade, on the theme of Christ's last days and death, was built between 1954 and 1978 based on surviving drawings by Gaudí, with four towers and a large, sculpture-bedecked portal. The sculptor, Josep Subirachs, worked on its decoration from 1986 to 2006. He did not attempt to imitate Gaudí; rather, he produced angular, controversial images of his own. The main series of sculptures, on three levels, are in an S-shaped sequence, starting with the Last Supper at the bottom left and ending with Christ's burial at the top right. Decorative work on the Passion Facade continues even today, as construction of the Glory Facade moves ahead.

To the right, in front of the Passion Facade, the Escoles de Gaudí is one of his simpler gems. Gaudí built this as a children's school, creating an original, undulating roof of brick that continues to charm architects to this day. Inside is a recreation of Gaudí's modest office as it was when he died, and explanations of the geometric patterns and plans at the heart of his building techniques.

> **☑ When to Go**
> There are always lots of people visiting the Sagrada Família, but if you can get there when it opens, you'll find fewer crowds.

ⓘ Did You Know?

Pope Benedict XVI consecrated the church in a huge ceremony in November 2010.

A Hidden Portrait

Careful observation of the Passion Facade will reveal a special tribute from sculptor Josep Subirachs to Gaudí. The central sculptural group (below Christ crucified) shows, from right to left, Christ bearing his cross, Veronica displaying the cloth with Christ's bloody image, a pair of soldiers and, watching it all, a man called the evangelist. Subirachs used a rare photo of Gaudí, taken a couple of years before his death, as the model for the evangelist's face.

Glory Facade

The Glory Facade is under construction and will, like the others, be crowned by four towers – the total of 12 representing the Twelve Apostles. Gaudí wanted it to be the most magnificent facade of the church. Inside will be the narthex, a kind of foyer made up of 16 'lanterns', a series of hyperboloid forms topped by cones. Further decoration will make the whole building a microcosmic symbol of the Christian church, with Christ represented by a massive 170m central tower above the transept and the five remaining planned towers symbolising the Virgin Mary and the four evangelists.

Museu Gaudí

Open the same times as the church, the Museu Gaudí, below ground level, includes interesting material on Gaudí's life and other works, as well as models and photos of La Sagrada Família. You can see a good example of his plumb-line models that showed him the stresses and strains he could get away with in construction. A side hall towards the eastern end of the museum leads to a viewing point above the simple crypt in which the genius is buried. The crypt, where Masses are now held, can also be visited from the Carrer de Mallorca side of the church.

What's Nearby?

Església de les Saleses   Church
(Map p254; ☎93 458 76 67; www.parroquia concepciobcn.org; Passeig de Sant Joan 90; ⏱7.30am-1pm & 5-9pm Mon-Fri, 7.30am-2pm & 5-9pm Sun; Ⓜ Tetuan) A singular neo-Gothic effort, this church is interesting because it was designed by Joan Martorell i Montells (1833–1906), Gaudí's architecture professor. The church was raised in 1878–85 with an adjacent convent; it was badly damaged in the civil war and is now used as a school. It offers hints of what was to come with Modernisme, with the use of brick, mosaics and sober stained glass.

Recinte Modernista de Sant Pau   Architecture
(☎93 553 78 01; www.santpaubarcelona.org; Carrer de Sant Antoni Maria Claret 167; adult/child €13/free; ⏱10am-6.30pm Mon-Sat, to 2.30pm Sun Apr-Oct, 10am-4.30pm Mon-Sat Nov-Mar; Ⓜ Sant Pau/Dos de Maig) Domènech i Montaner outdid himself as architect and philanthropist with the Modernista Hospital de la Santa Creu i de Sant Pau, redubbed in 2014 the 'Recinte Modernista'. It was long considered one of the city's most important hospitals. It has only recently been repurposed, its various spaces becoming cultural centres, offices and something of a monument. The complex, including 16 pavilions, is lavishly decorated and each pavilion is unique. Together with the Palau de la Música Catalana it is a World Heritage site.

Museu del Disseny de Barcelona   Museum
(☎93 256 68 00; www.museudeldisseny.cat; Plaça de les Glòries Catalanes 37; permanent/temporary exhibition €6/4.40, combination ticket €8; ⏱10am-8pm Tue-Sun; Ⓜ Glòries) Barcelona's design museum lies inside a new monolithic building with geometric facades and a rather brutalist appearance – which has already earned the nickname *la grapadora* (the stapler) by locals. Architecture aside, the museum houses a dazzling collection of ceramics, decorative arts and textiles, and is a must for anyone interested in the design world.

Detail from the Nativity Facade

135PIXELS/SHUTTERSTOCK ©

★ **Top Tip**

Audio guides – including some
tailored to children – are available for
an additional fee.

La Sagrada Família

A TIMELINE

1882 Construction begins on a neo-Gothic church designed by Francisco de Paula del Villar y Lozano.

1883 Antoni Gaudí takes over as chief architect and plans a far more ambitious church to hold 13,000 faithful.

1926 Gaudí dies; work continues under Domènec Sugrañes i Gras. Much of the **apse ❶** and **Nativity Facade ❷** is complete.

1930 Bell towers ❸ of the Nativity Facade completed.

1936 Construction is interrupted by Spanish Civil War; anarchists destroy Gaudí's plans.

1939–40 Architect Francesc de Paula Quintana i Vidal restores the crypt and meticulously reassembles many of Gaudí's lost models, some of which can be seen in the **museum ❹**.

1976 Passion Facade ❺ completed.

1986–2006 Sculptor Josep Subirachs adds sculptural details to the Passion Facade including the panels telling the story of Christ's last days, amid much criticism for employing a style far removed from what was thought typical of Gaudí.

2000 Central nave vault ❻ completed.

2010 Church completely roofed over; Pope Benedict XVI consecrates the church; work begins on a high-speed rail tunnel that will pass beneath the church's **Glory Facade ❼**.

2020s–40s Projected completion date.

TOP TIPS

➡ The best light through the stained-glass windows of the Passion Facade bursts into the heart of the church in the late afternoon.

➡ Visit at opening time on weekdays to avoid the worst of the crowds.

➡ Head up the Nativity Facade bell towers for the views, as long queues generally await at the Passion Facade towers.

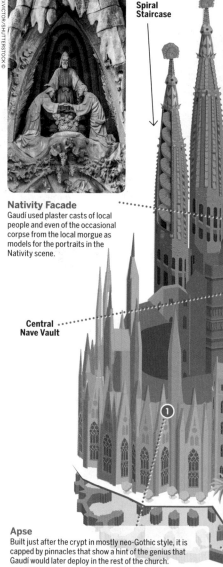

Spiral Staircase

Nativity Facade
Gaudí used plaster casts of local people and even of the occasional corpse from the local morgue as models for the portraits in the Nativity scene.

Central Nave Vault

Apse
Built just after the crypt in mostly neo-Gothic style, it is capped by pinnacles that show a hint of the genius that Gaudí would later deploy in the rest of the church.

Bell Towers
The towers of the three facades will represent the 12 Apostles. Eight are completed. Lifts whisk visitors up one tower of the Nativity and Passion Facades (the latter gets longer queues) for fine views.

NIKADA/GETTY IMAGES ©

Completed Church
Along with the Glory Facade and its four towers, six other towers remain to be completed. They will represent the four Evangelists, the Virgin Mary and, soaring above them all over the transept, a 170m colossus symbolising Christ.

Glory Facade
This will be the most fanciful facade of all, with a narthex boasting 16 hyperboloid lanterns topped by cones that will look something like an organ made of melting ice cream.

Museu Gaudí
Jammed with old photos, drawings and restored plaster models that bring Gaudí's ambitions to life, the museum also houses an extraordinarily complex plumb-line device he used to calculate his constructions.

Escoles de Gaudí

Crypt
The first completed part of the church, the crypt is in largely neo-Gothic style and lies under the transept. Gaudí's burial place here can be seen from the Museu Gaudí.

FOTOKON/SHUTTERSTOCK ©

Passion Facade
See the story of Christ's last days from Last Supper to burial in an S-shaped sequence from bottom to top of the facade. Check out the cryptogram in which the numbers always add up to 33, Christ's age at his death.

YURY DMITRIENKO/SHUTTERSTOCK ©

La Rambla

Barcelona's most famous street is both tourist magnet and window into Catalan culture, with arts centres, theatres and intriguing architecture. The middle is a broad pedestrian boulevard, crowded daily with a wide cross-section of society. A stroll here is pure sensory overload, with souvenir hawkers, buskers, pavement artists and living statues part of the ever-changing street scene.

Great For...

ℹ Need to Know

Map p250; Ⓜ Catalunya, Liceu, Drassanes
The Rambla stroll, from Plaça de Catalunya to Plaça del Portal de la Pau, is 1.5km.

★ **Top Tip**

Take an early morning stroll and another late at night to sample La Rambla's many moods.

History

La Rambla takes its name from a seasonal stream (derived from the Arabic word for sand, *raml*) that once ran here. From the early Middle Ages, it was better known as the Cagalell (Stream of Shit) and lay outside the city walls until the 14th century. Monastic buildings were then built and, subsequently, mansions of the well-to-do from the 16th to the early 19th centuries. Unofficially, La Rambla is divided into five sections, which explains why many know it as Las Ramblas.

La Rambla de Canaletes

The section of La Rambla north of Plaça de Catalunya is named after the **Font de Canaletes** (Map p250; M Catalunya), an inconspicuous turn-of-the-20th-century drinking fountain, the water of which supposedly emerges from what were once known as the springs of Canaletes. It used to be said that *barcelonins* 'drank the waters of Les Canaletes'. Nowadays people claim that anyone who drinks from the fountain will return to Barcelona, which is not such a bad prospect. Delirious football fans gather here to celebrate whenever the city's principal team, FC Barcelona, wins a cup or league title.

La Rambla dels Estudis

La Rambla dels Estudis, from Carrer de la Canuda running south to Carrer de la Portaferrissa, was formerly home to a twittering bird market, which closed in 2010 after 150 years in operation.

Església de Betlem

Just north of Carrer del Carme, this **church** (Map p250; J 93 318 38 23; www.mdbetlem.net;

Carrer d'en Xuclà 2; ⊙8.30am-1.30pm & 6-9pm; M Liceu) was constructed in baroque style for the Jesuits in the late 17th and early 18th centuries to replace an earlier church destroyed by fire in 1671. Fire was a bit of a theme for this site: the church was once considered the most splendid of Barcelona's few baroque offerings, but leftist arsonists torched it in 1936.

Palau Moja

Looming over the eastern side of La Rambla, **Palau Moja** (Map p250; ☎933 16 27 40; palaumoja.com; Carrer de Portaferrissa 1; ⊙info

> ### ⓘ Did You Know
> La Rambla saw plenty of action during the civil war. In *Homage to Catalonia*, George Orwell described the avenue gripped by revolutionary fervour.

MAURO BIGHIN/SHUTTERSTOCK ©

centre/shop 10am-9pm, cafe 9am-midnight Mon-Fri, 11am-midnight Sat & Sun; M Liceu) FREE is a neoclassical building dating from the second half of the 18th century. Its clean, classical lines are best appreciated from across La Rambla. Unfortunately, interior access is limited, as it houses mostly government offices.

La Rambla de Sant Josep

From Carrer de la Portaferrissa to Plaça de la Boqueria, La Rambla de Sant Josep (named after a 16th-century convent that was located there) is lined with flower stalls, which give it the alternative name La Rambla de les Flors.

Palau de la Virreina

The **Palau de la Virreina** (Map p250; La Rambla 99; M Liceu) is a grand 18th-century rococo mansion (with some neoclassical elements) that houses a municipal arts/entertainment information and ticket office run by the *ajuntament* (town hall). Built by Manuel d'Amat i de Junyent, the corrupt captain general of Chile (a Spanish colony that included the silver mines of Potosí), this is a rare example of postbaroque building in Barcelona. It's home to the **Centre de la Imatge** (Map p250; ☎93 316 10 00; www.ajuntament.barcelona.cat; Palau de la Virreina; ⊙noon-8pm Tue-Sun; M Liceu) FREE, which has rotating photography exhibits. Admission prices vary.

Mosaïc de Miró

At Plaça de la Boqueria, where four side streets meet just north of Liceu metro station, you can walk all over a Miró – the colourful **mosaic** (Map p250; Plaça de la Boqueria; M Liceu) in the pavement, with one tile signed by the artist. Miró chose this site

> ### ★ Local Knowledge
> While there are some decent eateries in the vicinity, the vast majority of cafes and restaurants along La Rambla are expensive, mediocre tourist traps.

as it's near the house where he was born on the Passatge del Crèdit. The mosaic's bold colours and vivid swirling forms are instantly recognisable to Miró fans, though plenty of tourists stroll right over it without realising.

La Rambla dels Caputxins

La Rambla dels Caputxins, named after a former monastery, runs from Plaça de la Boqueria to Carrer dels Escudellers. The latter street is named after the potters' guild, founded in the 13th century, the members of which lived and worked here. On the western side of La Rambla is the **Gran Teatre del Liceu** (p194; tour 45min/30min €9/6; ⊗45min tour hourly from 2pm-6pm Mon-Fri, from 9.30am Sat, 30min tour 1.30pm;); to the southeast is the entrance to the palm-shaded Plaça Reial. Below this point La Rambla gets seedier, with the occasional strip club and peep show.

La Rambla de Santa Mònica

The final stretch of La Rambla widens out to approach the Mirador de Colom overlooking Port Vell. La Rambla here is named after the Convent de Santa Mònica, which once stood on the western flank of the street and has since been converted into a cultural centre.

What's Nearby?
Església de
Santa Maria del Pi   Church
(Map p250; ☎93 318 47 43; www.basilicadelpi. com; Plaça del Pi; adult/concession/under 6yr €4/3/free; ⊗10am-6pm; MLiceu) This striking 14th-century church is a classic of Catalan Gothic, with an imposing facade, a wide interior and a single nave. The simple decor in the main sanctuary contrasts with the gilded chapels and exquisite stained-glass windows that bathe the interior in ethereal light. The beautiful rose window above its entrance is one of the world's largest. Occasional concerts are staged here (classical guitar, choral groups and chamber orchestras).

Plaça Reial   Square
(Map p250; MLiceu) One of the most photogenic squares in Barcelona, the Plaça Reial is a delightful retreat from the traffic and pedestrian mobs on the nearby Rambla. Numerous eateries, bars and nightspots lie beneath the arcades of 19th-century neoclassical buildings, with a buzz of activity at all hours.

Via Sepulcral
Romana   Archaeological Site
(Map p250; ☎93 256 21 00; www.museuhistoria. bcn.cat; Plaça de la Vila de Madrid; adult/concession/child €2/1.50/free; ⊗11am-2pm Tue & Thu, to 7pm Sat & Sun; MCatalunya) Along Carrer de la Canuda, a block east of the top end of La Rambla, there is a sunken garden where a series of Roman tombs lie exposed. A smallish display in Spanish and Catalan

by the tombs explores burial and funerary rites and customs. A few bits of pottery (including a burial amphora with the skeleton of a three-year-old Roman child) accompany the display.

Mirador de Colom   Viewpoint

(☎93 302 52 24; www.barcelonaturisme.com; Plaça del Portal de la Pau; adult/concession €6/4; ☺8.30am-8.30pm; ⓂDrassanes) High above the swirl of traffic on the roundabout below, Columbus keeps permanent watch, pointing vaguely out to the Mediterranean. Built for the Universal Exhibition in 1888, the monument allows you to zip up 60m in a lift for bird's-eye views back up La Rambla and across the ports of Barcelona.

Centre d'Art
Santa Mònica   Arts Centre

(Map p250; ☎93 567 11 10; artssantamonica. gencat.cat; La Rambla 7; ☺11am-9pm Tue-Sat, 11am-5pm Sun; ⓂDrassanes) **FREE** The Convent de Santa Mònica, which once stood on the western flank of the street, has since been converted into the Centre d'Art Santa Mònica, a cultural centre that mostly exhibits modern multimedia installations; admission is free.

☑ **Don't Miss**

Strolling the whole Rambla from end to end, keeping an eye on the architecture alongside.

★ **Top Tip**

Things have improved in recent years, but pickpockets still prey on head-in-air tourists along here.

KAVALENKAVA/SHUTTERSTOCK ©

Casa Batlló

One of the strangest residential buildings in Europe, this is Gaudí at his hallucinatory best. To some, Casa Batlló appears like a mythical creature, frozen in place. It has numerous intriguing design elements, both on the striking exterior and in the dreamlike, exuberant interior.

Great For...

❶ Need to Know

Map p254; ☎93 216 03 06; www.casabatllo. es; Passeig de Gràcia 43; adult/concession/ under 7yr €23.50/20.50/free; ☺9am-9pm, last admission 8pm; Ⓜ Passeig de Gràcia

The building is remarkable in every respect. The facade, sprinkled with bits of blue, mauve and green tiles and studded with wave-shaped window frames and balconies, rises to an uneven blue-tiled roof with a solitary tower. Casa Batlló and neighbouring Casa Amatller (p53) and Casa Lleó Morera (p53) were all renovated between 1898 and 1906; together, they demonstrate Modernisme's eclecticism.

Bones & Dragons

Locals know Casa Batlló variously as the *casa dels ossos* (house of bones) or *casa del drac* (house of the dragon). It's easy enough to see why. The balconies look like the bony jaws of some strange beast and the roof represents Sant Jordi (St George) and the dragon. Even the roof was built to represent the shape of an animal's back,

with shiny scales – the 'spine' changes colour as you walk around.

The Interior

When Gaudí was commissioned to refashion this building, he went to town inside and out. The internal light wells shimmer with tiles of deep sea blue. Gaudí eschewed the straight line, so the staircase wafts you up to the 1st (main) floor, where the salon looks on to Passeig de Gràcia. Everything swirls: the ceiling is twisted into a vortex around its sunlike lamp; the doors, window and skylights are dreamy waves of wood and coloured glass. The attic is characterised by Gaudí's trademark hyperboloid arches. Twisting, tiled chimney pots add a surreal touch to the roof.

Casa Batlló's Modernista roofline

Manzana de la Discordia

Despite the Catalanisation of most Barcelona street names since 1980, the Manzana de la Discordia is still known by its Spanish name to preserve a pun on *manzana*, which means 'block' and 'apple'. In Greek mythology, the original Apple of Discord was tossed onto Mt Olympus by Eris (Discord), with orders that it be given to the most beautiful goddess, sparking jealousies that were the catalyst for the Trojan War.

☑ Don't Miss

Before going inside, take a look at the pavement. Each paving piece carries stylised images of an octopus and a starfish, designs that Gaudí originally cooked up for Casa Batlló.

CATWALKER/SHUTTERSTOCK ©

What's Nearby?

Casa Amatller   Architecture

(Map p254; ☑93 461 74 60; www.amatller.org; Passeig de Gràcia 41; adult/child 6-12yr/under 6yr 1hr tour €17/8.50/free, 30min tour €14/7/free; ☺11am-6pm; Ⓜ Passeig de Gràcia) One of Puig i Cadafalch's most striking bits of Modernista fantasy, Casa Amatller combines Gothic window frames with a stepped gable borrowed from Dutch urban architecture. But the busts and reliefs of dragons, knights and other characters dripping off the main facade are pure caprice.

Casa Lleó Morera   Architecture

(Map p254; ☑93 676 27 33; www.casalleomorera.com; Passeig de Gràcia 35; guided tour adult/concession/under 12yr €15/13.50/free, express tour adult/under 12yr €12/free; ☺10am-1.30pm & 3-7pm Tue-Sun; Ⓜ Passeig de Gràcia) Domènech i Montaner's 1905 contribution to the Manzana de la Discordia, with Modernista carving outside and a bright, tiled lobby, is perhaps the least odd-looking of the three main buildings on the block. Since 2014 part of the building has been open to the public (by guided tour only – a one-hour tour in English at 11am and 'express' tours every 30 minutes), so you can appreciate the 1st floor, giddy with swirling sculptures, rich mosaics and whimsical decor.

Fundació Antoni Tàpies   Gallery

(Map p254; ☑93 487 03 15; www.fundaciotapies.org; Carrer d'Aragó 255; adult/concession €7/5.60; ☺10am-7pm Tue-Sun; Ⓜ Passeig de Gràcia) The Fundació Antoni Tàpies is both a pioneering Modernista building (completed in 1885) and the major collection of leading 20th-century Catalan artist Antoni Tàpies. A man known for his esoteric work, Tàpies died in February 2012, aged 88; he left behind a powerful range of paintings and a foundation intended to promote contemporary artists.

✕ Take A Break

Tapas 24 (p142), a modern basement tapas joint, opens all day.

ROMAN BABAKIN/SHUTTERSTOCK ©

Museu Nacional d'Art de Catalunya

From across Barcelona, the flamboyant neobaroque silhouette of the Palau Nacional can be seen on the slopes of Montjuïc. It houses a vast collection of mostly Catalan art.

Great For...

☑ Don't Miss

The fantastic assemblage of Romanesque frescoes from churches around Catalonia.

The Romanesque Masterpieces

The Romanesque art section is considered the most important concentration of early medieval art in the world. Rescued from neglected country churches across northern Catalonia in the early 20th century, the collection consists of 21 frescoes, woodcarvings and painted altar frontals (low-relief wooden panels that were the forerunners of the elaborate altarpieces that adorned later churches). The insides of several churches have been recreated and the frescoes – in some cases fragmentary, in others extraordinarily complete and alive with colour – have been placed as they were when in situ.

The first of the two most striking frescoes, in Sala 7, is a magnificent image of Christ in Majesty painted around 1123. Based on the text of the Apocalypse, we see Christ

ℹ Need to Know

MNAC; Map p256; ☎93 622 03 76; www.
museunacional.cat; Mirador del Palau
Nacional; adult/student/child €12/8.40/
free, after 3pm Sat & 1st Sun of month free;
⊙10am-8pm Tue-Sat, to 3pm Sun May-Sep, to
6pm Tue-Sat Oct-Apr; 🛜; Ⓜ Espanya

✕ Take a Break

On-site, there's a restaurant, cafeteria
and rooftop bar with great vistas.

★ Top Tip

The collection is huge, so just pick a
few sections and take your time.

The Gothic Collection

Opposite the Romanesque collection on
the ground floor is the museum's Gothic art
section. In these halls you can see Catalan
Gothic painting and works from other
Spanish and Mediterranean regions. Look
out especially for the work of Bernat Martorell in Sala 25 and Jaume Huguet in Sala
26. Among Martorell's works are images of
the martyrdom of St Vincent and St Llúcia.
Huguet's *Consagració de Sant Agustí,* in
which St Augustine is depicted as a bishop,
is dazzling in its detail.

The Cambó Bequest & the
Thyssen-Bornemisza Collection

As the Gothic collection draws to a close,
you pass through two separate and
equally eclectic private collections. The
Cambó Bequest, donated by Francesc
Cambó, spans the history of European
painting between the 14th century and
the beginning of the 19th century; the

enthroned with the world at his feet. He
holds a book open with the words *Ego Sum
Lux Mundi* (I am the Light of the World) and
is surrounded by the four evangelists. The
images were taken from the apse of the
Església de Sant Climent de Taüll in northwest Catalonia. Nearby in Sala 9 are frescoes painted around the same time in the
nearby Església de Santa Maria de Taüll. This
time the central image taken from the apse
is of the Virgin Mary and Christ Child. These
images were not mere decoration, but tools
of instruction in the basics of Christian faith
for the local population – try to set yourself
in the mind of the average medieval citizen:
illiterate, ignorant, fearful and in most cases
eking out a subsistence living. These images
transmitted the basic personalities and
tenets of the faith and were accepted at face
value by most.

Thyssen-Bornemisza Collection presents a selection of European painting and sculpture produced between the 13th and the 18th centuries, on loan to the MNAC by the Museo Thyssen-Bornemisza in Madrid. The Thyssen-Bornemisza Collection's highlight is Fra Angelico's *Madonna of Humility*, whereas the Cambó Bequest holds wonderful works by masters Veronese, Titian and Canaletto. Cranach, Titian, El Greco, Rubens and even Gainsborough also feature, but the collection's finale includes works by Francisco de Goya.

Modern Catalan Art

Up on the next floor, the collection turns to modern art, mainly but not exclusively Catalan. This collection is arranged thematically: Modernisme, Noucentisme, Art and the Civil War and so on. Among the many highlights: an early Salvador Dalí painting (*Portrait of My Father*), Juan Gris' collage-like paintings, the brilliant portraits of Marià Fortuny, and 1930s call-to-arms posters against the Francoist onslaught (nearby you'll find photos of soldiers and bombed-out city centres). There are works by Modernista painters Ramon Casas and Santiago Rusiñol, as well as Catalan luminary Antoni Tàpies.

The Fresco Strippers

Among the little known curiosities inside MNAC, you'll find a video (in Sala 3) depicting the techniques used by the 'Fresco Strippers' to preserve the great Romanesque works. The Stefanoni brothers, Italian art restorers, brought the secrets of *strappo* (stripping of frescoes from walls) to Catalonia in the early 1900s.

★ Top Tip

Within the modern art collection, look for items of Modernista furniture and decoration, which include a mural by Ramon Casas (the artist and Pere Romeu on a tandem bicycle). It once adorned the legendary bar and restaurant Els Quatre Gats (p134).

The Stefanoni would cover frescoes with a sheet of fabric, stuck on with a glue made of cartilage. When dry, this allowed the image to be stripped off the wall and rolled up. For three years the Stefanoni roamed the Pyrenean countryside, stripping churches and chapels and sending the rolls back to Barcelona, where they were eventually put back up on walls and inside purpose-built church apses to reflect how they had appeared in situ.

What's Nearby?

Museu d'Arqueologia de Catalunya   Museum

(MAC; Map p256; ☑93 423 21 49; www.mac. cat; Passeig de Santa Madrona 39-41; adult/ student €4.50/3.50; ☺9.30am-7pm Tue-Sat, 10am-2.30pm Sun; ⓂPoble Sec) This archaeology museum, housed in what was the

Poble Espanyol

Graphic Arts palace during the 1929 World Exhibition, covers Catalonia and cultures from elsewhere in Spain. Items range from copies of pre-Neanderthal skulls to lovely Carthaginian necklaces and jewel-studded Visigothic crosses.

Museu Etnològic　　Museum

(Map p256; www.museuetnologic.bcn.cat; Passeig de Santa Madrona 16-22; adult/child €5/3.50; ☉10am-7pm Tue-Sat, to 8pm Sun; ☐55) Barcelona's ethnology museum presents an intriguing permanent collection that delves into the rich heritage of Catalunya. Exhibits cover origin myths, religious festivals, folklore, and the blending of the sacred and the secular (along those lines, don't miss the Nativity scene with that quirky Catalan character *el caganer*, aka 'the crapper').

Poble Espanyol　　Cultural Centre

(Map p256; www.poble-espanyol.com; Avinguda de Francesc Ferrer i Guàrdia 13; adult/child €14/7; ☉9am-8pm Mon, to midnight Tue-Thu & Sun, to 3am Fri, to 4am Sat; ☐13, 23, 150, Ⓜ Espanya) Welcome to Spain! All of it! This 'Spanish Village' is both a cheesy souvenir hunters' haunt and an intriguing scrapbook of Spanish architecture built for the 1929 World Exhibition. You can meander from Andalucía to the Balearic Islands in the space of a couple of hours, visiting surprisingly good copies of Spain's characteristic buildings.

---

❶ Did You Know?

An emblematic building, the Palau Nacional was built for the 1929 World Exhibition and restored in 2005. The formidable collection of the gallery spans the early Middle Ages to the early 20th century.

Personnage, 1970, by Joan Miró

ALIONABIRUKOVA/SHUTTERSTOCK ©

Fundació Joan Miró

Joan Miró, the city's best-known 20th-century artistic progeny, bequeathed this art foundation to his home town in 1971. Its light-filled buildings are crammed with seminal works.

Great For...

☑ **Don't Miss**

The central highlights of the collection, Miró's masterworks in Rooms 18 and 19.

Sert's Temple to Miró's Art

Designed by Josep Lluís Sert, this shimmering white temple to one of Spain's artistic luminaries is considered one of the world's most outstanding museum buildings. The architect designed it after spending many of Franco's dictatorship years in the USA as the head of the School of Design at Harvard University. The foundation rests amid the greenery of the mountains and holds the greatest single collection of Miró's work, containing around 220 of his paintings, 180 sculptures, some textiles and more than 8000 drawings spanning his entire life. Only a small portion is ever on display.

The Collection

The exhibits give a broad impression of Miró's artistic development. The first

Fundació
Joan Miró

Jardins de
Laribal

Av de Miramar

Estació
Parc
Montjuïc

ℹ Need to Know

Map p256; 📞 93 443 94 70; www.fmirobcn. org; Parc de Montjuïc; adult/child €12/free; ⏱10am-8pm Tue-Wed & Fri, to 9pm Thu, to 3pm Sun Apr-Oct, shorter hours rest of the year; 🚗; 🚌55, 150, 🚇Paral·lel

✖ Take a Break

Pack a picnic and eat it in the shady sculpture garden.

★ Top Tip

The Articket Barcelona (www.articket bcn.org) gives entry to several major galleries and can be bought online.

couple of rooms (11 and 12) hold various works, including a giant tapestry in his trademark primary colours. Along the way, you'll pass *Mercury Fountain* by Alexander Calder, a rebuilt work that was originally made for the 1937 Paris Fair and represented Spain at the Spanish Republic's Pavilion. Room 13, a basement space called Espai 13, leads you downstairs to a small room for temporary exhibitions.

After Room 13, climb back up the stairs and descend to two other basement rooms, 14 and 15. Together labelled Homenatge a Joan Miró (Homage to Joan Miró), this space is dedicated to photos of the artist, a 15-minute video on his life and a series of works from some of his contemporaries, including Henry Moore, Antoni Tàpies, Eduardo Chillida, Yves Tanguy, Fernand Léger and others.

Returning to the main level, you'll find Room 16, the Sala Joan Prats, with works spanning the early years until 1919. Here, you can see how the young Miró moved away, under surrealist influence, from his relative realism (for instance his 1917 painting *Ermita de Sant Joan d'Horta*, with obvious Fauvist influences) toward his own unique style that uses primary colours and morphed shapes symbolising the moon, the female form and birds.

This theme is continued upstairs in Room 17, the Sala Pilar Juncosa (named after his wife), which covers the his surrealist years of 1932 to 1955. Rooms 18 and 19 contain masterworks of the years 1956 to 1983, and Room 20 a series of paintings done on paper. Room 21 hosts a selection of the private Katsuta collection of Miró works from 1914 to 1974. Room 22 rounds off the permanent exhibition with some major paintings and bronzes from the 1960s and '70s. The museum library contains Miró's personal book collection.

The Garden

Outside on the eastern flank of the museum is the Jardí de les Escultures, a small garden with various pieces of modern sculpture. The green areas surrounding the museum, together with the garden, are perfect for a picnic in the shade, after a hard day's sightseeing.

Take a Break

Enjoy a picnic in the shady sculpture garden, or head to the ornamental **Jardins de Mossèn Cinto de Verdaguer** (Map p256; www.bcn.cat/parcsijardins; ☺10am-sunset; ☐55, 150). These sloping, verdant gardens are home to various kinds of bulbs and aquatic plants.

What's Nearby?

Estadi Olímpic Lluís Companys   Stadium

(Map p256; ☎93 426 20 89; www.estadiolimpic.cat; Avinguda de l'Estadi; ☺8am-8pm May-Sep, 10am-6pm Oct-Apr; ☐150) **FREE** The Estadi Olímpic was the main stadium of Barcelona's Olympic Games. If you saw the Olympics on TV, the 65,000-capacity stadium may seem surprisingly small. So might the Olympic flame holder into which an archer spectacularly fired a flaming arrow during the opening ceremony. The stadium was opened in 1929 and restored for the 1992 Olympics.

Museu Olímpic i de l'Esport   Museum

(Map p256; ☎93 292 53 79; www.museuolimpic bcn.com; Avinguda de l'Estadi 60; adult/student

Castell de Montjuïc

€5.80/3.60; ⊙10am-8pm Tue-Sat, 10am-2.30pm Sun; ☐55, 150) The Museu Olímpic i de l'Esport is an information-packed interactive museum dedicated to the history of sport and the Olympic Games. Pick up tickets and wander down a ramp that snakes below ground level. It is lined with displays on the history of sport, starting with the ancients.

Jardins de Joan Maragall   Gardens

(Map p256; Avinguda dels Montanyans 48; ⊙10am-3pm Sat & Sun; Ⓜ Espanya) **FREE**
Near the Estadi Olímpic, make a detour to explore the lovely but little-visited Jardins de Joan Maragall. Lush lawns, ornamental

☑ **Don't Miss**
The central highlights of the collection, Miró's masterworks in Rooms 18 and 19.

SERGII ZINKO/SHUTTERSTOCK ©

fountains, photogenic sculptures and a neoclassical palace (the Spanish royal family's residence in Barcelona) set these gardens apart from the other green spaces on Montjuïc. The catch: the grounds are only open on weekends.

Jardí Botànic   Gardens

(Map p256; www.museuciencies.cat; Carrer del Doctor Font i Quer 2; adult/child €3.50/free, after 3pm Sun free; ⊙10am-7pm Apr-Sep, to 5pm Oct-Mar; ☐55, 150) This botanical garden is dedicated to Mediterranean flora and has a collection of some 40,000 plants and 1500 species that thrive in areas with a climate similar to that of the Mediterranean, such as the Eastern Mediterranean, Spain (including the Balearic and Canary Islands), North Africa, Australia, California, Chile and South Africa.

Castell de Montjuïc   Fortress

(Map p256; 📞93 256 44 45; www.bcn.cat/castelldemontjuic; Carretera de Montjuïc 66; adult/child €5/free, after 3pm Sun free; ⊙10am-8pm Apr-Oct, to 6pm Nov-Mar; ☐150, Telefèric de Montjuïc, Castell de Montjuïc) This forbidding *castell* (castle or fort) dominates the southeastern heights of Montjuïc and enjoys commanding views over the Mediterranean. It dates, in its present form, from the late 17th and 18th centuries. For most of its dark history, it has been used to watch over the city and as a political prison and killing ground.

Teleférico del Puerto   Cable Car

(Map p256; www.telefericodebarcelona.com; Av de Miramar, Jardins de Miramar; one way/return €11/16.50; ⊙11am-7pm Mar-Oct, to 5.30pm Nov-Feb; ☐50, 153) The quickest way from the beach to the mountain is via the cable car that runs between Torre de Sant Sebastiá in La Barceloneta and the Miramar stop on Montjuïc (from mid-June to mid-September only). From Estació Parc Montjuïc, the separate **Telefèric de Montjuïc** (Map p256; www.telefericdemontjuic.cat; Av de Miramar 30; adult/child one way €8/6.20; ⊙10am-9pm Jun-Sep, to 7pm Oct-May; ☐55, 150) cable car carries you to the Castell de Montjuïc via the *mirador* (lookout point).

Montjuïc

A ONE-DAY ITINERARY

Montjuïc, perhaps once the site of pre-Roman settlements, is today a hilltop green lung looking over city and sea. Interspersed across varied gardens are major art collections, a fortress, an Olympic stadium and more. A solid one-day itinerary can take in the key spots.

Alight at Espanya metro stop and make for ❶ **CaixaForum**, always host to three or four free top-class exhibitions. The nearby ❷ **Pavelló Mies van der Rohe** is an intriguing study in 1920s futurist housing by one of the 20th century's greatest architects. Uphill, the Romanesque art collection in the ❸ **Museu Nacional d'Art de Catalunya** is a must, and its restaurant is a pleasant lunch stop. Escalators lead further up the hill towards the ❹ **Estadi Olímpic**, scene of the 1992 Olympic Games. The road leads east to the ❺ **Fundació Joan Miró**, a shrine to the master surrealist's creativity. Contemplate ancient relics in the ❻ **Museu d'Arqueologia de Catalunya**, then have a break in the peaceful ❼ **Jardins de Mossèn Cinto Verdaguer**, the prettiest on the hill, before taking the cable car to the ❽ **Castell de Montjuïc**. If you pick the right day, you can round off with the gorgeously kitsch ❾ **La Font Màgica** sound and light show, followed by drinks and dancing in an open-air nightspot in ❿ **Poble Espanyol**.

CaixaForum
This former factory and barracks designed by Josep Puig i Cadafalch is an outstanding work of Modernista architecture; like a Lego fantasy in brick.

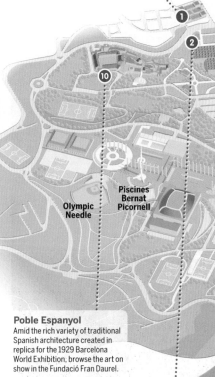

Piscines Bernat Picornell

Olympic Needle

Poble Espanyol
Amid the rich variety of traditional Spanish architecture created in replica for the 1929 Barcelona World Exhibition, browse the art on show in the Fundació Fran Daurel.

Pavelló Mies van der Rohe
Admire the inventiveness of the great German architect Ludwig Mies van der Rohe in this recreation of his avant garde German pavillion for the 1929 World Exhibition.

TOP TIPS

➤ Ride the Transbordador Aeri from Barceloneta for a bird's eye approach to Montjuïc. Or take the Teleféric de Montjuïc cable car to the Castell for more aerial views.

➤ The Castell de Montjuïc features outdoor summer cinema and concerts (see http://salamontjuic.org).

➤ Bursting with colour and serenity, the Jardins de Mossèn Cinto Verdaguer are exquisitely laid out with bulbs, especially tulips, and aquatic flowers.

La Font Màgica
Take a summer evening to behold the Magic Fountain come to life in a unique 15-minute sound and light performance, when the water glows like a cauldron of colour.

Museu Nacional d'Art de Catalunya
Make a beeline for the Romanesque art selection and the 12th-century polychrome image of Christ in majesty, which was recovered from the apse of a country chapel in northwest Catalonia.

Fundació Joan Miró
Take in some of Joan Miró's giant canvases, and discover little-known works from his early years in the Sala Joan Prats and Sala Pilar Juncosa.

9

3

Museu Etnològic

6

Teatre Grec

5

7

Museu Olímpic i de l'Esport

4

Estadi Olímpic

Jardí Botànic

8

Jardins de Mossèn Cinto Verdaguer

Museu d'Arqueologia de Catalunya
This archaeology museum, housed in what was the Graphic Arts palace during the 1929 World Exhibition, covers Catalonia and cultures from elsewhere in Spain. Items range from copies of pre-Neanderthal skulls to lovely Carthaginian necklaces and jewel-studded Visigothic crosses.

Castell de Montjuïc
Enjoy the sweeping views of the sea and city from atop this 17th-century fortress, once a political prison and long a symbol of oppression.

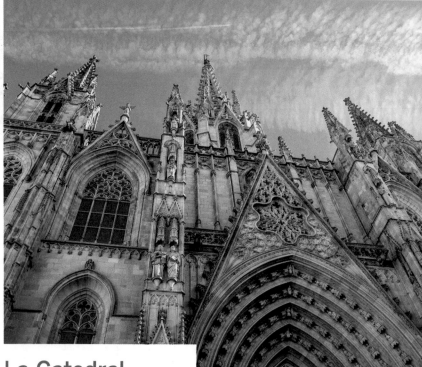

ALBERTO ZAMORANO/SHUTTERSTOCK ©

La Catedral

The richly decorated Gothic main facade of Barcelona's central place of worship, laced with gargoyles and stone intricacies, sets it quite apart from other churches in Barcelona.

Great For...

☑ Don't Miss

The *claustre* and its 13 geese, plus the views from the roof.

The key treasure of the Barri Gòtic, the cathedral was built between 1298 and 1460, though the facade was added in 1870.

The Interior

The interior is a broad, soaring space divided into a central nave and two aisles by lines of elegant, slim pillars. The cathedral was one of the few churches in Barcelona spared by the anarchists in the civil war, so its ornamentation, never overly lavish, is intact.

The Coro

In the middle of the central nave is the late-14th-century, exquisitely sculpted timber *coro* (choir stalls). The coats of arms on the stalls belong to members of the Barcelona chapter of the Order of the Golden Fleece. Emperor Carlos V presided over the order's meeting here in 1519.

Sculptures on the facade

CARLOS AMARILLO/SHUTTERSTOCK ©

Plaça d'Antoni Maura

Plaça de la Seu

Via Laietana

La Catedral

Ⓜ Jaume I

C de Jaume I

❶ Need to Know

Map p250; ☏ 93 342 82 62; www.catedralbcn. org; Plaça de la Seu; free, 'donation entrance' €7, choir €3, roof €3; ⏰ 8am-12.45pm & 5.15-7.30pm Mon-Fri, 8am-8pm Sat & Sun, entry by donation 1-5.30pm Mon, 1-5pm Sat, 2-5pm Sun; Ⓜ Jaume I

✕ Take a Break

For a special Japanese meal head to nearby Koy Shunka (p134).

★ Top Tip

If you want to see the lot, it's marginally cheaper entering between 1pm and 5pm.

Crypt

A broad staircase before the main altar leads you down to the crypt, which contains the tomb of Santa Eulàlia, one of Barcelona's two patron saints and more affectionately known as Laia. The reliefs on the alabaster sarcophagus recount some of her tortures and, along the top strip, the removal of her body to its present resting place.

Sant Crist de Lepant

In the first chapel on the right from the northwest entrance, the main Crucifixion figure above the altar is Sant Crist de Lepant. It is said Don Juan's flagship bore it into battle at Lepanto and that the figure acquired its odd stance by dodging an incoming cannonball. Left from the main entrance is the baptismal font where,

according to one story, six Native Americans brought to Europe by Columbus after his voyage of accidental discovery were bathed in holy water.

The Roof

For a bird's-eye view (mind the poo) of medieval Barcelona, visit the cathedral's roof and tower by taking the lift (€3) from the Capella de les Animes del Purgatori near the northeast transept.

The Claustre

From the southwest transept, exit by the partly Romanesque door (one of the few remnants of the present church's predecessor) to the leafy *claustre* (cloister), with its fountains and flock of 13 geese. The geese supposedly represent the age of Santa Eulàlia at the time of her martyrdom and have, generation after generation, been squawking here since medieval days. One of the cloister chapels commemorates 930 priests, monks and nuns killed during the civil war.

In the northwest corner of the cloister is the **Capella de Santa Llúcia** (Map p250; ☉8am-7.30pm Mon-Fri, to 8pm Sat & Sun; Ⓜ Jaume I) ᴳᴿᴱᴱ, one of the few reminders of Romanesque Barcelona (although the interior is largely Gothic).

Casa de l'Ardiaca

Upon exiting the Capella de Santa Llúcia, wander across the lane into the 16th-century **Casa de l'Ardiaca** (Arxiu Històric; Map p250; Carrer de Santa Llúcia 1; ☉9am-9pm Mon-Fri, 9am-2pm Sat; Ⓜ Jaume I) ᴳᴿᴱᴱ, which houses the city's archives. Stroll around the supremely serene courtyard, cooled by trees and a fountain; it was renovated by Lluís Domènech i Montaner in 1902, when the building was owned by the

lawyers' college. Domènech i Montaner also designed the postal slot, which is adorned with swallows and a tortoise, said to represent the swiftness of truth and the plodding pace of justice. You can get a good glimpse at a stout Roman wall in here. Upstairs, you can look down into the courtyard and across to La Catedral.

Palau Episcopal

Across Carrer del Bisbe is the 17th-century **Palau Episcopal** (Palau del Bisbat; Bishop's Palace; Map p250; Carrer del Bisbe; Ⓜ Jaume I). Virtually nothing remains of the original 13th-century structure. The Roman city's northwest gate was here and you can see the lower segments of the Roman towers that stood on either side of the gate at the base of the Palau Episcopal and Casa de l'Ardiaca. In fact, the lower part of the entire

Mailbox on the wall of Casa de l'Ardiaca

northwest wall of the Casa de l'Ardiaca is of Roman origin – you can also make out part of the first arch of a Roman aqueduct.

What's Nearby?

Temple Romà d'August   Ruins
(Map p250; ☎93 256 21 22; Carrer del Paradis 10; ⏱10am-2pm Mon, to 7pm Tue-Sat, to 8pm Sun; Ⓜ Jaume I) **FREE** Opposite the southeast end of La Catedral, narrow Carrer del Paradis leads towards Plaça de Sant Jaume. Inside No 10, an intriguing building with Gothic and baroque touches, are four columns and the architrave of Barcelona's main Roman temple, dedicated to Caesar Augustus and built to worship his imperial highness in the 1st century AD.

Museu Diocesà   Museum
(Casa de la Pia Almoina; Map p250; ☎93 315 22 13; www.gaudiexhibitioncenter.com; Plaça de la Seu 7; adult/concession/under 8yr €15/12/ free; ⏱10am-6pm Nov-Feb, to 8pm Mar-Oct; Ⓜ Jaume I) Next to the cathedral, the Diocesan Museum has a handful of exhibits on Gaudí (including a fascinating documentary on his life and philosophy) on the upper floors. There's also a sparse collection of medieval and Romanesque religious art, usually supplemented by a temporary exhibition or two.

Palau del Lloctinent   Historic Site
(Map p250; Carrer dels Comtes; ⏱10am-2pm & 4-8pm Mon-Sat; Ⓜ Jaume I) **FREE** This converted 16th-century palace has a peaceful courtyard worth wandering through. Have a look upwards from the main staircase to admire the extraordinary timber *artesonado*, a sculpted ceiling made to seem like the upturned hull of a boat. Temporary exhibitions, usually related in some way to the archives, are often held here.

Roman Walls   Ruins
(Map p250; Ⓜ Jaume I) From Plaça del Rei it's worth a detour to see the two best surviving stretches of Barcelona's Roman walls, which once boasted 78 towers (as much a matter of prestige as of defence). One section is on the southern side of Plaça de Ramon Berenguer el Gran, with the Capella Reial de Santa Àgata atop. The other is a little further south, by the northern end of Carrer del Sotstinent Navarro.

> ✕ **Take a Break**
> A short walk away, local favourite Cafè de l'Acadèmia (p133) serves great lunch specials and tasty traditional dishes at night.

LVIV/SHUTTERSTOCK ©

> ★ **Top Tip**
> Outside La Catedral there's always entertainment afoot, from *sardana* dancing (Catalonia's folk dance) on weekends to periodic processions and open-air markets; street musicians are never far from the scene.

Park Güell

Park Güell – north of Gràcia and about 4km from Plaça de Catalunya – is where Gaudí turned his hand to landscape gardening. It's a strange, enchanting place, where this iconic Modernista's passion for natural forms really took flight, to the point that the artificial almost seems more natural than the natural.

Great For...

❶ Need to Know

Map p254; ☏93 409 18 31; www.parkguell. cat; Carrer d'Olot 7; adult/child €8/6; ☺8am- 9.30pm May-Aug, to 8pm Sep-Apr; 🚌24, Ⓜ Lesseps, Vallcarca

★ **Top Tip**
Access to the central area is limited by numbers; it's wise to prebook online.

A City Park

Park Güell originated in 1900, when Count Eusebi Güell bought the tree-covered hillside of El Carmel (then outside Barcelona) and hired Gaudí to create a miniature city of houses for the wealthy, surrounded by landscaped grounds. The project was a commercial flop and was abandoned in 1914 – but not before Gaudí had created, in his inimitable manner, steps, a plaza, two gatehouses and 3km of roads and walks. In 1922 the city bought the estate for use as a public park. The park became a Unesco World Heritage site in 2004. The idea was based on the English 'garden cities' much admired by Güell – hence the spelling of 'Park'.

Just inside the main entrance on Carrer d'Olot, immediately recognisable by the two Hansel-and-Gretel gatehouses, is the park's newly refurbished Centre d'Interpretació, in the Pavelló de Consergeria, which is a typically curvaceous former porter's home that hosts a display on Gaudí's building methods and the history of the park. There are nice views from the top floor.

Sala Hipóstila

The steps up from the entrance, guarded by a mosaic dragon/lizard, lead to the Sala Hipóstila (aka the Doric Temple). This forest of 88 stone columns – some leaning like mighty trees bent by the weight of time – was originally intended as a market. To the left curves a gallery, the twisted stonework columns and roof of which give the effect of a cloister beneath tree roots – a motif repeated in several places in the park. On top of the Sala Hipóstila is a broad open space. Its centrepiece is the Banc de Trencadís, a tiled bench curving sinuously around

Gaudí's mosaic guard for the Sala Hipóstila

its perimeter, which was designed by one of Gaudí's closest colleagues, architect Josep Maria Jujol (1879–1949). With Gaudí, however, there is always more than meets the eye. This giant platform was designed as a kind of catchment area for rainwater washing down the hillside. The water is filtered through a layer of stone and sand, and it drains down through the columns to an underground cistern.

Casa-Museu Gaudí

The spired house above and to the right of the entrance is the **Casa-Museu Gaudí** (Map p254; www.casamuseugaudi.org; Park Güell; adult/student/child €5.50/4.50/free;

> ☑ **Don't Miss**
>
> The undulating tiled bench with views across the city.

LENA SERDITOVA/SHUTTERSTOCK ©

⊙9am-8pm Apr-Sep, 10am-6pm Oct-Mar; ☐24, 92, 116, Ⓜ Lesseps), where Gaudí lived for almost the last 20 years of his life (1906–26). It contains furniture he designed (including items that once lived in La Pedrera, Casa Batlló and Casa Calvet) along with other memorabilia. The house was built in 1904 by Francesc Berenguer i Mestres as a prototype for the 60 or so houses that were originally planned here.

Much of the park is still wooded, but it's laced with pathways. The best views are from the cross-topped Turó del Calvari in the southwest corner.

What's Nearby?

Gaudí Experience
Theatre

(Map p254; ☎93 285 44 40; www.gaudiexperi encia.com; Carrer de Larrard 41; adult/child €9/7.50; ⊙10.30am-7pm Apr-Sep, to 5pm Oct-Mar; ℗; Ⓜ Lesseps, Vallcarca) This fun-filled look at the life and work of Barcelona's favourite son is just a stone's throw from Park Güell. There are models of his buildings and interactive exhibits, but the highlight is the stomach-churning 4D presentation in its tiny screening room. Not recommended for the frail or children aged under six years.

Bunkers del Carmel
Viewpoint

(Map p254; Ⓜ El Carmel, then bus 86) For a magnificent view over the city that's well off the beaten path, head to the neighbourhood of El Carmel and make the ascent up the hill known as Turó de la Rovira to the Bunkers del Carmel viewpoint. Above the weeds and dusty hillside, you'll find the old concrete platforms that were once part of anti-aircraft battery during the Spanish Civil War (after the war it was a shanty town until the early 1990s and it has lain abandoned since then).

> ✗ **Take A Break**
>
> **Las Delicias** (Map p254; ☎93 429 22 02; www.barrestarantedelicias.com; Carrer de Mühlberg 1; tapas €6-14, mains €8-17; ⊙10am-4pm Tue-Sun & 7-10.30pm Tue-Thu, 8-11pm Fri & Sat; Ⓜ El Carmel, then bus 86), just east of the park, is a fine choice.

An FC Barcelona match

CHRISTIAN BERTRAND/SHUTTERSTOCK ©

Camp Nou

A pilgrimage site for football fans from around the world, Camp Nou, home to FC Barcelona, is one of the sport's most hallowed grounds.

Great For...

☑ Don't Miss

A live match, or if not, the museum's footage of the team's best goals.

Museum

The Camp Nou Experience begins in FC Barcelona's museum, which provides a high-tech view into the club. Massive touch-screens allow visitors to explore arcane aspects of the legendary team. You can also watch videos of particularly artful goals. Displays delve into the club's history, its social commitment and connection to Catalan identity, and in-depth stats of on-field action. Sound installations include the club's anthem and the match-day roar of the amped-up crowds.

You can admire the golden boots of celebrated goal scorers of the past and learn about the greats who have played for Barça over the years, including Maradona, Cruyff, Kubala and many others. There's a special area devoted to Lionel Messi,

❶ Need to Know

Camp Nou Experience (📞902 189900; www.fcbarcelona.com; Gate 9, Avinguda de Joan XXIII; adult/child €25/20; ⏱9.30am-7.30pm daily Apr-Sep, 10am-6.30pm Mon-Sat, to 2.30pm Sun Oct-Mar; ⓂPalau Reial)

✖ Take a Break

Just inside the gates (but outside the stadium) are a handful of open-air eating spots.

★ Top Tip

You can purchase tickets from vending machines at gate 9. No need to wait in line.

generally considered the world's greatest current footballer.

Stadium

The stadium, built in 1957 and enlarged for the 1982 World Cup, is one of the world's biggest, holding 99,000 people. The club has a world-record membership of 173,000.

The self-guided tour of the stadium takes in the team's dressing rooms, heads out through the tunnel onto the pitch and winds up in the presidential box. You'll also get to visit the television studio, the press room and the commentary boxes. Set aside about 2½ hours for the whole visit.

To make the tour, enter via Gate 9 (Avinguda de Joan XXIII near Carrer de Martí i Franquès).

Getting to a Game

Tickets to FC Barcelona matches are available at Camp Nou, online (through FC Barcelona's official website), and through various city locations. Tourist offices sell them – the branch at **Plaça de Catalunya** (Map p254; 📞93 285 38 34; www.barcelonaturisme.com; Plaça de Catalunya 17-S, underground; ⏱8.30am-9pm; ⓂCatalunya) is a centrally located option – as do FC Botiga stores. Tickets can cost anything from €39 to upwards of €250, depending on the seat and match. On match day the ticket windows (at gates 9 and 15) open from 9.15am until kick off. Tickets are not usually available for matches with Real Madrid.

You will almost definitely find scalpers lurking near the ticket windows. They are often club members and can sometimes get you in at a significant reduction. Don't pay until you are safely seated.

If you attend a game, go early so you'll have ample time to find your seat and soak up the atmosphere.

La Pedrera

This undulating beast is another madcap Gaudí masterpiece, built from 1905 to 1910 as a combined apartment and office block. Formally called Casa Milà after the businessman who commissioned it, it is better known as La Pedrera (the Quarry) because of its uneven grey stone facade, which ripples around the corner of Carrer de Provença.

Great For...

ⓘ Need to Know

Casa Milà; Map p254; ☎902 202138; www.lapedrera.com; Passeig de Gràcia 92; adult/concession/under 13yr/under 7yr €22/16.50/11/free; ☺9am-6.30pm & 7pm-9pm Mon-Sun; Ⓜ Diagonal

★ **Top Tip**
For a few extra euros, a 'Premium'
ticket means you don't have to queue.

History

Pere Milà had married the older – and far richer – Roser Guardiola, the widow of Josep Guardiola, and he clearly knew how to spend his new wife's money. When commissioned to design this apartment building, Gaudí wanted to top anything else done in L'Eixample. Milà was one of the city's first car owners and Gaudí built a parking space into the building, itself a first.

Top Floors

The Fundació Caixa Catalunya has opened the top-floor apartment, attic and roof, together called the Espai Gaudí (Gaudí Space), to visitors. The roof is the most extraordinary element, with its giant chimney pots looking like multicoloured medieval knights. Gaudí wanted to put a tall statue of the Virgin up here, too: when the Milà family said no, fearing it might make the building a target for anarchists, Gaudí resigned from the project in disgust.

One floor below the roof, where you can appreciate Gaudí's taste for parabolic arches, is a museum dedicated to his work.

Apartment

The next floor down is the apartment (El Pis de la Pedrera). It is fascinating to wander around this elegantly furnished home, done up in the style a well-to-do family might have enjoyed in the early 20th century. There are sensuous curves and unexpected touches in everything from light fittings to bedsteads, from door handles to balconies.

What's Nearby?

Casa de les Punxes   Architecture
(Casa Terrades; Map p254; ☏93 016 01 28; www.casadelespunxes.com; Avinguda Diagonal 420; ⊙9am-8pm; Ⓜ Diagonal) Puig i Cadafalch's Casa Terrades is better known as the Casa de les Punxes (House of Spikes) because

of its pointed turrets. This apartment block, completed in 1905, looks like a fairy-tale castle and has the singular attribute of being the only fully detached building in L'Eixample.

Palau del Baró Quadras   Architecture
(Map p254; ☏93 467 80 00; www.llull.cat; Avinguda Diagonal 373; ⊙8am-8pm Mon-Fri; Ⓜ Diagonal) ꜰꜱᴇᴇ Puig i Cadafalch designed Palau del Baró Quadras (built 1902–06) in an exuberant Gothic-inspired style. The main facade is the most intriguing, with a soaring, glassed-in gallery. Take a closer look at the gargoyles and reliefs – the pair of toothy fish and the sword-wielding knight clearly have the same artistic signature as that of the architect behind Casa Amatller. Decor inside is eclectic, but dominated by Middle Eastern and East Asian themes.

> ✗ **Take A Break**
> Stop by for a gourmet sandwich at Entrepanes Díaz (p142).

Museu Egipci   Museum

(Map p254; ☑93 488 01 88; www.museuegipci. com; Carrer de València 284; ☉10am-2pm & 4-8pm Mon-Fri, 10am-8pm Sat, to 2pm Sun; ⓂPasseig de Gràcia) Hotel magnate Jordi Clos has spent much of his life collecting ancient Egyptian artefacts, brought together in this private museum. It's divided into different thematic areas (the pharaoh, religion, funerary practices, mummification, crafts etc) and boasts an interesting variety of exhibits.

Església de la Puríssima Concepció i Assumpció de Nostra Senyora   Church

(Map p254; ☑93 457 65 52; www. parroquiaconcepciobcn.org; Carrer de Roger de Llúria 70; ☉7.30am-1pm & 5-9pm Mon-Fri, 7.30am-2pm & 5-9pm Sun; ⓂPasseig de Gràcia) One hardly expects to run into a medieval church on the grid-pattern streets of the late-19th-century city extension, yet that is just what this is. Transferred stone by stone from the old centre in 1871–88, this 14th-century church has a pretty 16th-century cloister with a peaceful garden.

Fundació Suñol   Gallery

(Map p254; ☑93 496 10 32; www.fundaciosunol. org; Passeig de Gràcia 98; ☉11am-2pm & 4-8pm Mon-Fri, 4-8pm Sat; ⓂDiagonal) Rotating exhibitions of portions of this private collection of mostly 20th-century art offer anything from Man Ray's photography to sculptures by Alberto Giacometti. Over two floors, you are most likely to run into Spanish artists (anyone from Picasso to Jaume Plensa), along with a sprinkling of international artists.

☑ **Don't Miss**
The marvellous roof.

Bar Hopping in El Born

If there's one place that distils Barcelona's enduring cool to its essence and captures all that's irresistible about this city, it has to be the tangle of streets that is El Born.

Great For...

☑ Don't Miss

Not all tapas are on view – look out for lists of hot tapas from the kitchen, they are often the best.

Passeig del Born

Most nights, and indeed most things, in El Born begin along the Passeig del Born, one of the prettiest little boulevards in Europe. It's a place to sit as much as to promenade. It's the graceful setting beneath the trees from which El Born's essential appeal is obvious – thronging people, brilliant bars and architecture that springs from a medieval film set.

Catalan Tapas

Push through the crowd, order a *cava* (sparkling wine) and an assortment of tapas at El Xampanyet (p178), one of the city's best-known *cava* bars, in business since 1929. Star dishes include tangy *boquerones en vinagre* (white anchovies in vinegar) and there's high-quality seafood served from a can in the Catalan way.

❶ Need to Know

Get the Metro to Jaume I and it's a short stroll into the heart of this barrio.

✖ Take a Break

Take a break from the decadent tapas-hopping by admiring the stern exterior of the Basílica de Santa Maria del Mar (p116).

★ Top Tip

For the best atmosphere, don't get here until at least 8pm.

Best of Basque

Having taken your first lesson in Barcelona-style tapas it's time to compare it with the *pintxos* (Basque tapas of food morsels perched atop pieces of bread) lined up along the bar at Euskal Etxea (p138), a real slice of San Sebastián.

Spain with a Twist

The detour to **Bar del Pla** (Map p250; ☎93 268 30 03; www.bardelpla.cat; Carrer de Montcada 2; mains €12-16; ⓢnoon-11pm Mon-Thu, to midnight Fri & Sat; Ⓜ Jaume I) on the northern limits of El Born is worth the walk. The tapas may look traditionally Spanish but a confident hand in the kitchen bestows deft touches of originality.

Tapas with Vistas

Back in the heart of El Born, in the shadow of Basílica de Santa Maria del Mar, pastry chef Carles Mampel operates **Bubó** (Map p250; ☎93 268 72 24; www.bubo.es; Carrer de les Caputxes 6 & 10; tapas from €5; ⓢ10am-9pm Mon-Thu & Sun, to 11pm Fri & Sat; Ⓜ Barceloneta). If you're not already sated, try the salted cod croquettes at one of the outdoor tables inching onto the lovely square.

Cal Pep

Boisterous Cal Pep (p139) is one of Barcelona's enduring stars. It can be difficult to snaffle a bar stool from which to order gourmet bar snacks such as *cloïsses amb pernil* (clams with ham); so if it's full, order a drink and wait. It's always worth it.

The Last Mojito

So many Barcelona nights end with a mojito, and El Born's biggest and best are to be found at **Cactus Bar** (☎93 310 63 54; www.cactusbar.cat; Passeig del Born 30; ⓢ3pm-3am; Ⓜ Jaume I). The outdoor tables next to Passeig del Born are the perfect way to wind down the night.

The cloister of the Palau Aguilar

Museu Picasso

Picasso's itchy feet and his extraordinary artistic output mean that his works fill several museums in Europe. Though his best-known works aren't here, the setting alone, in five contiguous medieval stone mansions, makes the Museu Picasso unique. The pretty courtyards, galleries and staircases preserved in these buildings are as delightful as the collection inside.

Great For...

❶ Need to Know

Map p250; ☎93 256 30 00; www.museupicasso.bcn.cat; Carrer de Montcada 15-23; adult/concession/child all collections €14/7.50/free, permanent collection €11/7/free, temporary exhibitions €4.50/3/free, 3-7pm Sun & 1st Sun of month free; ⊗9am-7pm Tue-Sun, to 9.30pm Thu; 🛜; Ⓜ Jaume I

★ Top Tip
Queues here can be very long; the people strolling to the front booked online. Be one of them.

The permanent collection is housed in Palau Aguilar, Palau del Baró de Castellet and Palau Meca, all dating to the 14th century. The 18th-century Casa Mauri, built over medieval remains (even some Roman leftovers have been identified), and the adjacent 14th-century Palau Finestres accommodate temporary exhibitions. The first three of these buildings are particularly splendid.

History of the Museum

Allegedly it was Picasso himself who proposed the museum's creation, to his friend and personal secretary Jaume Sabartés, a Barcelona native, in 1960. Three years later, the 'Sabartés Collection' was opened, since a museum bearing Picasso's name would have been met with censorship – Picasso's opposition to the Franco regime

was well known. The Museu Picasso we see today opened in 1983. It originally held only Sabartés' personal collection of Picasso's art and a handful of works hanging at the Barcelona Museum of Art, but the collection gradually expanded with donations from Salvador Dalí and Sebastià Junyer Vidal, among others; most artworks were bequeathed by Picasso himself. His widow, Jacqueline Roque, also donated 41 ceramic pieces and the *Woman With Bonnet* painting after Picasso's death.

Sabartés' contribution and years of service are honoured with an entire room devoted to him, including Picasso's famous Blue Period portrait of him wearing a ruff.

The Collection

This collection concentrates on the artist's formative years, yet there is enough

One of the museum's courtyards

material from subsequent periods to give you a thorough impression of the man's versatility and genius. Above all, you come away feeling that Picasso was the true original, always one step ahead of himself (and everyone else, of course) in his search for new forms of expression. The collection includes more than 3500 artworks, largely pre-1904, which is apt considering the artist spent his formative creative years in Barcelona.

It is important, however, not to expect a parade of his well-known works, or even works representative of his best-known periods. The holdings at the museum reflect Picasso's years in Barcelona and elsewhere in Spain, and what makes this collection truly impressive – and unique among the many Picasso museums around the world – is the way in which it displays his extraordinary talent at such a young age. Faced with the technical virtuosity of a painting such as *Ciència i Caritat* (*Science and Charity*), for example, it is almost inconceivable that such a work could have been created by the hands of a 15-year-old. Some of his self-portraits and the portraits of his parents, which date from 1896, are also evidence of his precocious talent.

Las Meninas through the Prism of Picasso

From 1954 to 1962 Picasso was obsessed with the idea of researching and 'rediscovering' the greats, in particular Velázquez. In 1957 he created a series of renditions of the latter's masterpiece *Las Meninas*, now displayed in rooms 12–14. It is as though Picasso has looked at the original Velázquez painting through a prism reflecting all the styles he had worked through until then, creating his own masterpiece in the process. This is a wonderful opportunity to see *Las Meninas* in its entirety, in this beautiful space.

Ceramics

What is also special about the Museu Picasso is its showcasing of his work in lesser-known mediums. The last rooms contain engravings and some 40 ceramic pieces completed throughout the latter years of his unceasingly creative life. You'll see plates and bowls decorated with simple, single-line drawings of fish, owls and other animal shapes, typical of Picasso's daubing on clay.

☑ **Don't Miss**

El Foll (*The Madman*) and *Retrato de la Tía Pepa* (*Portrait of Aunt Pepa*).

MAXISPORT/SHUTTERSTOCK ©

✗ **Take A Break**

Euskal Etxea (p138) is a formidably good spot for authentic Basque pintxos.

What's Nearby?

Parc de la Ciutadella — Park
(Map p250; Passeig de Picasso; ☺8am-9pm May-Sep, to 7pm Oct-Apr; Ⓜ Arc de Triomf) Come for a stroll, a picnic, a visit to the zoo or to inspect Catalonia's regional parliament, but don't miss a visit to this, the most central green lung in the city. Parc de la Ciutadella is perfect for winding down.

Museu de Cultures del Món — Museum
(☎93 256 23 00; museuculturesmon.bcn.cat; Carrer de Montcada 12; adult/concession/child €5/3.50/free, temporary exhibition €2.20/1.50/free, 3-8pm Sun & 1st Sun of month free; ☺10am-7pm Tue-Sat, to 8pm Sun; ☏; Ⓜ Jaume I) The Palau Nadal and the Palau Marquès de Lliò reopened in 2015 as the site of the Museum of World Cultures. Exhibits from private and public collections, including many from the Museu Etnològic on Montjuïc, take the visitor on a trip through ancient cultures. There's a combined ticket with Museu Egipci (p77) and the Museu Etnològic (p57) for €12.

Castell dels Tres Dragons — Architecture
(Ⓜ Arc de Triomf) The Passeig de Picasso side of the Parc de la Ciutadella is lined by several buildings constructed for the Universal Exhibition of 1888. The medieval-looking caprice at the top end is the most engaging. Known as the Castell dels Tres Dragons (Castle of the Three Dragons), it long housed the Museu de Zoologia, which has since been transferred to the Fòrum area.

Espai Santa Caterina — Archaeological Site
(☎93 256 21 22; www.museuhistoria.bcn.cat; Carrer de Joan Capri; ☺7.30am-3.30pm Mon-Sat; Ⓜ Jaume I) **FREE** The Mercat de Santa Caterina's 1848 predecessor was built over the remains of the demolished 15th-century Gothic Monestir de Santa Caterina, a powerful Dominican monastery. A small section of the church foundations is glassed over in one corner as an archaeological reminder (with explanatory panels) – the Espai Santa Caterina.

Born Centre de Cultura i Memòria — Historic Building
(Map p250; ☎93 256 68 51; elbornculturaimemoria.barcelona.cat; Plaça Comercial 12; centre free, exhibition spaces adult/concession/child €4.40/3/free; ☺10am-8pm Tue-Sun Mar-Oct, 10am-7pm Tue-Sat, to 8pm Sun Nov-Feb; Ⓜ Barceloneta) Launched to great fanfare in 2013, as part of the events held for the tercentenary of the Catalan defeat in the War of the Spanish Succession, this cultural space is housed in the former Mercat del Born, a handsome 19th-century structure of slatted iron and brick. Excavation in 2001 unearthed remains of whole streets flattened to make way for the much-hated citadel (*ciutadella*) – these are now on show on the exposed subterranean level.

Carrer de Montcada — Street
(Map p250; Ⓜ Jaume I) An early example of town planning, this medieval high street was driven towards the sea from the road that in the 12th century led northeast from the city walls. It was the city's most coveted address for the merchant classes. The bulk of the great mansions that remain today mostly date to the 14th and 15th centuries.

Fundació Gaspar — Gallery
(Map p250; ☎93 887 42 48; www.fundaciogaspar.org; Carrer de Montcada 25; adult/concession/under 12yr €5/3/free; ☺10am-8pm Tue-Sun, to 9.30pm Sat; ☏; Ⓜ Jaume I) Set in a stunning Gothic palazzo next to the Museu Picasso, the Fundació Gaspar opened in November 2015 with the intention of complementing the works of other galleries and museums around town by bringing contemporary artists who have yet to exhibit here or whose work explores new concepts and styles.

ⓘ Annual Pass

Though ostensibly aimed at residents, the Museu Picasso Card, valid for 12 months, is also available to visitors on presentation of ID. It's cheaper than a day pass.

Castell dels Tres Dragons

VENIAMIN KRASKOV/SHUTTERSTOCK ©

❶ Did You Know?

Picasso's full name: Pablo Diego José Francisco de Paula Juan Nepomuceno María de los Remedios Cipriano de la Santísima Trinidad Ruiz y Picasso.

Walking Tour: Barri Gòtic

This scenic walk through the Barri Gòtic will take you back in time, from the early days of Roman-era Barcino through to the medieval era.

Start: La Catedral
Distance: 1.5km
Duration: 1½ hours

Classic Photo: Stop 1 La Catedral

1 Before entering the cathedral, look at three Picasso friezes on the building facing the square. Next, wander through the magnificence of **La Catedral** (p64).

PERESANZ/SHUTTERSTOCK ©

2 Pass through the city gates; turn right into **Plaça de Sant Felip Neri**. The shrapnel-scarred church was damaged by pro-Franco bombers in 1939.

3 Head west to the looming 14th-century **Església de Santa Maria del Pi** (p48), famed for its magnificent rose window.

IAKOV FILIMONOV/SHUTTERSTOCK ©

C d'en Roca
C del Petritxol
Plaça del Pi
Plaça de St Josep Oriol
La Rambla de Sant Josep
C del Cardenal Cassañas
La Rambla
Plaça de Sant Josep Oriol **3**
C de la Boqueria
C d'en Quintana
Plaça de la Boqueria
M Liceu
C d'en Aroles
C de Sant Pau
La Rambla dels Caputxins
C de la Unió

4 Follow the curving road to pretty **Plaça Reial** (p48). Flanking the fountain are Gaudí-designed lamp posts.

ENGINEERVOSHKIN/SHUTTERSTOCK ©

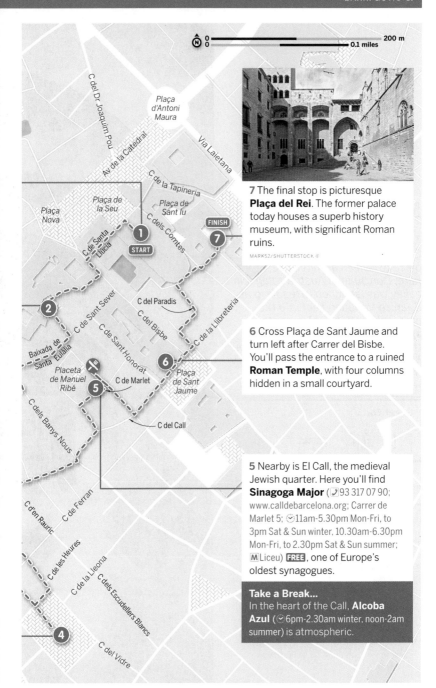

Plaça d'Antoni Maura

C del Dr Joaquín Pou

Av. de la Catedral

Via Laietana

C de la Tapineria

Plaça Nova

Plaça de la Seu

Plaça de Sant Iu

C dels Comtes

FINISH

7 The final stop is picturesque **Plaça del Rei**. The former palace today houses a superb history museum, with significant Roman ruins.

MARK52/SHUTTERSTOCK ©

START

C de Santa Llúcia

1

2

C del Paradís

C de Sant Sever

C del Bisbe

C de la Llibreteria

Baixada de Santa Eulàlia

C de Sant Honorat

6

Placeta de Manuel Ribé

C de Marlet

Plaça de Sant Jaume

5

C del Call

C dels Banys Nous

6 Cross Plaça de Sant Jaume and turn left after Carrer del Bisbe. You'll pass the entrance to a ruined **Roman Temple**, with four columns hidden in a small courtyard.

C d'en Rauric

C de Ferran

C de les Heures

C de la Lleona

C dels Escudellers Blancs

4

C del Vidre

5 Nearby is El Call, the medieval Jewish quarter. Here you'll find **Sinagoga Major** (📞 93 317 07 90; www.calldebarcelona.org; Carrer de Marlet 5; ⏰ 11am-5.30pm Mon-Fri, to 3pm Sat & Sun winter, 10.30am-6.30pm Mon-Fri, to 2.30pm Sat & Sun summer; Ⓜ Liceu **FREE**, one of Europe's oldest synagogues.

Take a Break...
In the heart of the Call, **Alcoba Azul** (⏰ 6pm-2.30am winter, noon-2am summer) is atmospheric.

Replica of Don Juan of Austria's flagship

Museu Marítim

The mighty Reials Drassanes (Royal Shipyards) are an extraordinary piece of civilian architecture. From here, Don Juan of Austria's flagship galley was launched to lead a joint Spanish-Venetian fleet into the momentous Battle of Lepanto against the Turks in 1571. Today, the broad arches shelter the Museu Marítim, the city's seafaring-history museum and one of Barcelona's most intriguing institutions.

Great For...

❶ Need to Know

☎93 342 99 20; www.mmb.cat; Avinguda de les Drassanes; adult/child €5/2.50, 3-8pm Sun free; ☉10am-8pm; 📶; Ⓜ Drassanes

★ **Top Tip**

With your museum ticket, visit the **Pailebot de Santa Eulàlia** (www.mmb. cat; Moll de la Fusta; adult/child €3/free; ⏱10am-8.30pm Tue-Fri & Sun, 2-8.30pm Sat; Ⓜ Drassanes), **docked nearby.**

Royal Shipyards

The shipyards were, in their heyday, among the greatest in Europe. Begun in the 13th century and completed by 1378, the long, arched bays (the highest arches reach 13m) once sloped off as slipways directly into the water, which lapped the seaward side of the Drassanes until at least the end of the 18th century. Shipbuilding was later moved to southern Spain and the Drassanes became a barracks for artillery.

Replica of Don Juan of Austria's Flagship

The centre of the shipyards is dominated by a full-sized replica of Don Juan of Austria's flagship. A clever audiovisual display aboard the vessel brings to life the ghastly existence of the slaves, prisoners and volunteers (!)

who, at full steam, could haul this vessel along at 9 knots. They remained chained to their seats, four to an oar, at all times. Here they worked, drank (fresh water was stored below decks, where the infirmary was also located), ate, slept and went to the loo. You could smell a galley like this from miles away.

Exhibitions

Fishing vessels, old navigation charts, models and dioramas of the Barcelona waterfront make up the rest of this engaging museum. Temporary exhibitions are also held. The museum, which has seen major renovations in recent years, is scheduled to finally reopen in its entirety by early 2017. When it reopens, visitors will encounter a greatly expanded collection with multimedia exhibits evoking more of Spain's epic history on the high seas.

Inside L'Aquàrium

Ictíneo

In the courtyard, you can have a look at a swollen replica of the *Ictíneo*, one of the world's first submarines. It was invented and built in 1858 by Catalan polymath Narcis Monturiol and was operated by hand-cranked propellers turned by friends of Monturiol who accompanied him on dozens of successful short dives in the harbour. He later developed an even larger submarine powered by a combustion engine that allowed it to dive to 30m and remain submerged for seven hours. Despite impressive demonstrations to awestruck crowds he never attracted the interest of the navy and remains largely forgotten today.

☑ Don't Miss
The replica of Don Juan of Austria's flagship.

SHILER/SHUTTERSTOCK ©

What's Nearby?

L'Aquàrium
Aquarium

(Map p250; ☎93 221 74 74; www.aquariumbcn. com; Moll d'Espanya; adult/child €20/15, dive €300; ⏰9.30am-11pm Jul & Aug, to 9pm Sep-Jun; Ⓜ Drassanes) It is hard not to shudder at the sight of a shark gliding above you, displaying its toothy, wide-mouthed grin. But this, the 80m shark tunnel, is the highlight of one of Europe's largest aquariums. It has the world's best Mediterranean collection and plenty of colourful fish from as far off as the Red Sea, the Caribbean and the Great Barrier Reef. All up, some 11,000 fish (including a dozen sharks) of 450 species reside here.

Museu d'Història de Catalunya
Museum

(Museum of Catalonian History; Map p250; ☎93 225 47 00; www.mhcat.net; Plaça de Pau Vila 3; adult/child €4.50/3.50, last Tue of the month Oct-Jun free; ⏰10am-7pm Tue & Thu-Sat, to 8pm Wed, to 2.30pm Sun; Ⓜ Barceloneta) Inside the Palau de Mar, this worthwhile museum takes you from the Stone Age through to the early 1980s. It is a busy hotchpotch of dioramas, artefacts, videos, models, documents and interactive bits: all up, an entertaining exploration of 2000 years of Catalan history. Signage is in Catalan/Spanish.

Passeig Marítim de la Barceloneta
Waterfront

(Ⓜ Barceloneta, Ciutadella Vila Olímpica) On La Barceloneta's seaward side are the first of Barcelona's **beaches**, which are popular on summer weekends. The pleasant Passeig Marítim de la Barceloneta, a 1.25km promenade from La Barceloneta to Port Olímpic, is a haunt for strollers and runners, with cyclists zipping by on a separate path nearby.

✗ Take a Break
The pleasant museum cafe offers courtyard seating, set lunches and a small assortment of bites.

AUGUSTCINDY/SHUTTERSTOCK ©

Palau Güell

This extraordinary neo-Gothic mansion, one of few major buildings of that era raised in the old city, is a magnificent example of the early days of Gaudí's fevered architectural imagination.

Great For...

☑ Don't Miss

The music room, the basement stables and the tiled chimney pots.

Gaudí & Güell

Gaudí built the palace just off La Rambla in the late 1880s for his wealthy and faithful patron, the industrialist Eusebi Güell, without whose support it is unlikely he'd have left a fraction of the creative legacy that is now so celebrated, but at the time was viewed with deep suspicion by much of Catalan society. Although a little sombre compared with some of his later whims, the Palau is still a characteristic riot of styles and materials. After the civil war the police occupied it and tortured political prisoners in the basement. The building was then abandoned, leading to its long-term disrepair. It finally reopened in 2012 after lengthy renovations.

The Building

The tour begins on the ground floor, which
was once the coach house, and from there
moves down to the basement, with squat
mushroom-shaped brick pillars; this is
where horses were stabled. Back upstairs
admire the elaborate wrought iron of the
main doors from the splendid vestibule
and the grand staircase lined with sand-
stone columns. Up another floor are the
main hall and its annexes; check out the
rosewood coffered ceilings and the gallery
behind trelliswork, from where the family
could spy on their guests as they arrived.
Central to the structure is the magnificent
music room with a rebuilt organ played
during opening hours; the choir would sing
from the mezzanine up on the other side.
Alongside the alcove containing the organ
is another that opened out to become the

family chapel, with booths to seat nobility
and, above them, the servants. The main
hall is a parabolic pyramid – each wall an
arch stretching up three floors and coming
together to form a dome, giving a magnificent sense of space in what is a surprisingly narrow building, constructed on a site
of just 500 sq m.

Above the main floor are the family
rooms, which are sometimes labyrin-
thine and dotted with piercings of light or
grand, stained-glass windows. The bright,
diaphanous attic used to house the servants' quarters, but now houses a detailed
exhibition on the history and renovation
of the building. The roof is a tumult of tiled
mosaics and fanciful chimney pots. The
audio guide (included) is worth getting
not only for the detailed description of
the architecture, but also for the pieces of
music and its photographic illustrations of
the Güell family's life.

Mercat de la Boqueria

One of the greatest sound, smell and colour sensations is Barcelona's central produce market, the Mercat de la Boqueria, slap bang on the Rambla, but still used by locals.

Great For...

☑ Don't Miss

Picking up fresh produce for a beach picnic.

The vibrant market spills over with all the rich and varied colour of fruit and vegetable stands, seemingly limitless varieties of sea critters, sausages, cheeses, meat (including the finest Jabugo ham) and sweets.

The Historic Market

Some chronicles place a market here as early as 1217. As much as it has become a modern-day attraction, this has always been the place where locals come to shop.

Between the 15th and 18th centuries a pig market known as Mercat de la Palla (Straw Market) stood here; it was considered part of a bigger market extending to Plaça del Pi. What we now know as La Boqueria didn't come to exist until the 19th century, when the local authorities decided to build a structure that would house fishmongers and butchers, as well as fruit and

BORJA LARIA/SHUTTERSTOCK ©

⊙ Need to Know

Map p250; ☑93 412 13 15; www.boqueria.
info; La Rambla 91; ⊘8am-8.30pm Mon-Sat;
Ⓜ Liceu

✕ Take a Break

Take your pick from one of the many
eateries dotted through the market.

★ Top Tip

Stallholders aren't here for tourists:
give way to purchasers and ask per-
mission for photos.

vegetable sellers. The iron Modernista gate
was constructed in 1914.

Many of Barcelona's top restaurateurs
buy their produce here, although it's no
easy task getting past the crowds of tourists
to snare a slippery slab of sole or a tempting
piece of *queso de cabra* (goat's cheese).

What to Try?

La Boqueria is dotted with unassuming
places to eat, and eat well, with stallholders
opening up at lunchtime. Whether you eat
here or you're self-catering, it's worth trying
some of Catalonia's gastronomic specialities, such as *bacallà salat* (dried salted cod),
which usually comes in an *esqueixada*, a
tomato, onion and black olive salad with
frisée lettuce; *calçots* (a cross between a
leek and an onion), which are chargrilled
and the insides eaten as a messy whole;

cargols (snails), a Catalan staple that is best
eaten baked as *cargols a la llauna*; *peus de
porc* (pig's trotters), which are often stewed
with snails; or *percebes* (goose-necked
barnacles). Much loved across Spain, these
crustaceans look like witches' fingers and
are eaten with a garlic and parsley sauce.

What's Nearby?

Antic Hospital
de la Santa Creu   Historic Building
(Former Hospital of the Holy Cross; Map p249;
☑93 270 16 21; www.bcn.cat; Carrer de l'Hospital
56; ⊘9am-8pm Mon-Fri, to 2pm Sat; Ⓜ Liceu)
Behind La Boqueria stands what was
once the city's main hospital. Begun in
1401, it functioned until the 1930s and was
considered one of the best in Europe in its
medieval heyday. It is the place where Antoni
Gaudí died in 1926. Today it houses the
Biblioteca de Catalunya (National Library
of Catalonia) and the **Institut d'Estudis
Catalans** (Institute for Catalan Studies).
The hospital's Gothic chapel, **La Capella**
(☑93 256 20 44; www.bcn.cat/lacapella; ⊘noon-
8pm Tue-Sat, 11am-2pm Sun & holidays) shows
temporary exhibitions.

MACBA

Designed by Richard Meier and opened in 1995, MACBA (Museu d'Art Contemporani de Barcelona) has become the city's foremost contemporary art centre, with captivating exhibitions for the serious art lover.

The ground and 1st floors of this great white bastion of contemporary art are generally given over to exhibitions from the gallery's own collections. There are some 3000 pieces centred on three periods: post-WWII; around 1968; and the years since the fall of the Berlin Wall in 1989, right up until the present day.

The Permanent Collection

The permanent collection is on the ground floor and dedicates itself to Spanish and Catalan art from the second half of the 20th century, with works by Antoni Tàpies, Joan Brossa and Miquel Barceló, among others, though international artists, such as Paul Klee, Bruce Nauman and John Cage, are also represented.

The gallery, across two floors, is dedicated to temporary visiting exhibitions that are

Great For...

☑ Don't Miss

The permanent collection dedicated to 20th-century Spanish and Catalan art.

🛈 Need to Know

Museu d'Art Contemporani de Barcelona; Map p249; ☑93 481 33 68; www.macba.cat; Plaça dels Àngels 1; adult/concession/under 12yr €10/8/free; ⏱11am-7.30pm Mon & Wed-Fri, 10am-9pm Sat, 10am-3pm Sun & holidays; Ⓜ Universitat

✕ Take a Break

Stop in for tacos and homemade ginger beer at Caravelle (p137).

★ Top Tip

Before visiting, check the website for events that might coincide.

almost always challenging and intriguing. MACBA's 'philosophy' is to do away with the old model of a museum where an artwork is a spectacle and to create a space where art can be viewed critically, so the exhibitions are usually tied in with talks and events. This is food for the brain as well as the eyes.

Capella Macba

Across the square in front, where the city's skateboarders gather, the renovated 400-year-old Convent dels Àngels houses the Capella MACBA, where MACBA regularly rotates selections from its permanent collection. The Gothic framework of the one-time convent-church remains intact.

Fringe Attractions

The library and auditorium stage regular concerts, talks and events, all of which are either reasonably priced or free. The extensive art bookshop is fantastic for stocking up on art and art theory books, as well as quirky gifts and small design objects.

What's Nearby?

Centre de Cultura Contemporània de Barcelona
Notable Building

(CCCB; Map p249; ☑93 306 41 00; www.cccb. org; Carrer de Montalegre 5; adult/concession/ under 12yr for 1 exhibition €6/4/free, 2 exhibitions €8/6/free, Sun 3-8pm free; ⏱11am-8pm Tue-Sun; Ⓜ Universitat) A complex of auditoriums, exhibition spaces and conference halls opened here in 1994 in what had been an 18th-century hospice, the Casa de la Caritat. The courtyard, with a vast glass wall on one side, is spectacular. With 4500 sq metres of exhibition space in four separate areas, the centre hosts a constantly changing program of exhibitions, film cycles and other events.

Museu-Monestir de Pedralbes

This peaceful old monastery is now a museum of monastic life; it's full of architectural treasures and provides a fascinating glimpse into centuries past. Perched at the top of busy Avinguda de Pedralbes in what was once unpeopled countryside, the museum remains a divinely quiet corner of Barcelona. The heart of the former monastery is the cloister, an excellent example of Catalan Gothic.

Great For...

❶ Need to Know

📞93 256 34 34; monestirpedralbes.bcn. cat; Baixada del Monestir 9; adult/child €5/ free, 3-8pm Sun free; ⏱10am-5pm Tue-Fri, to 7pm Sat, to 8pm Sun; 🚌22, 63, 64, 75, 🚉FGC Reina Elisenda

★ **Top Tip**

To make the most of your visit, be sure to pick up an audio guide, which gives crucial historical details.

The Cloister & Chapel

The large, elegant cloister is a jewel of Catalan Gothic, built in the early 14th century. Following its course to the right, stop at the first chapel, the Capella de Sant Miquel, and see murals done in 1346 by Ferrer Bassá, one of Catalonia's earliest documented painters. A few steps on is the ornamental grave of Queen Elisenda, who founded the convent. It is curious, as it is divided in two: the side in the cloister shows her dressed as a penitent widow, while the other part, an alabaster masterpiece inside the adjacent church, shows her dressed as queen.

The Refectory & Sleeping Quarters

As you head around the ground floor of the cloister, you can peer into the restored

refectory, kitchen, stables, stores and a reconstruction of the infirmary – all giving a good idea of convent life. Eating in the refectory must not have been a whole lot of fun, judging by the inscriptions around the walls exhorting *Silentium* (Silence) and *Audi Tacens* (Listen and Keep Quiet).

Upstairs is a grand hall that was once the *dormidor* (sleeping quarters). It was lined by tiny night cells, but they were long ago removed. Today this space is graced by a modest collection of the monastery's art, especially Gothic devotional works, and furniture.

Parc de l'Orenata

A little-visited park lies just behind the Museu-Monestir de Pedralbes. Set amid woodlands, the compact oak- and pine-filled Parc de l'Orenata has fine lookouts and the

Giant tree display at CosmoCaixa

ruins of an old castle. On weekends, families arrive for pony rides and short rides on a mini locomotive. To get there, take the stairs leading past the monastery and continue uphill along Carrer de Montevideo.

What's Nearby?

CosmoCaixa Museum

(Museu de la Ciència; 📞93 212 60 50; www. fundacio.lacaixa.es; Carrer d'Isaac Newton 26; adult/child €4/free; 🕙10am-8pm Tue-Sun; 🚌60, 🚊FGC Avinguda Tibidabo) Kids (and kids at heart) are fascinated by displays here and this science museum remains one of the city's most popular attractions. The

---

☑ **Don't Miss**

Ferrer Bassá's murals, the three-storey Gothic cloister or the refectory's admonishing inscriptions.

JUAN AUNION/SHUTTERSTOCK ©

highlight is the re-creation of over 1 sq km of flooded **Amazon** rainforest (Bosc Inundat). More than 100 species of Amazon flora and fauna (including anacondas, colourful poisonous frogs, and caimans) prosper in this unique, living diorama in which you can even experience a tropical downpour.

In another original section, the Mur Geològic, seven great chunks of rock (90 metric tons in all) have been assembled to create a **Geological Wall**.

These and other displays on the lower 5th floor (the bulk of the museum is underground) cover many fascinating areas of science, from fossils to physics and from the alphabet to outer space. To gain access to other special sections, such as the **Planetari** (Planetarium), check for guided visits. Most of these activities are inter-active and directed at children, and cost €4. The planetarium has been adapted so that people with visual and hearing impairments may also enjoy it.

Outside, there's a nice stroll through the extensive Plaça de la Ciència, whose modest garden flourishes with Mediterranean flora.

Tibidabo Mountain

(🚋T2A) Framing the north end of the city, the forest-covered mountain of Tibidabo, which tops out at 512m, is the highest peak in Serra de Collserola. Aside from the superb views from the top, the highlights of Tibidabo include the 8000-hectare **Parc del Collserola**, a telecommunications tower with a viewing platform, an old-fashioned amusement park and a looming church that's visible from many parts of the city.

Tibidabo gets its name from the devil, who, trying to tempt Christ, took him to a high place and said, in Latin: '*Haec omnia tibi dabo si cadens adoraberis me*' ('All this I will give you if you fall down and worship me').

✗ **Take a Break**

A kilometre northeast, next door to Sar-rià's pretty 18th-century church, cheery **Santamasa** (📞93 676 35 74; Carrer Major de Sarrià 97; mains €7-12; 🕘9am-midnight; 🚊FGC Reina Elisenda) is open all day.

Palau de la Música Catalana

This concert hall is a high point of Barcelona's Modernista architecture: a symphony in tile, brick, sculpted stone and stained glass conceived as a temple for the Catalan Renaixença *(Renaissance).*

Great For...

☑ **Don't Miss**

The principal facade's mosaics and columns and the foyer and pillars in the restaurant.

Built by Domènech i Montaner between 1905 and 1908 for the Orfeo Català musical society, the *palau* (palace) was built with the help of some of the best Catalan artisans of the time, in the cloister of the former Convent de Sant Francesc. Since 1990 it has undergone several major changes.

The Facade

The *palau*, like a peacock, shows off much of its splendour on the outside. Take in the principal facade with its mosaics, floral capitals and the sculpture cluster representing Catalan popular music.

The Interior

Wander inside the foyer and restaurant areas to admire the spangled, tiled pillars. Best of all, however, is the richly colourful auditorium upstairs, with its ceiling of

SOPOTNICKI/SHUTTERSTOCK ©

❶ Need to Know

Map p254; ☑93 295 72 00; www.
palaumusica.cat; Carrer de Palau de la Música
4-6; adult/concession/child €18/11/free;
☺guided tours 10am-3.30pm, to 6pm Easter,
Jul & Aug; MUrquinaona

✕ Take a Break

Le Cucine Mandarosso (☑93 269 07
80; www.lecucinemandarosso.com; Carrer de
Verdaguer i Callís 4; mains €12-14, menú del
día €11; ☺1.30pm-1am Tue-Sat, 1.30-5pm &
8pm-midnight Sun; MUrquinaona) is tops
for Italian comfort food.

★ Top Tip

Under 30? Take ID to the ticket office
to bag a discount.

blue-and-gold stained glass and shimmering skylight that looks like a giant,
crystalline, downward-thrusting nipple.
Above a bust of Beethoven on the stage
towers a wind-blown sculpture of Wagner's
Valkyries (Wagner was top of the Barcelona
charts at the time it was created). This can
only be savoured on a guided tour or by
attending a performance – either is highly
recommended. Admission is by tour only,
and tickets can be bought up to a week
in advance by phone or online. Space is
limited to a maximum of 55 people.

Performances

This is the city's most traditional venue for
classical and choral music, although it has a
wide-ranging program, including flamenco,
pop and – particularly – jazz. Just being
here for a performance is an experience.

A Controversial History

The original Modernista creation, now a
World Heritage site, did not meet with universal approval in its day. The doyen of Catalan literature, Josep Pla, did not hesitate
to condemn it as 'horrible' (although few
share his sentiments today). Domènech i
Montaner himself was also in a huff – he
failed to attend the opening ceremony in
response to unsettled bills.

The *palau* (palace) was at the centre of
a fraud scandal from 2009 to 2012, as its
president, Felix Millet, who subsequently
resigned, admitted to having siphoned off
millions of euros of its funds. He and his
partner were ordered to repay the embez-
zled money to the *palau* in March 2012.

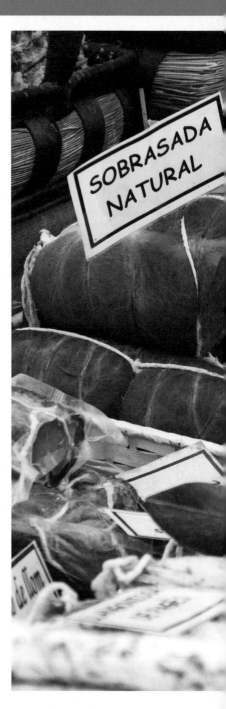

SOBRASADA NATURAL

Foodie Trails in La Ribera

Gourmands and gastronomes will be thoroughly beguiled by the choice in La Ribera, home to a fabulous market and gourmet shops offering all sorts of delicacies. It's almost impossible to walk into its enticing pedestrian zone and come out without having tried, tasted or bought something.

Great For...

ℹ Need to Know

Buying smallgoods? The Spanish phrase for 'vacuum pack' is *'envasar al vacío'*.

Mercat de Santa Caterina   Market

(Map p250; 📞93 319 57 40; www.mercatsanta
caterina.com; Avinguda de Francesc Cambó 16;
🕐7.30am-3.30pm Mon, Wed & Sat, to 8.30pm
Tue, Thu & Fri, closed afternoons Jul & Aug; 📶;
Ⓜ Jaume I) This extraordinary-looking produce market was designed by Enric Miralles
and Benedetta Tagliabue to replace its
19th-century predecessor. Finished in 2005,
it is distinguished by its kaleidoscopic and
undulating roof, held up above the bustling
produce stands, restaurants, cafes and bars
by twisting slender branches of what look
like grey steel trees.

Museu de la Xocolata   Museum

(📞93 268 78 78; www.museuxocolata.cat; Carrer
del Comerç 36; adult/under 7yr €6/free; 🕐10am-
8pm Mon-Sat, 10am-3pm Sun; 📶; Ⓜ Arc de Triomf)
Chocoholics have a hard time containing
themselves in this museum dedicated to
the fundamental foodstuff – particularly
when faced with the cocoa-based treats in
the cafe at the exit. The displays trace the
origins of chocolate, its arrival in Europe and
the many myths and images associated with
it. Kids and grown-ups can join guided tours
and occasionally take part in chocolate-
making and tasting sessions.

Hofmann Pastisseria   Food

(Map p250; 📞93 268 82 21; www.hofmann-bcn.
com; Carrer dels Flassaders 44; 🕐9am-2pm
& 3.30-8pm Mon-Thu, 9am-8.30pm Fri & Sat,
9am-2.30pm Sun; Ⓜ Barceloneta) This bite-
sized gourmet patisserie, linked to the
prestigious Hofmann cooking school,
tempts with jars of delicious chocolates, its
renowned croissants and an array of cakes
and other sweet treats.

Mercat de Santa Caterina

Casa Gispert — Food

(Map p250; 93 319 75 35; www.casagispert.com; Carrer dels Sombrerers 23; 10am-8.30pm Mon-Sat; Jaume I) The wonderful wood-fronted Casa Gispert has been toasting nuts and selling all manner of dried fruit since 1851. Pots and jars piled high on the shelves contain an unending variety of crunchy tidbits: some roasted, some honeyed, all of them moreish. Your order is shouted over to the till, along with the price, in a display of old-world accounting.

La Botifarreria — Food

(Map p250; 93 319 91 23; www.labotifarreria.com; Carrer de Santa Maria 4; 8.30am-2.30pm & 5-8.30pm Mon-Sat; Jaume I) Say it with a sausage! Although this delightful deli sells all sorts of goodies, the mainstay is an astounding variety of handcrafted sausages – the *botifarra*. Not just the regular pork variety either – these sausages are stuffed with anything from green pepper and whisky to apple curry.

El Magnífico — Coffee

(Map p250; 93 319 60 81; www.cafeselmagnifico.com; Carrer de l'Argenteria 64; 10am-8pm Mon-Sat; Jaume I) All sorts of coffee has been roasted here since the early 20th century. The variety of coffee (and tea) available is remarkable – and the aromas hit you as you walk in.

Vila Viniteca — Wine

(Map p250; 902 327777; www.vilaviniteca.es; Carrer dels Agullers 7; 8.30am-8.30pm Mon-Sat; Jaume I) One of the best wine stores in Barcelona (and there are a few...), this place has been searching out the best local and imported wines since 1932. On a couple of November evenings it organises what has become an almost riotous wine-tasting event in Carrer dels Agullers and surrounding lanes, at which cellars from around Spain present their young new wines.

Olisoliva — Food

(Map p250; 93 268 14 72; www.olisoliva.com; Mercat de Santa Caterina; 9.30am-3.30pm Mon, Wed & Sat, to 7pm Tue, to 8pm Thu-Fri; Jaume I) Inside the Mercat de Santa Caterina, this simple, glassed-in store is stacked with olive oils and vinegars from all over Spain. Taste some of the products before deciding.

Sans i Sans — Drinks

(Map p250; 93 310 25 18; www.sansisans.com; Carrer de l'Argenteria 59; 10am-8pm Mon-Sat; Jaume I) This exquisite tea shop is run by the same people who run El Magnífico across the road.

☑ Don't Miss
The Mercat de Santa Caterina: what a place.

Mercat de Santa Caterina

JOAN BAUTISTA/SHUTTERSTOCK ©

★ Top Tip
In the Museu de la Xocolata, look for chocolate models of emblematic buildings such as La Sagrada Família.

Underground ruins at the museum

Museu d'Història de Barcelona

This fascinating museum in the Barri Gòtic takes you back through the centuries to the very foundations of Roman Barcino. It's an impressive display of archaeology and a most intriguing place to wander in the bowels of the old city and observe the layers of history spread out before you.

Great For...

❶ Need to Know

MUHBA; Map p250; ☑93 256 21 00; www.museuhistoria.bcn.cat; Plaça del Rei; adult/concession/child €7/5/free, 3-8pm Sun & 1st Sun of month free; ⊗10am-7pm Tue-Sat, to 2pm Mon, to 8pm Sun; 🛜; Ⓜ Jaume I

★ **Top Tip**

Entry here includes admission to other MUHBA-run sites, such as the **Domus de Sant Honorat** (Map p250; ☏ 93 256 21 00; www.museuhistoria.bcn.cat; Carrer de la Fruita 2; adult/concession/child €2/1.50/free, 1st Sun of month free; ☺10am-2pm Sun; Ⓜ Jaume I) and the **MUHBA Refugi 307** (Map p256; ☏ 93 256 21 22; www.museuhistoria.bcn.cat; Carrer Nou de la Rambla 169; adult/child incl tour €3.40/free; ☺tours 10.30am, 11.30am & 12.30pm Sun; Ⓜ Paral·lel).

At the museum, you'll stroll amid extensive ruins of the town that flourished here following its founding by Emperor Augustus around 10 BC. Equally impressive is the setting inside the former Palau Reial Major (Grand Royal Palace), among the key locations of medieval princely power in Barcelona.

Casa Padellàs

Enter through Casa Padellàs, just south of Plaça del Rei. Casa Padellàs was built for a 16th-century noble family in Carrer dels Mercaders and moved here, stone by stone, in the 1930s. It has a courtyard typical of Barcelona's late-Gothic and baroque mansions, with a graceful external staircase up to the 1st floor. Today it leads to a restored Roman tower and a section of Roman wall (the exterior of which faces Plaça Ramon de Berenguer el Gran), as well as a section of the house set aside for temporary exhibitions.

Underground Ruins

Below ground is a remarkable walk through about 4 sq km of excavated Roman and Visigothic Barcelona. After the display on the typical Roman *domus* (villa), you reach a public laundry (outside in the street were containers for people to urinate into, as the urine was used as disinfectant). You pass more laundries and dyeing shops, a 6th-century public cold-water bath and more dye shops. As you hit the Cardo Minor (a main street), you turn right then left and reach various shops dedicated to the making of *garum*. This paste, a favourite food across the Roman Empire, was made of mashed-up fish intestines, eggs and blood. Occasionally prawns, cockles and herbs were added to create other flavours. Further on are fish-preserve stores. Fish

were sliced up (and all innards removed for making *garum*), laid in alternate layers using salt for preservation, and sat in troughs for about three weeks before being ready for sale and export.

Next come remnants of a 6th- to 7th-century church and episcopal buildings, followed by wine-making stores, with ducts for allowing the must to flow off, and ceramic, round-bottomed *dolia* for storing and ageing wine. Ramparts then wind around and upward, past remains of the gated patio of a Roman house, the medieval Palau Episcopal (Bishops' Palace) and into two broad vaulted halls with displays on medieval Barcelona.

In Columbus' Footsteps

You eventually emerge at a hall and ticket office set up on the north side of Plaça del

Plaça del Rei

✕ Take a Break

For a vegan burger and artisanal beer, hit **Cat Bar** (Carrer de la Bòria 17; mains €6.50-8.50; ⊙6-11.30pm Mon-Wed, 1-11pm Thu-Sat).

Rei. To your right is the Saló del Tinell, the banqueting hall of the royal palace and a fine example of Catalan Gothic (built 1359–70). Its broad arches and bare walls give a sense of solemnity that would have made an appropriate setting for Fernando and Isabel to hear Columbus' first reports of the New World. The hall is sometimes used for temporary exhibitions, which may cost extra and mean that your peaceful contemplation of its architectural majesty is somewhat obstructed.

A Chapel

As you leave the *saló* you come to the 14th-century Capella Reial de Santa Àgata, the palace chapel. Outside, a spindly bell tower rises from the northeast side of Plaça del Rei. Inside, all is bare except for the 15th-century altarpiece and the magnificent *techumbre* (decorated timber ceiling). The altarpiece is considered to be one of Jaume Huguet's finest surviving works.

Out to the Square

Head down the fan-shaped stairs into Plaça del Rei and look up to observe the Mirador del Rei Martí (lookout tower of King Martin), built in 1555, long after the king's death. It is part of the Arxiu de la Corona d'Aragón; the magnificent views over the old city are now enjoyed only by a privileged few.

☑ **Don't Miss**
The public laundry and the wine-making stores.

EYE UBIQUITOUS/ STEPHEN RAFFE/AGEFOTOSTOCK ©

Museu Frederic Marès

One of the wildest collections of historical curios lies inside this vast medieval complex, once part of the royal palace of the counts of Barcelona.

Great For...

☑ Don't Miss

Displays from the collector's cabinet.

The building holding the museum is an intriguing one. A rather worn coat of arms on the wall indicates that it was also, for a while, the seat of the Spanish Inquisition in Barcelona.

Sculpture

Frederic Marès i Deulovol (1893–1991) was a rich sculptor, traveller and obsessive collector. He specialised in medieval Spanish sculpture, huge quantities of which are displayed in the basement and on the ground and 1st floors – including some lovely polychrome wooden sculptures of the Crucifixion and the Virgin. Among the most eye-catching pieces is a reconstructed Romanesque doorway with four arches, taken from a 13th-century country church in the Aragonese province of Huesca.

Exterior detail

RICHARD CUMMINS/GETTY IMAGES ©

Plaça de la Seu
Via Laietana
🚇 **Museu Frederic Marès**
Jaume I Ⓜ
C. del Bisbe
C. de Jaume I

❶ Need to Know

Map p250; ✆93 256 35 00; www.museu
mares.bcn.cat; Plaça de Sant lu 5; adult/con-
cession/child €4.20/2.40/free, after 3pm Sun
& 1st Sun of month free; ⏰10am-7pm Tue-Sat,
11am-8pm Sun; ⓂJaume I

✕ Take a Break

The museum's likeable cafe is the
handiest place for refreshments.

★ Top Tip

This museum is very close to
La Catedral (p64): kill two birds with
one stone.

Collector's Cabinet

The top two floors comprise 'the
collector's cabinet', a mind-boggling
array of knick-knacks, including medieval
weaponry, finely carved pipes, delicate
ladies' fans, intricate 'floral' displays made
of seashells and 19th-century daguerreo-
types and photographs. A room that once
served as Marès' study and library is now
crammed with sculptures. The shady
courtyard houses a pleasant summer cafe
(Cafè de l'Estiu).

What's Nearby?

Plaça de Sant Jaume   Square

(Map p250; ⓂLiceu, Jaume I) In the 2000 or
so years since the Romans settled here,
the area around this square (often remodelled), which started life as the forum, has
been the focus of Barcelona's civic life.

This is still the central staging area for
Barcelona's traditional festivals. Facing
each other across the square are the seat
of Catalonia's regional government, the
Palau de la Generalitat (Map p250; www.
president.cat; Plaça de Sant Jaume; ⏰2nd & 4th
weekend of month; ⓂJaume I), on the north
side, and the town hall, or **Ajuntament**
(Casa de la Ciutat; Map p250; ✆93 402 70 00;
www.barcelonaturisme.com; Plaça de Sant
Jaume; ⏰10.30am-1.30pm Sun; ⓂJaume I)
FREE, to the south.

Palau Centelles   Architecture

(Plaça de Sant Miquel; ⓂLiceu, Jaume I)
A rare 15th-century gem, Palau Centelles
is on the corner of Baixada de Sant
Miquel. You can wander into the fine
Gothic-Renaissance courtyard if the gates
are open.

Walking Tour: Gràcia's Squares

One of Barcelona's most vibrant districts, Gràcia was an independent town until the 1890s. Explore the *barrio*'s picturesque squares and experience its beauty, history and culture.

Start: Plaça de Joan Carles I
Distance: 1.9km
Duration: 50 minutes

7 Busy, elongated **Plaça de la Revolució de Setembre de 1868** commemorates the toppling of Queen Isabel II.

Take a Break...
La Nena (p146) is a chaotic, exuberant gem of a cafe.

Fontana Ⓜ

4 Plaça de la Llibertat (Liberty Sq) is home to a Modernista produce market, designed by Francesc Berenguer i Mestres, Gaudí's long-time assistant.

GLEB SOLOGUB/SHUTTERSTOCK ©

Gràcia 🚇

3 Plaça de Galla Placidia recalls the brief sojourn of the Roman empress-to-be Galla Placidia in the 5th century AD.

C de Regàs
Via Augusta
Travessera de Gràcia
C de Vic

2 Where Carrer Gran de Gràcia leads you into Gràcia proper, the grand **Modernista Casa Fuster** rises in all its glory.

TUPUNGATO/SHUTTERSTOCK ©

GRÀCIA

N

0   400 m
0   0.2 miles

FINISH

C d'Asturies
C de l'Or
C de Torrijos
C de la Perla
C de Terol
C de Ramón y Cajal
Travessera de Gràcia

8

7

6

C de Maspons
C del Torrent de l'Olla

SANT GERVASI

5

C de Goya
C de Martínez de la Rosa
C de Francisco Giner
C de Mozart
C Gran de Gràcia

2

C de Bonavista

C de la Riera de Sant Miquel
C de Sèneca
C de Còrsega

START   1

Av Diagonal

Diagonal M

Pg de Gràcia

Rambla de Catalunya

Diagonal M

8 Pleasant terraces adorn pedestrianised **Plaça de la Virreina**, presided over by the 17th-century Església de Sant Joan.

ULLSTEIN BILD/GETTY IMAGES ©

6 Possibly the rowdiest of Gràcia's squares, **Plaça del Sol** (Sun Sq) is lined with bars and eateries, which buzz on summer nights.

5 Popular **Plaça de la Vila de Gràcia** is home to the Torre del Rellotge (Clock Tower), long a symbol of Republican agitation.

ULISES PFI/SHUTTERSTOCK ©

1 The obelisk at **Plaça de Joan Carles I** honours Spain's former king for stifling an attempted coup d'état in 1981.

TAKASHI IMAGES/ SHUTTERSTOCK ©

STEVE LOVEGROVE/SHUTTERSTOCK ©

Basílica de Santa Maria del Mar

At the southwest end of Passeig del Born stands the apse of Barcelona's finest Catalan Gothic church, Santa Maria del Mar (Our Lady of the Sea).

Built in the 14th century with record-breaking alacrity for the time (it took just 54 years), the church is remarkable for its architectural harmony and simplicity.

The People's Church

Its construction started in 1329, with Berenguer de Montagut and Ramon Despuig as the architects in charge. During construction the city's *bastaixos* (porters) spent a day each week carrying on their backs the stone required to build the church from royal quarries in Montjuïc. Their memory lives on in reliefs of them in the main doors and stone carvings elsewhere in the church. The walls, the side chapels and the facades were finished by 1350 and the entire structure was completed in 1383.

Great For...

☑ **Don't Miss**

The church's architects in memorial stone relief.

Exterior detail

JOLANTA WOJCICKA/SHUTTERSTOCK ©

Jaume I Ⓜ **Basílica de**
Santa Maria ➊
del Mar

Via Laietana

Av del Marquès de l'Argentera

Barceloneta Ⓜ

❶ Need to Know

Map p250; ☎93 310 23 90; www.
santamariadelmarbarcelona.org; Plaça de
Santa Maria del Mar; €8; ⊙guided tours
1.15pm, 2pm, 3pm, 5.15pm; Ⓜ Jaume I

✖ Take a Break

Head to the unsigned Passadís Del Pep
(p139) for top seafood.

★ Top Tip

Use the website www.classictic.com
and filter by venue to find upcoming
concerts here.

The Interior

The exterior gives an impression of stern-
ness and the narrow streets surrounding it
are restrictive and claustrophobic. It may
come as a (pleasant) surprise then to find
a spacious and light interior – the central
nave and two flanking aisles separated by
slender octagonal pillars give an enormous
sense of lateral space.

The interior is almost devoid of imagery
of the sort to be found in Barcelona's other
large Gothic churches, but Santa Maria
was lacking in superfluous decoration even
before anarchists gutted it in 1909 and
1936. Keep an ear out for music recitals,
often baroque and classical.

Old Flame

Opposite Basílica de Santa Maria del Mar's
southern flank, an eternal flame burns

brightly over an apparently anonymous
sunken square. This is El Fossar de les
Moreres (The Mulberry Cemetery), the
site of a Roman cemetery. It's also where
Catalan resistance fighters were buried
after the siege of Barcelona ended in defeat
in September 1714; it is for them that the
flame burns.

What's Nearby?

Museu Europeu
d'Art Modern
Museum

(MEAM; Map p250; ☎93 319 56 93; www.meam.es;
Carrer Barra de Ferro 5; adult/concession/under
10yr €9/7/free; ⊙10am-8pm Tue-Sun; Ⓜ Jaume I)
The European Museum of Modern Art
opened in the summer of 2011 in the Palau
Gomis, a handsome 18th-century mansion
around the corner from the Museu Picasso.
The art within is strictly representational
(the 'Modern' of the name simply means
'contemporary') and is mostly from young
Spanish artists, though there are some
works from elsewhere in Europe.

Walking Tour: Modernisme

Catalan modernism (Modernisme) abounds in Barcelona's L'Eixample district. This walk introduces you to the movement's main form of expression: the architecture.

Start: Casa Calvet
Finish: Casa Macaya
Length: 4km; one hour

5 Completed in 1912, **Casa Thomas** was one of Domènech i Montaner's earlier efforts; the wrought-iron decoration is magnificent.

ALFRED ABAD/AGEFOTOSTOCK ©

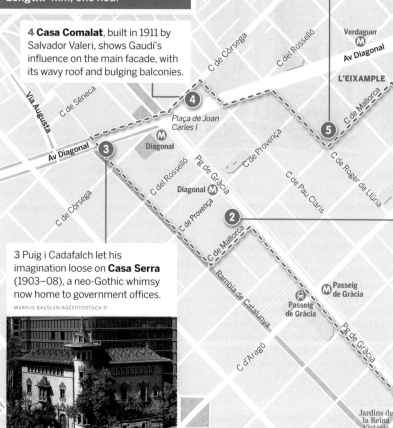

4 Casa Comalat, built in 1911 by Salvador Valeri, shows Gaudí's influence on the main facade, with its wavy roof and bulging balconies.

3 Puig i Cadafalch let his imagination loose on **Casa Serra** (1903–08), a neo-Gothic whimsy now home to government offices.

MARKUS BASSLER/AGEFOTOSTOCK ©

Verdaguer Ⓜ
Av Diagonal
L'EIXAMPLE
C de Mallorca
C del Rosselló
C de Còrsega
Via Augusta
C de Sèneca
Plaça de Joan Carles I
Av Diagonal
Diagonal Ⓜ
Pg de Gràcia
C del Rosselló
Diagonal Ⓜ
C de Provença
C de Provença
C de Mallorca
Rambla de Catalunya
C de Còrsega
C de Pau Claris
C de Roger de Llúria
Passeig de Gràcia Ⓜ
Passeig de Gràcia
Pg de Gràcia
C d'Aragó
Jardins de la Reina Victòria

7 Puig i Cadafalch's **Casa Macaya** (1901) features the typical playful, pseudo-Gothic decoration that characterises many of the architect's projects.

**Classic Photo: Stop 4
Casa Comalat**

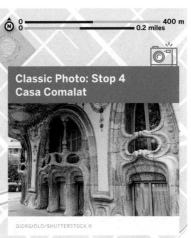

GIORGIOLO/SHUTTERSTOCK ©

Monumental Ⓜ

6 Casa Llopis i Bofill, designed by Antoni Gallissà in 1902, has a particularly striking graffiti-covered facade.

Take a Break...
Seek out **Casa Amalia** (⊙1-3.30pm & 9-10.30pm Tue-Sat, 1-3.30pm Sun) for hearty Catalan cooking.

2 Casa Enric Batlló, today part of the Comtes de Barcelona hotel, was completed in 1896 by Josep Vilaseca.

1 Antoni Gaudí's most conventional contribution to L'Eixample is **Casa Calvet**, built in 1900. Inside, admire the staircase from the swanky restaurant.

YURY DMITRIENKO/SHUTTERSTOCK ©

Pg de Sant Joan
Ⓜ **7** FINISH
Verdaguer
Av Diagonal

Plaça de
Mossèn Jacint
Verdaguer

Pg de Sant Joan

SANT
GERVASI
C de València
6
C de Bailén
C d'Aragó

C de Girona

Gran Via de les Corts Catalanes
C de Casp
1
START
Via Laietana
Ronda de Sant Pere

Plaça
de Joan
Carles I
Plaça
Urquinaona Ⓜ d'Urquinaona

Colònia Güell

Apart from La Sagrada Família, Gaudí's last big project was the creation of a utopian textile workers' complex for magnate patron Eusebi Güell outside Barcelona at Santa Coloma de Cervelló.

Great For...

☑ **Don't Miss**

The church crypt built by Gaudí.

Gaudí's main role here was to erect the colony's church, Colònia Güell. Work began in 1908, but the idea fizzled eight years later when Eusebi Güell's business ventures took a downturn due to the First World War. In the end, Gaudí only finished the crypt, which still serves as a working church. It's 24km west of central Barcelona and a quick journey on the train. The complex has been designated a Unesco World Heritage site and is well worth the trip out here for lovers of Gaudí's work.

The Structure

This structure is a key to understanding what the master had in mind for his magnum opus, La Sagrada Família. The mostly brick-clad columns that support the ribbed vaults in the ceiling are inclined at all angles in much the way you might expect trees in a forest to lean. That effect was deliberate,

★ **Top Tip**

FGC trains zip very regularly from Plaça d'Espanya station, taking 20 minutes.

but also grounded in physics. Gaudí worked out the angles so that their load would be transmitted from the ceiling to the earth without the help of extra buttressing. Similar thinking lay behind his plans for La Sagrada Família, the Gothic-inspired structure that would tower above any medieval building, without requiring a single buttress. Gaudí's hand is visible even down to the wavy design of the pews. The primary colours in the curvaceous plant-shaped stained-glass windows are another reminder of the era in which the crypt was built. The broken mosaic tiling known as *trencadis* is typical of other Gaudí works. It was an elegant solution to the problem of using normal-sized tiles on his characteristically uneven, fluid surfaces.

Other Factory Buildings

The cute brick houses, designed for the factory workers and still inhabited today,

🛈 **Need to Know**

📋 93 630 58 07; www.gaudicoloniaguell.org; Carrer de Claudi Güell; adult/student €7/5.50; ⏰10am-7pm Mon-Fri, to 3pm Sat & Sun, shorter hours outside of summer; 🚆FGC lines S4, S8, S33 to Colònia Güell

✕ **Take a Break**

There are some eating options in the former workers' cottages.

are spread near the church. A short stroll away, the 23 factory buildings of a Modernista industrial complex, idle since the 1970s, were brought back to life in the early 2000s, with shops and businesses moving into the renovated complex.

In a five-room display with audiovisual and interactive material, the history and life of the industrial colony and the story of Gaudí's church are told in colourful fashion.

Platja de la Nova Icària

NITO/SHUTTERSTOCK ©

Beaches of Barcelona

A series of pleasant beaches stretches northeast from the Port Olímpic marina. They are largely artificial, but this doesn't stop an estimated seven million bathers from piling in every year.

Great For...

☑ Don't Miss

The vibrant bustle of Platja de la Nova Icària.

Platja de la Nova Icària

The southernmost of these beaches, Platja de la Nova Icària, is the busiest. Behind it, across the Avinguda del Litoral highway, is the Plaça dels Campions, site of the rusting three-tiered platform used to honour medallists in the sailing events of the 1992 games. Much of the athletes' housing-turned-apartments are in the blocks immediately behind Carrer de Salvador Espriu.

Platja de Bogatell

The next beach is Platja de Bogatell. Just in from the beach is **Cementiri del Poblenou** (Poblenou Cemetery; ☎93 225 16 61; Av d'Icària, near Carrer del Taulat; ⊗8am-6pm; ⓂLlacuna), created in 1773. It was positioned outside the then city limits for health reasons. Its central monument commemorates the

❶ Need to Know

Line 4 (yellow) is the handiest Metro line, though it's a fair stroll to some beaches.

✕ Take a Break

The beaches are dotted with *chiringuitos*, snack bars that stay open until the wee hours.

★ Top Tip

The broad beachside boulevard is great for strolling, cycling or skating.

victims of a yellow-fever epidemic that swept across Barcelona in 1821. The cemetery is full of bombastic family memorials, but an altogether disquieting touch is the sculpture *El Petó de la Mort* (the Kiss of Death), in which a winged skeleton kisses a young kneeling lifeless body.

There's a good skateboard area with half-pipes at the north end of the beach.

Other Beaches

Platja de la Mar Bella (with its brief nudist strip and sailing school) and Platja de la Nova Mar Bella follow, leading into the new residential and commercial waterfront strip, the Front Marítim, part of the Diagonal Mar project in the Fòrum district. It is fronted by the last of these artificial beaches to be created, Platja del Llevant.

What's Nearby?

Museu Blau   Museum

(Blue Museum; ☏ 93 256 60 02; www.museu ciencies.cat; Parc del Fòrum; adult/child €6/ free; ⊙10am-7pm Tue-Sat, to 8pm Sun Mar-Sep, to 6pm Tue-Fri Oct-Feb; Ⓜ El Maresme Fòrum) Set inside the futuristic Edifici Fòrum, the Museu Blau takes visitors on a journey all across the natural world. Multimedia and interactive exhibits explore topics like the history of evolution, Earth's formation and the great scientists who have helped shaped human knowledge. There are also specimens from the animal, plant and mineral kingdoms – plus dinosaur skeletons – all rather dramatically set amid the sprawling 9000 sq metres of exhibition space.

El Fòrum   Area

(Ⓜ El Maresme Fòrum) Once an urban wasteland, this area has seen dramatic changes in the last 20 years, with sparkling new buildings, open plazas and waterfront recreation areas. The most striking element is the eerily blue, triangular *2001: A Space Odyssey*–style **Edifici Fòrum** building by Swiss architects Herzog & de Meuron.

WESTEND61 PREMIUM/SHUTTERSTOCK ©

Shopping in the Quadrat

While visitors to L'Eixample do the sights, locals go shopping in the Quadrat d'Or, the grid of streets either side of Passeig de Gràcia.

Great For...

☑ **Don't Miss**

Trying before you buy in the wine bar at Monvínic (p181).

The Retail Scene

This is Barcelona at its most fashion- and design-conscious, which also describes a large proportion of L'Eixample's residents. All the big names are here, alongside boutiques of local designers who capture the essence of Barcelona cool.

The New Wave

You could spend an entire day along Passeig de Gràcia but make sure you detour for a moment to **Lurdes Bergada** (Map p254; ☎93 218 48 51; www.lurdesbergada.es; Rambla de Catalunya 112; ⊙10.30am-8.30pm Mon-Sat; Ⓜ Diagonal), a boutique run by mother-and-son designer team Lurdes Bergada and Syngman Cucala. The classy men's and women's fashions use natural fibres and have attracted a cult following.

SORBIS/SHUTTERSTOCK ©

ℹ Need to Know

Passeig de Gràcia and Diagonal are your best Metro stops for these shops.

✕ Take a Break

Enjoy the plush interior and delicious pastries of **Mauri** (Map p254; ☎93 215 10 20; www.pasteleriasmauri.com; Rambla de Catalunya 102; pastries from €3.50; ⊙8am-midnight Mon-Sat, 9am-4pm Sun; Ⓜ Diagonal), capped by an ornate fresco dating back to the cafe's first days in 1929.

★ Top Tip

Live outside the EU? You can claim sales tax back on purchases over €90.

Modernista Jewellery

This is more than just any old jewellery store. The boys from **Bagués-Masriera** (Map p254; ☎93 216 01 74; www.bagues-masriera.com; Passeig de Gràcia 41; ⊙10am-8.30pm Mon-Fri, 11am-8pm Sat; Ⓜ Passeig de Gràcia) have been chipping away at precious stones and moulding metal since the 19th century and many of the classic pieces here have a flighty, Modernista influence. Bagués backs it up with service that can be haughty, but owes much to old-school courtesies.

Luxury Luggage

While bags and suitcases in every conceivable colour of buttersoft leather are the mainstay at **Loewe** (Map p254; ☎93 216 04 00; www.loewe.com; Passeig de Gràcia 35; ⊙10am-8.30pm Mon-Sat; Ⓜ Passeig de Gràcia), there is also a range of clothing for men and women, along with some stunning – and stunningly priced – accessories. The shop itself is worth a visit, housed in the Casa Lleó Morera (p53) and with some interior details by Domènech i Montaner.

Say it with Chocolate

A sleek and modern temple to the brown stuff, **Cacao Sampaka** (Map p254; ☎93 272 08 33; www.cacaosampaka.com; Carrer del Consell de Cent 292; ⊙9am-9pm Mon-Sat; Ⓜ Passeig de Gràcia) doubles as a shop and cafe and is the perfect place to stock up with gifts to take back home. Select from every conceivable flavour (rosemary, anyone, or curry?), either in bar form or as individual choccies to fill your own elegant little gift box.

Fine Wines

For superior souvenirs in liquid form, head to the state-of-the-art Monvínic (p181), a veritable palace of wine with more than 3000 wines in its cellar, including some extremely rare finds. Ask them to make you up a gift box for someone special back home.

DINING OUT

From tapas to world-renowned restaurants

Dining Out

Barcelona has a celebrated food scene fuelled by a combination of world-class chefs, imaginative recipes and magnificent ingredients fresh from farms and the sea. Catalan culinary masterminds like Ferran Adrià and Carles Abellan have become international icons, reinventing the world of haute cuisine, while classic old-world Catalan recipes continue to earn accolades in dining rooms and tapas bars across the city.

In This Section

Price Ranges

The following price symbols represent the cost of a main course:

€	less than €10
€€	€10 to €20
€€€	over €20

Tipping

Service is rarely included in the bill. Locals aren't big tippers, but if you're particularly happy, 5% is generally fine.

Gràcia & Park Güell
Hip and characterful
tapas bars and taverns
(p146)

**Camp Nou, Pedralbes
& La Zona Alta**
Culinary gems well worth the trip
(p147)

**La Sagrada Família
& L'Eixample**
Some of Barcelona's
best restaurants
(p142)

La Ribera
Atmospheric and
avant-garde restaurants
(p138)

*Port
Olímpic*

El Raval
Classic, budget and
artful newcomers
(p135)

**La Rambla &
Barri Gòtic**
Both touristy and
well-respected eateries
(p132)

**Barceloneta &
the Waterfront**
Top choice for
seafood and paella
(p141)

*Mediterranean
Sea*

*Port
Vell*

**Montjuïc, Poble Sec
& Sant Antoni**
Historic taverns, famed tapas bars,
new trendsetters
(p144)

Useful Phrases

The bill, please.	*La cuenta, por favor.*	la *kwen*·ta por fa·*vor.*
I'd/We'd like...	*Quería/ queríamos...*	ke·*ria*/ ke·*ria*·mos
A dish of... chicken	*Una de... pollo*	oo·na de... pol·yo
I'm allergic to...	*Tengo alergía a...*	ten·go al·er·hi·ya a
I don't eat... meat	*No como... carne*	No ko·mo... kar·ne
Very good, thank you!	*Muy rico, gracias!*	Mwee *ri*·ko gra·thyas!

Classic Dishes

Calçots Barbecued leek/spring onion cross.

Escalivada Grilled and cooled sliced vegetables with oil.

Esqueixada Salad of salt cod with vegetables and beans.

Botifarra amb mongetes Pork sausage with white beans.

Cargols/Caracoles Snails, often stewed with rabbit.

Fideuà Like seafood paella, but with vermicelli noodles.

The Best...

Experience Barcelona's top restaurants and cafes

By Budget

€

La Cova Fumada (p141) Barceloneta hole-in-the-wall with excellent small plates.

Bormuth (p138) Tasty tapas in an old-city setting.

€€

Suculent (p137) Carles Abellan's bistro serves excellent Catalan cooking.

Casa Delfín (p139) Delicious Mediterranean fare in an atmospheric setting.

€€€

Disfrutar (p143) Expect the unexpected – this is Catalan cooking at its most experimental.

Koy Shunka (p134) Avant-garde Japanese fare, probably Barcelona's best.

For Brunch

Black Remedy (p132) All-day Sunday brunch to burn off the hangover.

Federal (p145) Excellent brunches and a small roof terrace.

Milk (p133) Serves brunch daily (till 4.30pm).

Benedict (p133) True to the name, it's all about the eggs here.

For Vegetarians

Aguaribay (p141) First-rate prix fixe lunches and a small but well-executed evening à la carte menu.

Green Spot (p141) Upmarket modern fare with some great flavours.

Flax & Kale (p136) Vast, colourful salads and a truly creative approach.

Rasoterra (p134) Airy vegetarian charmer in Barri Gòtic.

For Tapas

Bormuth (p138) Serves both the classic and the new wave, plus tasty vermouths.

Quimet i Quimet (p144) Mouth-watering morsels served to a standing crowd.

Palo Cortao (p144) A new star in Poble Sec with outstanding sharing plates.

Bar Pinotxo (p136) Pull up a bar stool at this legendary Boqueria joint.

Tapas 24 (p142) Everyone's favourite gourmet tapas bar.

For Seafood

Barraca (p141) A sparkling waterfront restaurant with unique and flavour-rich seafood combinations.

Cal Pep (p139) Brilliant seafood tapas at this legendary spot.

Can Ros (p141) A family-run Barceloneta classic.

Can Maño (p141) An unfussy place with great dishes at low prices.

Cafes

Els Quatre Gats (p134) Soak up the atmosphere at this majestic Modernista spot.

Black Remedy (p132) Top coffee and buzzy hipstery character.

Federal (p133) Unnervingly hip, but the food is excellent and the service friendly.

Čaj Chai (p135) Teas and lively chatter in Barri Gòtic.

Spice (p144) Quite simply Catalonia's best carrot cake.

For Carnivores

Patagonia Beef & Wine (p143) Feast on Argentine steaks.

Roig Robí (p147) Exquisitely treated meat dishes are a highlight here.

El Asador de Aranda (p147) Roast lamb in a Modernista setting.

★ For Catalan Cuisine

Vivanda (p147) Magnificent Catalan cooking with year-round garden dining.

Mam i Teca (p136) Intimate venue for quality market cuisine.

Roig Robí (p147) A pillar of traditional Catalan cooking.

Cafè de l'Acadèmia (p133) High-quality dishes that never disappoint.

Can Culleretes (p133) The city's oldest restaurant, with great-value traditional dishes.

⊗ La Rambla & Barri Gòtic

Belmonte   Tapas €

(Map p250; ✏93 310 76 84; Carrer de la Mercè 29; tapas €4-10, mains €12; ⊙8pm-midnight Tue-Sat, plus 1-3.30pm Sat; 🛜; Ⓜ Jaume I) This tiny tapas joint in the southern reaches of Barri Gòtic whips up beautifully prepared small plates – including an excellent *truita* (tortilla), rich *patatons a la sal* (salted new potatoes with *romesco* sauce) and tender *carpaccio de pop* (octopus carpaccio). Wash it down with the housemade *vermut* (vermouth).

Black Remedy   Cafe €

(Map p250; ✏93 461 92 12; www.blackremedy. com; Carrer de la Ciutat 5; mains €8-11; ⊙8.30am-8pm Mon-Wed, 8.30am-11pm Thu-Sat, 11am-5.30pm Sun; Ⓜ Jaume I) Craft beer? Check. Pulled-pork sandwiches? Check. Half the clientele tapping into MacBooks? Check. Black Remedy is the latest hipster joint in the slow transformation of the Barri Gòtic. This is a gallery-like space with floor-to-ceiling windows for those who like to see and be seen. Pluses include great coffee, cold-pressed juices and bottled artisanal beers, and an all-day brunch on Sundays.

Xurreria   Churros €

(Map p250; ✏93 318 76 91; Carrer dels Banys Nous 8; cone €1.20; ⊙7.30am-1.30pm & 3.30-8.15pm; Ⓜ Jaume I) It doesn't look much from the outside, but this brightly lit street joint is Barcelona's best spot for paper cones of piping-hot churros – long batter sticks fried and sprinkled with sugar and best enjoyed dunked in hot chocolate.

La Vinateria del Call   Spanish €€

(Map p250; ✏93 302 60 92; www.lavinateria delcall.com; Carrer de Sant Domènec del Call 9; raciones €7-12; ⊙7.30pm-1am; Ⓜ Jaume I) In a magical setting in the former Jewish quarter, this tiny jewel box of a restaurant serves up tasty Iberian dishes including Galician octopus, cider-cooked chorizo and the Catalan *escalivada* (roasted peppers, aubergine and onions) with anchovies. Portions are small and made for sharing, and there's a good and affordable selection of wines.

VISIONSI/SHUTTERSTOCK ©

Cafè de l'Acadèmia
Catalan €€

(Map p250; 📞93 319 82 53; Carrer dels Lledó 1; mains €15-20; ⏱1-3.30pm & 8-11.30pm Mon-Fri; 📶; MJaume I) Expect a mix of traditional Catalan dishes with the occasional creative twist. At lunchtime, local *ajuntament* (town hall) office workers pounce on the *menú del día* (daily set menu; €15.70). In the evening it is rather more romantic, as low lighting emphasises the intimacy of the beamed ceiling and stone walls. On warm days you can also dine on the pretty square at the front.

Federal
Cafe €€

(Map p250; 📞93 280 81 71; www.federalcafe.es; Passatge de la Pau 11; mains €9-12; ⏱9am-midnight Mon-Thu, to 1am Fri & Sat, 9am-5.30pm Sun; 📶; MDrassanes) Don't be intimidated by the industrial chic, the sea of open MacBooks or the stack of design mags – this branch of the Poble Sec Federal mothership is incredibly welcoming, with healthy, hearty, good-value food. Choose a salad and a topping (poached eggs, strips of chicken) or a yellow curry, say, and follow it up with a moist slab of carrot cake.

Can Culleretes
Catalan €€

(Map p250; 📞93 317 30 22; www.culleretes.com; Carrer Quintana 5; mains €10-18; ⏱1.30-4pm & 9-11pm Tue-Sat, 1.30-4pm Sun; MLiceu) Founded in 1786, Barcelona's oldest restaurant is still going strong, with tourists and locals flocking here to enjoy its rambling interior, old-fashioned tile-filled decor and enormous helpings of traditional Catalan food, including fresh seafood and sticky stews.

Milk
American €€

(Map p250; 📞93 268 09 22; www.milkbarcelona.com; Carrer d'en Gignàs 21; mains €9-12; ⏱9am-2am Thu-Mon, to 1.30am Fri & Sat; 📶; MJaume I) Also known to many as an enticing cocktail spot, Irish-run Milk's key role for Barcelona night owls is providing morning-after brunches (served till 4.30pm). Avoid direct sunlight and tuck into pancakes, eggs Benedict and other hangover dishes in a cosy lounge-like setting complete with ornate wallpaper, framed prints on the wall

🍽 Seafood Heaven

There is a wealth of restaurants specialising in seafood. Not surprisingly Barceloneta, which lies near the sea, is packed with eateries of all shapes and sizes doling out decadent paellas, cauldrons of bubbling molluscs, grilled catches of the day and other delights. Nearest the sea, you'll find pricier open-air places with Mediterranean views; plunge into the narrow lanes to find the real gems, including bustling family-run places that serve first-rate plates at great prices.

Mussels at a street stall near La Catedral (p64)
ELIJAH LOVKOFF/SHUTTERSTOCK ©

and cushion-lined seating. The musical selection is also notable.

Benedict
Brunch €€

(Map p250; 📞93 250 75 11; www.benedictbcn.com; Carrer de Gignás 23; mains €10-11; ⏱9am-4pm Mon, 9am-4pm & 7pm-2am Tue-Fri, 9am-2.30am Sat & Sun; 📶; MJaume I) As the name suggests, brunch is the main event at friendly little Benedict, with eggs prepared every which way and an option for the full English fry-up. There's also a list of handmade burgers and club sandwiches. In the evening various tapas are served, along with onion rings, deep-fried brie, chicken wings and other American favourites.

Opera Samfaina
Catalan €€

(Map p250; 📞93 481 78 71; www.operasamfaina.com; La Rambla 51; Opera Prima adult/under 12yr €19/€12, Odissea adult/under 12yr €33/€20; ⏱7pm-midnight Mon-Wed, to 1.30am Thu, 1pm-1.30am Fri & Sat, to midnight Sun; MLiceu)

Markets

Barcelona has some fantastic food markets. Foodies will enjoy the sounds, smells and most importantly tastes of the **Mercat de la Boqueria** (p94). This is probably Spain's biggest and best market, and it's conveniently located right off La Rambla. Here you can find temptations of all sorts – plump fruits and veggies, fresh-squeezed juices, artisanal cheeses, smoked meats, seafood and pastries. The best feature: an array of tapas bars and food stalls where you can sample amazingly fresh ingredients cooked to perfection. Some other great market options:

Mercat de Sant Antoni (p164)
Mercat de Santa Caterina (p106)
Mercat del Ninot (p163)
Mercat de l'Abaceria Central (p167)

A surreal sensory experience deep in the bowels of the Liceu opera house. Enter through the Vermuteria, a tenebrous tapas bar, then go to the Odissea and try traditional Catalan dishes at a shared table, surrounded by audiovisuals. Or you could head down to the Opera Prima, a dreamlike labyrinth of wine and tapas bars and psychedelic installations.

Rasoterra Vegetarian €€
(Map p250; ☎93 318 69 26; www.rasoterra.cat; Carrer del Palau 5; tapas €6-10, lunch menu €13; ⏰1-4pm & 7-11pm Tue-Sun; 🛜🌿; Ⓜ Jaume I) A delightful addition to the Gothic quarter, Rasoterra cooks up first-rate vegetarian dishes in a Zen-like setting with tall ceilings, low-playing jazz and fresh flowers on the tables. The creative, globally influenced menu changes regularly and might feature Vietnamese-style coconut pancakes with tofu and vegetables, beluga lentils with basmati rice, and pear and goat cheese quesadillas. Good vegan and gluten-free options.

Pla Fusion €€
(Map p250; ☎93 412 65 52; www.restaurantpla. cat; Carrer de la Bellafila 5; mains €16-21; ⏰7-11.30pm Sun-Thu, to midnight Fri & Sat; 🛜; Ⓜ Jaume I) One of Gòtic's long-standing favourites, Pla is a stylish, romantically lit medieval dining room where the cooks churn out such temptations as oxtail braised in red wine, seared tuna with oven-roasted peppers and polenta with seasonal mushrooms.

Koy Shunka Japanese €€€
(Map p250; ☎93 412 79 39; www.koyshunka. com; Carrer de Copons 7; multicourse menu €89-132; ⏰1.30-3pm & 8.30-10.30pm Tue-Sat, 1.30-3pm Sun; Ⓜ Urquinaona) Down a narrow lane north of the cathedral, Koy Shunka opens a portal to exquisite dishes from the East – mouth-watering sushi, sashimi, seared Wagyu beef and flavour-rich seaweed salads are served alongside inventive cooked fusion dishes such as steamed clams with sake or tempura of scallops and king prawns with Japanese mushrooms. Don't miss the house speciality of tender *toro* (tuna belly).

Els Quatre Gats Catalan €€€
(Map p250; ☎93 302 41 40; www.4gats.com; Carrer de Montsió 3; mains €23-29; ⏰12.30-4.30pm & 6.30pm-1am; 🛜; Ⓜ Urquinaona) Once the lair of Barcelona's Modernista artists, Els Quatre Gats is a stunning example of the movement, inside and out, with its colourful tiles, geometric brickwork and wooden fittings. The restaurant is not quite as thrilling as its setting, though you can just have a coffee and a croissant in the cafe (open from 9am to 1am) at the front.

La Granja Cafe €
(Map p250; ☎617 37 02 90; Carrer dels Banys Nous 4; ⏰9am-9pm; Ⓜ Jaume I) This long-running cafe serves up thick, rich cups of chocolate, in varying formats, but it doesn't make its own churros. Buy them a few doors down at Xurreria (p132) and bring them here for the perfect combo of churros dipped in chocolate. Also worth a look is the section of Roman wall visible at the back.

Tapas at the Mercat de la Boqueria

Caelum   Cafe €

(Map p250; 📞93 302 69 93; www.caelum barcelona.com; Carrer de la Palla 8; desserts around €3; ⊙10am-8.30pm Mon-Thu, 10.30am-10pm Fri & Sat, to 9pm Sun; MLiceu) Centuries of heavenly gastronomic tradition from across Spain are concentrated in this exquisite medieval space in the heart of the city. The upstairs cafe is a dainty setting for decadent cakes and pastries, while descending into the underground chamber with its stone walls and flickering candles is like stepping into the Middle Ages.

Cafè de l'Òpera   Cafe €

(Map p250; 📞93 317 75 85; www.cafeoperabcn. com; La Rambla 74; desserts around €2; ⊙8.30am-2.30am; 🛜; MLiceu) Opposite the Gran Teatre del Liceu is La Rambla's most intriguing cafe. Operating since 1929, it is pleasant enough for an early evening libation or coffee and croissants. Head upstairs for an elevated seat above the busy boulevard. Can you be tempted by the *cafè de l'Òpera* (coffee with chocolate mousse)?

Čaj Chai   Cafe €

(Map p250; 📞93 301 95 92; www.cajchai.com; Carrer de Sant Domènec del Call 12; ⊙3pm-10pm Mon, from 10.30am Thu-Sun; MJaume I) Inspired by Prague's bohemian tearooms, this bright and buzzing cafe in the heart of the old Jewish quarter is a tea connoisseur's paradise. Čaj Chai stocks around 200 teas from China, India, Korea, Japan, Nepal, Morocco and beyond. It's a much-loved local haunt.

El Raval

El Colectivo   Cafe €

(Map p249; 📞93 318 63 80; Carrer del Pintor Fortuny 22; bocadillos from €4; ⊙9am-9pm Mon-Wed, 9am-midnight Thu, 9am-2am Fri & Sat; 🛜; MCatalunya) A relaxed little cafe on a quiet Raval street, El Colectivo makes excellent cake, creative *bocadillos* (filled rolls) and good coffee. The shop-window seating is perfect for street watching, the decor is simple and minimal with a single row of wooden tables, and there's always good jazz playing in the background. Tapas are served on Thursdays and Fridays.

Sésamo — Vegetarian €

(Map p249; ☑93 441 64 11; Carrer de Sant Antoni Abat 52; tapas €6; ⊗8pm-midnight Tue-Sun; ☑; Ⓜ Sant Antoni) Widely held to be the best vegie restaurant in the city (admittedly not as great an accolade as it might be elsewhere), Sésamo is a cosy, fun place. The menu is mainly tapas and most people go for the seven-course tapas menu (€25, wine included), but there are a few more substantial dishes. Nice touches include the home-baked bread and cakes.

Mam i Teca — Catalan €€

(Map p249; ☑93 441 33 35; Carrer de la Lluna 4; mains €10-12; ⊗1-4pm & 8pm-midnight Mon, Wed-Fri & Sun, 8pm-midnight Sat; Ⓜ Sant Antoni) A tiny place with half a dozen tables, Mam i Teca is as much a lifestyle choice as a restaurant. Locals drop in and hang at the bar, and diners are treated to Catalan dishes made with locally sourced products that adhere to Slow Food principles (such as cod fried in olive oil with garlic and red pepper, or pork ribs with chickpeas).

Bar Pinotxo — Tapas €€

(Map p250; www.pinotxobar.com; Mercat de la Boqueria; mains €8-17; ⊗7am-4pm Mon-Sat; Ⓜ Liceu) Bar Pinotxo is arguably La Boqueria's, and even Barcelona's, best tapas bar. It sits among the half-dozen or so informal eateries within the market. The popular owner, Juanito, might serve up chickpeas with pine nuts and raisins, a soft mix of potato and spinach sprinkled with salt, soft baby squid with cannellini beans, or a quivering cube of caramel-sweet pork belly.

Flax & Kale — Vegetarian €€

(Map p249; ☑93 317 56 64; www.teresacarles. com; Carrer dels Tallers 74; mains €12.50-16.50; ⊗9.30am-11.30pm Mon-Fri, from 10am Sat & Sun; ☎☑; Ⓜ Universitat) A far cry from the veggie restaurants of old, Flax & Kale marks a new approach (for Barcelona, at least) that declares that going meat-free does not mean giving up on choice or creativity, and is entirely possible in stylish surroundings. There are gluten-free and vegan options, and dishes include tacos with guacamole, aubergine, shiitake mushrooms with sour cashew cream, or Penang red curry.

From left: Cheese croquettes; Bar Pinotxo; Quimet i Quimet (p144)

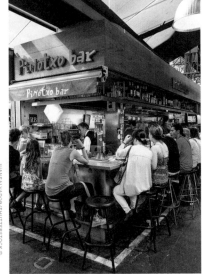

JUANSALVADOR/SHUTTERSTOCK ©

CAMESASCA DAVIDE/AGEFOTOSTOCK ©

Suculent
Catalan €€

(Map p250; 📞93 443 65 79; www.suculent.com; Rambla del Raval 43; mains €16-22; ⏱1-4pm & 8-11.30pm Wed-Sun; Ⓜ Liceu) Michelin-starred chef Carles Abellan adds to his stable with this old-style bistro, which showcases the best of Catalan cuisine. From the cod brandade to the oxtail stew with truffled sweet potato, only the best ingredients are used. Be warned that the prices can mount up a bit, but this is a great place to sample regional highlights.

Caravelle
International €€

(Map p249; 📞93 317 98 92; www.caravelle. es; Carrer del Pintor Fortuny 31; mains €10-13; ⏱9.30am-5.30pm Mon, 9.30am-1am Tue-Fri, 10am-1am Sat, 10am-5.30pm Sun; Ⓜ Liceu) A bright little joint, beloved of the hipster element of El Raval and anyone with a discerning palate. It dishes up tacos as you've never tasted them (cod, lime *alioli* and radish, and pulled pork with roast corn and avocado), a superior steak sandwich on homemade brioche with pickled celeriac and all manner of soul food.

El Quim
Tapas €€

(Map p250; 📞93 301 98 10; www.elquimdelabo queria.com; Mercat de la Boqueria; mains €15-20; ⏱7am-4pm Tue-Thu, to 5pm Fri & Sat; Ⓜ Liceu) This classic counter bar in the Mercat de la Boqueria is ideal for trying traditional Catalan dishes such as fried eggs with baby squid (the house speciality) or *escalivada* (smoky grilled vegetables). Daily specials are prepared using whatever is in season and might include artichoke chips or sautéed wild mushrooms.

Granja M Viader
Cafe €

(Map p250; 📞93 318 34 86; www.granjaviader. cat; Carrer d'en Xuclà 6; desserts around €2; ⏱9am-1.15pm & 5-9.15pm Mon-Sat; Ⓜ Liceu) For more than a century, people have flocked down this alley to get to the cups of homemade hot chocolate and whipped cream (ask for a *suís*) ladled out in this classic Catalan-style milk-bar-cum-deli. The Viader clan invented Cacaolat, a forerunner of kids' powdered-chocolate beverages. The interior here is delightfully vintage and the atmosphere always upbeat.

MICHAEL HEFFERNAN/LONELY PLANET ©

⊗ La Ribera

El Casal — Modern French €

(Map p250; 🖉 93 268 40 04; www.elcasalcafe.com; Plaça Victor Balaguer 5; menú del día €11.25, sandwiches €3.50-€4.50; ⊙7am-5pm Mon-Fri; M Jaume I) A French-run cafe serving excellent food for a great price in noisy but welcoming surroundings, adorned with *objets* from the motherland. The fixed lunch changes daily, but look out for the superior cauliflower cheese and an authentic tarte tatin. Breakfast is available until 1pm, and tapas and sandwiches are available throughout the day. Arrive early for a terrace table.

Paradiso — Smokery €

(Map p250; 🖉 639 310671; www.rooftopsmokehouse.com; Carrer de Rera Palau 4; mains €8; ⊙pastrami bar 7pm-2am Mon-Thu, to 3am Fri & Sat; M Barceloneta) A kind of Narnia-in-reverse, Paradiso is fronted with a snowy-white space, not much bigger than a wardrobe and in itself reason enough to linger. It serves pastrami sandwiches, smoked duck and other home-cured delights from the Rooftop Smokehouse team, best known for their food trucks. But this is only the portal – pull open the huge wooden fridge door, and step through into a glam, sexy speakeasy of a cocktail bar.

Bormuth — Tapas €

(Map p250; 🖉 93 310 21 86; Carrer del Rec 31; tapas €4-10; ⊙12.30pm-1.30am Sun-Thu, to 2.30am Fri & Sat; 🛜; M Jaume I) Located on the pedestrian Carrer del Rec, Bormuth has tapped into the vogue for old-school tapas with modern-day service and decor, and serves all the old favourites along with some less predictable and superbly prepared numbers (try the chargrilled red pepper with black pudding).

Euskal Etxea — Tapas €

(Map p250; 🖉 93 310 21 85; www.euskaletxeataberna.com; Placeta de Montcada 1; tapas €1.95; ⊙10am-12.30am Sun-Thu, to 1am Fri & Sat; M Jaume I) Barcelona has plenty of Basque and pseudo-Basque eateries, but this is the real deal. It captures the feel of San Sebastián better than many of its newer competitors. Choose your *pintxos* (Basque tapas piled on slices of bread), sip *txacolí*

(Basque white wine) and keep the toothpicks so the staff can count them up and work out your bill.

Cat Bar
Vegan €

(Map p250; Carrer de la Bòria 17; mains €6.50-8.50; ⏰1pm-11pm Thu-Mon; 📶🍴; Ⓜ Jaume I) This tiny little joint squeezes in a vegan kitchen, a great selection of local artisanal beers and a smattering of live music. The food mostly centres on a list of different burgers, plus a gluten-free dish of the day, tapas and hummus. The beers change regularly, but there is always one wheat, one porter, one gluten-free and an IPA.

Casa Delfín
Catalan €€

(Map p250; 📞93 319 50 88; www.tallerdetapas. com; Passeig del Born 36; mains €10-15; ⏰8am-midnight Sun-Thu, to 1am Fri & Sat; 📶; Ⓜ Barceloneta) One of Barcelona's culinary delights, Casa Delfín is everything you dream of when you think of Catalan (and Mediterranean) cooking. Start with the tangy and sweet *calçots* (a cross between a leek and an onion; February and March only) or salt-strewn Padrón peppers, moving on to grilled sardines speckled with parsley, then tackle the meaty monkfish roasted in white wine and garlic.

Cal Pep
Tapas €€

(Map p250; 📞93 310 79 61; www.calpep.com; Plaça de les Olles 8; mains €13-20; ⏰7.30-11.30pm Mon, 1-3.45pm & 7.30-11.30pm Tue-Sat, closed last 3 weeks Aug; Ⓜ Barceloneta) It's getting a foot in the door of this legendary fish restaurant that's the problem – there can be queues out into the square. And if you want one of the five tables out the back, you'll need to call ahead. Most people are happy elbowing their way to the bar for some of the tastiest seafood tapas in town.

Farigola
Mediterranean €€

(📞93 488 55 83; Carrer del Davant del Portal Nou 3; fixed-price lunch €10, mains €6-8; ⏰11am-1am; Ⓜ Arc de Triomf) Farigola is a bit of a gem, hidden on a quiet backstreet and known only to locals. Its small terrace and cosy dining room/bar are rarely full, but its lunch deal (two dishes for €10) is unbeatable. Dishes

🍽️ **New Catalan Cuisine**

Avant-garde chefs have made Catalonia famous throughout the world for their food laboratories, their commitment to food as art and their crazy riffs on the themes of traditional local cooking.

Here the notion of gourmet cuisine is deconstructed as chefs transform liquids and solid foods into foams, create 'ice cream' of classic ingredients by means of liquid nitrogen, freeze-dry foods to make concentrated powders and employ spherification to create unusual and artful morsels. This alchemical cookery is known as molecular gastronomy, and invention is the keystone of this technique.

Diners may encounter olive oil 'caviar', 'snow' made of gazpacho with anchovies, jellified Parmesan turned into spaghetti, and countless other concoctions.

The dining rooms themselves also offer a reconfiguration of the five-star dining experience. Restaurateurs generally aim to create warm and buzzing spaces, with artful design flourishes, and without the stuffiness and formality typically associated with high-end dining.

might include roast beef with rosemary potatoes, or beetroot couscous with ricotta, or sandwiches (the pastrami is superb), which are available all day.

Passadís Del Pep
Seafood €€€

(Map p250; 📞93 310 10 21; www.passadis. com; Plaça del Palau 2; mains €19-24, set menus €60-85; ⏰1.30-3.30pm & 8.15-11.30pm Mon-Sat; Ⓜ Barceloneta) There's no sign, but locals know where to head for a seafood feast. They say the restaurant's raw materials are delivered daily from fishing ports along the Catalan coast. There's no a la carte menu – what's on offer depends on what the sea has surrendered that day – but you can count on fresh seafood and/or fish, *jamón* (cured ham), tomato bread and grilled vegetables.

Barcelona on a Plate

Simply garnished is best: rock salt and quality olive oil

Traditional medley of chargrilled vegetables

The tastiest are cooked over coals or direct flame

Served either cold or lukewarm

Everyone's favourite was made by their grandmother

KABAND/SHUTTERSTOCK ©

Escalivada

Vegetable Delight

Colourful, slippery and full of flavour, escalivada is a Catalan classic. Order as a shared plate towards the beginning of a meal or tackle it alongside a meaty or fishy main. Catalans argue copiously about what ingredients should be present, so vegetables vary, but expect to find aubergine, onion, garlic and peppers at least, backed by a spicy undertone of cumin. Other additions might include goat's cheese or fresh anchovies.

★ Top Five for Escalivada

Can Recasens (p141) Romantic setting and a delicious array of delicacies.

Vinateria del Call (p132) A jewel box of a restaurant, serving up tasty dishes from around Spain.

El Quim (p137) A classic counter bar in the Mercat de la Boqueria.

Suculent (p137) Try your escalivada Michelin-starred.

Sésamo (p136) Widely held to be the best vegie restaurant in the city.

NITO/SHUTTERSTOCK ©

⊗ Barceloneta & the Waterfront

La Cova Fumada   Tapas €

(☏93 221 40 61; Carrer del Baluard 56; tapas €4-8; ⊙9am-3.20pm Mon-Wed, 9am-3.20pm & 6-8.15pm Thu & Fri, 9am-1pm Sat; Ⓜ Barceloneta) There's no sign and the setting is decidedly downmarket, but this tiny, buzzing family-run tapas spot always packs in a crowd. The secret? Mouthwatering *pulpo* (octopus), *calamar, sardines* and 15 or so other small plates cooked to perfection in the small open kitchen. The *bombas* (potato croquettes served with *alioli*) and grilled *carxofes* (artichokes) are good, and everything is amazingly fresh.

El 58   Tapas €

(Le cinquante huit; Rambla del Poblenou 58; sharing plates €4-11; ⊙1.30pm-11pm Tue-Sat; Ⓜ Llacuna) This French-Catalan eatery serves imaginative, beautifully prepared tapas dishes that earn rave reviews from both locals and expats. Solo diners can grab a seat at the marble-topped front bar and get dining tips from the friendly multilingual baristas. The back dining room with its exposed brick walls, industrial light fixtures and curious artworks is a lively place to linger over a long meal.

Can Recasens   Catalan €€

(☏93 300 81 23; www.canrecasens.com; Rambla del Poblenou 102; mains €8-15; ⊙9pm-1am Mon-Fri & 1-4pm & 9pm-1am Sat; Ⓜ Poblenou) One of Poblenou's most romantic settings, Can Recasens hides a warren of warmly lit rooms full of oil paintings, flickering candles, fairy lights and baskets of fruit. The food is outstanding, with a mix of salads, fondues, smoked meats, cheeses and open-faced sandwiches piled high with delicacies like wild mushrooms and brie, *escalivada* (grilled vegetables) and gruyere, and spicy chorizo.

Green Spot   Vegetarian €€

(Map p250; ☏93 802 55 65; www.encompa niadelobos.com/the-green-spot; Carrer de la Reina Cristina 12; mains €10-15; ⊙12.30pm-midnight Mon-Fri, 1pm-midnight Sat & Sun; ✍;

Ⓜ Barceloneta) The vegetarian's lot has vastly improved in Barcelona in recent years, and Green Spot is one of the places they can find sanctuary. It embraces all the latest food vogues (*dukkah, tempeh,* cold-pressed juices, black pizzas) and presents them in a beautifully stylish dining room, a far cry from the earnest veggie joints of yore.

Can Maño   Spanish €€

(Carrer del Baluard 12; mains €8-14; ⊙8.30am-4pm Tue-Sat & 8-11pm Mon-Fri; Ⓜ Barceloneta) It may look like a dive, but you'll need to be prepared to wait before being squeezed in at a packed table for a raucous night of *raciones* (full-plate-size tapas serving) over a bottle of *turbio* – a cloudy white plonk. The seafood is abundant with first-rate squid, prawns and fish served at rock-bottom prices.

Aguaribay   Vegetarian €€

(☏93 300 37 90; www.aguaribay-bcn.com; Carrer del Taulat 95; mains €9-12; ⊙1-4pm Mon-Wed & Sun, 1-4pm & 8.30-11pm Thu, to 11.30pm Fri & Sat; ✍; Ⓜ Llacuna) Step into this polished eatery in Poblenou and you can't help but feel that the vegetarian renaissance has arrived in Barcelona. Aguaribay serves a small well-executed a la carte menu by night: miso and smoked tofu meatballs, soba noodles with shiitake mushrooms, seasonal vegetables and a rich black rice. At lunchtime, stop in for the prix-fixe lunch specials, which change daily.

Barraca   Seafood €€€

(☏93 224 12 53; www.tribuwoki.com; Passeig Maritim de la Barceloneta 1; mains €19-24; ⊙1-11.30pm; Ⓜ Barceloneta) This buzzing space has a great location fronting the Mediterranean – a key reference point in the excellent seafood dishes served here. Start off with a cauldron of chilli-infused clams, cockles and mussels before moving on to the lavish paellas and other rice dishes, which steal the show.

Can Ros   Seafood €€€

(☏93 221 45 79; www.canros.cat; Carrer del Almirall Aixada 7; mains €16-30; ⊙1-4pm & 7-11pm Tue-Sun; 🚌45, 57, 59, 64, 157, Ⓜ Barceloneta) The fifth generation is now at the controls of this immutable seafood favourite, which first opened in 1908. In a restaurant where the decor is a reminder of simpler times, there's a straightforward guiding principle: serve juicy fresh fish cooked with a light touch.

Els Pescadors — Seafood €€€

(☎93 225 20 18; www.elspescadors.com; Plaça de Prim 1; mains €19-40; ⏰1-3.45pm & 8-11.30pm; ☞; 🚌6, ⓂPoblenou) Set on a picturesque square lined with low houses and *bella ombre* trees long ago imported from South America, this quaint family restaurant continues to serve some of the city's best grilled fish and seafood-and-rice dishes. There are three dining areas inside: two quite modern, while the main one preserves its old tavern flavour. On warm nights, try for a table outside.

❽ La Sagrada Família & L'Eixample

Tapas 24 — Tapas €

(Map p254; ☎93 488 09 77; www.carlesabellan. com; Carrer de la Diputació 269; tapas €4-9.50; ⏰9am-midnight; ☞; ⓂPasseig de Gràcia) Carles Abellan, master of the now-defunct Comerç 24 in La Ribera, runs this basement tapas haven known for its gourmet versions of old faves. Specials include the *bikini* (toasted ham and cheese sandwich – here the ham is cured and the truffle makes all the difference) and a thick black *arròs negre de sípia* (cuttlefish-ink black rice).

Cremeria Toscana — Gelato €

(☎93 539 38 25; www.cremeriatoscana.es; Carrer de Muntaner 161; ice cream from €2.80; ⏰1pm-midnight Mon-Thu, to 1am Fri & Sat, noon-midnight Sun Apr-Oct, 1-9pm Tue-Thu, to midnight Fri, to 1am Sat, noon-11pm Sun Nov-Mar; ⓂHospital Clínic) Yes, you can stumble across quite reasonable ice cream in Barcelona, but close your eyes and imagine yourself across the Mediterranean with the real ice-cream wizards. Creamy *stracciatella* and wavy *nocciola* and myriad other flavours await at the most authentic gelato outlet in town. Buy a cone or a tub.

Chicha Limoná — Mediterranean, Pizzeria €€

(Map p254; ☎93 277 64 03; www.chichalimona. com; Passeig de Sant Joan 80; mains €10-16; ⏰9.30am-1am Tue-Thu, to 2am Fri & Sat, 9.30am-5pm Sun; ☞; ⓂTetuan) Passeig de Sant Joan has become the newest haunt for the hussar-moustached, turned-up-cigarette-pants brigade, and bright, bustling Chicha Limoná has provided them with somewhere great to eat. Grilled octopus with quince jelly, pork with apple compote and pear tatin with crème anglaise are among the oft-changing dishes (set menu €13.90), along with homemade pizzas.

Entrepanes Díaz — Sandwiches €€

(Map p254; ☎93 415 75 82; Carrer de Pau Claris 189; sandwiches €6-8, salads €12; ⏰1pm-midnight Tue-Sat, to 6pm Sun; ⓂDiagonal) A new concept in upmarket gourmet sandwiches, from roast beef to suckling pig, along with sharing plates of Spanish specialities such as sea urchins and prawn fritters, in a sparkling old-style bar. The policy of only hiring experienced waiters over 50 lends a certain gravitas to the operation and some especially charming service.

Can Kenji — Japanese €€

(Map p254; ☎93 476 18 23; www.cankenji.com; Carrer del Rosselló 325; mains €10-14; ⏰1-3.30pm & 8.30-11pm; ⓂVerdaguer) If you want to go Japanese in Barcelona, this is the place. The chef of this understated little *izakaya* (a Japanese tavern) gets his ingredients fresh from the city's markets, with traditional Japanese recipes receiving a Mediterranean touch. This is fusion at its very best.

Cu-Cut! — Spanish €€

(Map p254; ☎93 667 79 69; www.cu-cut.cat; Carrer d'Enric Granados 68; mains €9-13, fixed lunch €12.90; ⏰10am-2am; 🚆FGC Provença) Named after a popular Catalan satirical magazine from the early 19th century, Cu-Cut! is an attractive beamed taberna, with a large covered porch out front, a bar groaning with tapas and a long romantically lit dining room. There are dishes from all over Spain

Food preparation at Tapas 24

and further afield, including octopus *a feira* (with paprika), roast Iberian pork and hake ceviche.

Casa Amalia
Catalan €€

(Map p254; ☑ 93 458 94 58; www.casamaliabcn. com; Passatge del Mercat 4-6; mains €9-20; ⏱1-3.30pm & 9-10.30pm Tue-Sat, 1-3.30pm Sun; Ⓜ Girona) This very local restaurant is popular for its hearty Catalan cooking that uses fresh produce, mainly sourced from the busy market next door. On Thursdays during winter it offers the mountain classic, *escudella*. Otherwise, you might try light variations on local cuisine, such as the *bacallà al allioli de poma* (cod in an apple-based aioli sauce). The three-course *menú del día* is €15.50.

Patagonia Beef & Wine
South American €€

(Map p254; ☑ 93 304 37 35; www.patagoniabw. com; Gran Via de les Corts Catalanes 660; mains €18-30; ⏱1.30-3.30pm & 7-11pm Mon-Thu, to 11.30pm Fri, to 10.30pm Sat; Ⓜ Passeig de Gràcia) This stylish restaurant does exactly what it says on the tin, which is offer an Argentinian

meat-fest. Start with *empanadas* (small pies filled with various meats), then head for a hearty meat main, such as a juicy beef *medallón con salsa de colmenillas* (medallion in a morel sauce) or such classics as the *bife de chorizo* (sirloin strip) or Brazilian *picanha* (rump).

Disfrutar
Modern European €€€

(☑ 93 348 68 96; www.en.disfrutarbarcelona.com; Carrer de Villarroel 163; tasting menus €110-180; ⏱1-2.30pm & 8-9.30pm Tue-Sat; Ⓜ Hospital Clínic) In its first few months of life, Disfrutar rose stratospherically to become the city's finest restaurant – book now while it's still possible to get a table. Run by alumni of Ferran Adrià's game-changing El Bulli restaurant, it operates along similar lines.

Cinc Sentits
International €€€

(Map p254; ☑ 93 323 94 90; www.cincsentits. com; Carrer d'Aribau 58; tasting menus €100-120; ⏱1.30-3pm & 8.30-10pm Tue-Sat; Ⓜ Passeig de Gràcia) Enter the realm of the 'Five Senses' to indulge in a jaw-dropping tasting menu consisting of a series of small, experimental dishes (there is no à la carte, although

Vegetarian Food

Vegetarians and vegans can have a hard time in Spain, but in Barcelona a growing battery of vegetarian restaurants offers welcome relief. Be careful when ordering salads (such as the *amanida catalana*), which may contain popular 'vegetables' such as ham or tuna.

dishes can be tweaked to suit diners' requests). There is a lunch *menú* for €55.

Lasarte Modern European €€€

(Map p254; ☏93 445 32 42; www.restaurantlasarte.com; Passeig de Gràcia 75; mains €46-53; ☉1.30-3.30pm, 8.30-11pm Tue-Sat; Ⓜ Diagonal) One of the best restaurants in Barcelona, overseen by triple-starred chef Martín Berasategui. From Duroc pigs' trotters with quince to his famous smoked eel terrine, this is sophisticated stuff, served in a modern, spacious dining room by waiting staff who could put the most overawed of diners at ease.

Casa Calvet Catalan €€€

(Map p254; ☏93 412 40 12; www.casacalvet.es; Carrer de Casp 48; mains €29-32, lunch menú €38; ☉1-3.30pm & 8.30-11pm Mon-Sat; Ⓜ Urquinaona) An early Gaudí masterpiece loaded with his trademark curvy features houses a swish restaurant (just to the right of the building's main entrance). Dress up and ask for an intimate *taula cabina* (wooden booth). You could opt for scallops and razor clams with pesto and buckwheat, or venison with juniper and porcini sauce.

⊗ Montjuïc, Poble Sec & Sant Antoni

Spice Cafe €

(Map p256; spicecafe.es; Carrer de Margarit 13; desserts around €4; ☉4-9pm Tue-Thu, 11am-9pm Fri-Sun; ☏; Ⓜ Poble Sec) Spice is a delightful cafe that's earned quite a following for its

delicious homemade desserts – especially its moist, creamy carrot cake (the best in town). Good coffees, loose-leaf teas, friendly English-speaking staff and heavenly temptations in the glass front counter may inspire multiple visits.

Palo Cortao Tapas €€

(Map p256; ☏93 188 90 67; www.palocortao.es; Carrer de Nou de la Rambla 146; mains €10-15; ☉8pm-1am Tue-Sun & 1-5pm Sat & Sun; Ⓜ Paral·lel) Palo Cortao has a solid reputation for its beautifully executed seafood and meat dishes, served at fair prices. Highlights include octopus with white bean hummus, skirt steak with foie armagnac, and tuna tataki tempura. You can order half sizes of all plates, allowing you to try more.

Quimet i Quimet Tapas €€

(Map p256; ☏93 442 31 42; Carrer del Poeta Cabanyes 25; tapas €4-10, montaditos around €3; ☉noon-4pm & 7-10.30pm Mon-Fri, noon-4pm Sat; Ⓜ Paral·lel) Quimet i Quimet is a family-run business that has been passed down from generation to generation. There's barely space to swing a *calamar* in this bottle-lined, standing-room-only place, but it is a treat for the palate, with *montaditos* (tapas on a slice of bread) made to order.

Malamén Modern Spanish €€

(Map p256; ☏93 252 77 63; Carrer de Blai 53; mains €14-25; ☉8pm-midnight Tue-Sun; Ⓜ Poble Sec) Carrer de Blai is now lined with bars and restaurants, but Malamén towers above most for its elegant deco design, immaculate service and superb food. A shortish menu runs a mighty range, from vegan 'tartare' of beetroot, fennel and mustard to a juicy steak with bacon and creamed mushrooms. The wine list is equally concise and well curated.

Juice House Health Food €€

(Map p256; ☏93 117 15 15; thejuicehouse.es; Carrer del Parlament 12; mains €8-10; ☉10am-11pm Sun-Thu, to midnight Fri & Sat; ☏; Ⓜ Poble Sec) Juice House ticks all the boxes in the healthy-living camp. Whether you're a vegetarian, vegan, flexitarian, raw-food fan or simply after a tasty, thoughtfully prepared meal, this cheery cafe should figure high on your itinerary. Oat and chia pancakes, açaí fruit bowls, and oven-baked eggs are fine ways to start the morning.

Bodega 1900 Tapas **€€**

(Map p256; ☎93 325 26 59; www.bodega1900.com; Carrer de Tamarit 91; tapas €6-15; ⏰1pm-10.30pm Tue-Sat; Ⓜ Sant Antoni) A venture from the world-famous Adrià brothers, Bodega 1900 mimics an old-school tapas and vermouth bar, but this is no ordinary spit-and-sawdust joint serving *patatas bravas*. Witness, for example, the 'spherified' false olives, or the *mollete de calamars*, probably the best squid sandwich in the world, hot from the pan and served with chipotle mayonnaise, kimchi and lemon zest.

Federal Cafe **€€**

(Map p256; ☎93 187 36 07; www.federalcafe.es; Carrer del Parlament 39; mains €9-12; ⏰8am-11pm Mon-Thu, 8am-1am Fri, 9am-1am Sat, 9am-5.30pm Sun; 📶✍; Ⓜ Sant Antoni) On a stretch that now teems with cafes, Australian-run Federal was the trailbazer, with its breezy chic and superb brunches. Later in the day there is healthy, tasty cooking from veggie burgers to grilled salmon with soba noodles, not to mention snacks (like prawn toast or polenta chips with gorgonzola) and good coffee (including a decent flat white).

Tickets Modern Spanish **€€€**

(Map p256; ☎606 225545; www.ticketsbar.es; Avinguda del Paral·lel 164; tapas €5-27; ⏰6.30-10.30pm Tue-Fri, 1-3pm & 7-10.30pm Sat, closed Aug; Ⓜ Paral·lel) This is one of the sizzling tickets in the restaurant world, a tapas bar opened by Ferran Adrià, of the legendary El Bulli, and his brother Albert. And unlike El Bulli, it's an affordable venture – if you can book a table, that is: you can only book online and two months in advance (or call for last-minute cancellations).

Lascar 74 Peruvian **€€**

(Map p256; ☎93 017 98 72; www.lascar.es; Carrer del Roser 74; mains €11-12; ⏰1-4pm & 7pm-midnight; Ⓜ Paral·lel) A self-styled 'ceviche and pisco bar', which does exactly what it says on the tin. In addition to the regular Peruvian ceviches, there are also renditions from Thailand, Japan and Mexico, and

Serving a dish at Tickets

oyster shooters with *leche de tigre* (the traditional ceviche marinade). Pisco sours are the real deal, frothy egg white and all.

⊗ Gràcia & Park Güell

La Nena   Cafe €

(Map p254; ☎93 285 14 76; www.chocolateri alanena.com; Carrer de Ramon i Cajal 36; desserts from €4.50; ⓢ9am-10pm; ⓜ; ⓂFontana) A French team has created this delightfully chaotic space for indulging in cups of *suïssos* (rich hot chocolate) served with a plate of heavy homemade whipped cream and *melindros* (spongy sweet biscuits), fine desserts and even a few savoury dishes. The place is strewn with books and you can play with the board games on the shelves.

TimeLine   Sandwiches €

(Map p254; ☎93 217 79 38; Carrer de la Providèn-cia 3; sandwiches €7-9; ⓢ7pm-2am Mon-Thu, to 3am Fri & Sat, from noon Sun; ⓧ; ⓂLesseps, Fontana) Like stepping into an enchanted cuckoo clock, TimeLine is a cosy candlelit eating-and-drinking cabin decked with

curious artwork (roller skates, twisted light sculptures), black-and-white tile floors and a tiny train set scuttling along the bar. It draws a fun and multilingual crowd, who come for cocktails, sandwiches (curry chicken, meatballs, veggie barbecue), hummus platters and goat's cheese–drizzled salads.

La Panxa del Bisbe   Tapas €€

(Map p254; ☎93 213 70 49; Carrer del Torrent de les Flors 156; tapas €8-14, tasting menus from €30; ⓢ1.30-3.30pm & 8.30pm-midnight Tue-Sat; ⓂJoanic) With low lighting and an artfully minimalist interior, the 'Bishop's Belly' serves up creative tapas that earn high praise from the mostly local crowd. Feast on grilled razor clams, foie gras with pine nuts and pumpkin, tender morsels of tuna tataki or *picanya* (grilled rump steak) served with chips and Béarnaise sauce.

Con Gracia   Fusion €€€

(Map p254; ☎93 238 02 01; www.congracia.es; Carrer de Martínez de la Rosa 8; set menu €65, with wine pairing €95; ⓢ7-11pm Tue-Sat; ⓂDiagonal) This teeny hideaway (seating about 20 in total) is a hive of originality, producing

delicately balanced Mediterranean cuisine with Asian touches. On offer is a regularly changing surprise tasting menu or the set 'traditional' one, with dishes such as squid stuffed with *jamón ibérico* and black truffle, and juicy black angus steak. Book ahead.

Botafumeiro   Seafood €€€

(☑93 218 42 30; www.botafumeiro.es; Carrer Gran de Gràcia 81; mains €20-48; ⊙noon-1am; MFontana) It is hard not to mention this classic temple of Galician shellfish and other briny delights, long a magnet for VIPs visiting Barcelona. You can bring the price down by sharing a few *medias raciones* (large tapas plates) to taste a range of marine offerings.

Roig Robí   Catalan €€€

(Map p254; ☑93 218 92 22; www.roigrobi.com; Carrer de Sènega 20; mains €20-35; ⊙1.30-4pm & 8.30-11.30pm Mon-Fri, 8.30-11.30pm Sat; MDiagonal) This is an altar to refined traditional cooking. The menu changes seasonally and serves as a showcase for beautifully presented creations with local and organic ingredients. Start off with sautéed baby squid with chickpeas or artichokes with foie gras, before moving on to outstanding seafood rice dishes, grilled market-fresh fish baked with salt or slow roasted young lamb.

⊗ Camp Nou, Pedralbes & La Zona Alta

Vivanda   Catalan €€

(☑93 203 19 18; www.vivanda.cat; Carrer Major de Sarrià 134; sharing plates €8-18; ⊙1.30-3.30pm Tue-Sun & 8.30-11pm Tue-Sat; ℝFGC Reina Elisenda) With a menu designed by celebrated Catalan chef Jordi Vilà, diners are in for a treat at this Sarrià classic. The changing dishes showcase seasonal fare (like eggs with truffles, rice with cuttlefish and artichokes with romesco sauce). One of Vivanda's best features is the gardenlike terrace hidden behind the restaurant. With heat lamps, it's open year-round – blankets and hot broth are distributed to diners in winter.

Ajoblanco   Tapas €€

(☑93 667 87 66; www.ajoblancorestaurant.com; Carrer de Tuset 20; sharing plates €6-21; ⊙noon-1am Sun-Wed, to 3am Thu-Sat; ☑; ℝFGC Gràcia) This beautifully designed space serves up a mix of classic and creative tapas plates that go nicely with the imaginative cocktail menu. Sip the house vermouth while munching on crispy artichoke hearts with romesco sauce, slow-roasted lamb shoulder, or wild sea bass ceviche with mango and chilli.

ABaC   Catalan €€€

(☑93 319 66 00; www.abacbarcelona.com; Avinguda del Tibidabo 1; tasting menus €140-170; ⊙1.30-4pm & 8.30-11pm; ℝFGC Av Tibidabo) Led by celebrated chef Jordi Cruz, ABaC offers one of Barcelona's most memorable dining experiences (and also one of its priciest). Expect creative, mouth-watering perfection in dishes like sea-urchin curry with lime, guinea fowl with Norway lobster, and roasted sea bass with artichokes and oysters. Reservations essential.

El Asador de Aranda   Spanish €€€

(☑93 417 01 15; www.asadordearanda.com; Avinguda del Tibidabo 31; mains €17-24; ⊙1-4.30pm daily, 8-11.30pm Mon-Sat; ☎; ℝFGC Avinguda Tibidabo) A great place for a meal after visiting Tibidabo, El Asador de Aranda is set in a striking art-nouveau building, complete with stained-glass windows, Moorish-style brick arches and elaborate ceilings. You'll find a fine assortment of tapas plates for sharing, though the speciality is the meat (roast lamb, spare ribs, beef), beautifully prepared in a wood oven.

La Balsa   Mediterranean €€€

(☑93 211 50 48; www.labalsarestaurant.com; Carrer de la Infanta Isabel 4; mains €20-28; ⊙1.30-4pm Tue-Sun & 8.30-11pm Tue-Sat; ☎; ℝFGC Avinguda Tibidabo) With its grand ceiling and the scented gardens that surround the main terrace dining area, La Balsa is one of the city's top dining experiences. The menu changes frequently and is a mix of traditional Catalan and off-centre inventiveness. Lounge over a cocktail at the bar before you're ushered to your table.

TREASURE HUNT

Begin your shopping adventure

Treasure Hunt

If your doctor has prescribed an intense round of retail therapy to deal with the blues, then Barcelona is the place. Across Ciutat Vella (Barri Gòtic, El Raval and La Ribera), L'Eixample and Gràcia is spread a thick mantle of boutiques, historic shops, original one-off stores, gourmet corners, wine dens and more designer labels than you can shake your gold card at. You name it, you'll find it here.

In This Section

Useful Phrases

I'd like to buy...	*Quería comprar...*	ke·*ria* kom·prar...
I'm just looking	*Sólo estoy mirando*	so·lo es·*toy* mee·*ran*·do
Can I look at it?	*¿Puedo verlo?*	pwe·do ver·lo
Do you have other sizes?	*¿Tienes más tallas?*	tyen·es mas·tie·yas
How much is it?	*¿Cuanto cuesta?*	kwan·to kwes·ta

Gràcia & Park Güell
A bit of everything in this
intriguing, locally focused district
(p164)

**Camp Nou, Pedralbes
& La Zona Alta**
Large-scale shops and the
FC Barcelona stadium store
(p167)

**La Sagrada Família
& L'Eixample**
Big-name designers and
upmarket boutiques
(p162)

La Ribera
Great market and numerous
gourmet food outlets
(p159)

*Port
Olímpic*

El Raval
Alternative, bohemian
design, clothing and
vintage stores
(p156)

**La Rambla &
Barri Gòtic**
Intriguing quirky shops
on narrow lanes among
tourist traps
(p154)

**Barceloneta &
the Waterfront**
Great flea market and
craft market choices
(p160)

**Montjuïc, Poble Sec
& Sant Antoni**
Small, quirky boutiques,
pop-ups and cutting-edge streetwear
(p164)

*Port
Vell*

*Mediterranean
Sea*

Opening Hours

In general, shops open between 10am
and 2pm and then again from around
4.30pm to 8pm Monday to Friday,
though some fashion boutiques, design
stores and the like don't close at
lunchtime. Many open on Saturdays too,
sometimes only in the morning, and a
few open on Sundays and holidays.

Large supermarkets, malls and department stores open from 10am to 10pm
Monday to Saturday.

Sales

The winter sales start after El Dia
dels Reis/Epifanía (6 January) and,
depending on the shop, can go on well
into February. Summer sales start in
July, with shops trying to entice locals
in before they flood out of the city on
holiday in August. Some shops prolong
sales to August's end.

The Best...

Experience Barcelona's best shopping

Markets

Mercat de Santa Caterina (p106) A colourful alternative to La Boqueria, with fewer crowds and lower prices.

Els Encants Vells (p160) A sprawling flea market in a spanking new building.

El Bulevard dels Antiquaris (p163) A labyrinth of tiny antique shops that merits a morning's browsing.

For Vintage

L'Arca (p154) Ethereal gowns, often used for film sets, in the heart of the Barri Gòtic.

El Bulevard dels Antiquaris (p163) A quirky hotchpotch of antique shops.

Els Encants Vells (p160) Stunningly remodelled flea market, where you can unearth retro homeware and kitschy bric-a-brac.

Port Antic (p163) A quirky street market with finds from vintage toys to tiny oil paintings.

For Fashion

Coquette (p160) Offbeat women's clothes that share an ethereal elegance.

Holala! Plaza (p159) These days vintage is the new designer, and nowhere has a better selection than Holala!

Bagués-Masriera (p125) Exquisite jewellery from a company with a long tradition.

Custo Barcelona (p160) Quirky, colourful clothes that are not for the shy.

Loisaida (p159) Cute, smart and somewhat retro clothing for men and women.

For Design & Craft

Drap Art (p155) Weird and wonderful recycled art and accessories.

Arlequí Màscares (p159) Handmade masks to rival any in Venice; the perfect souvenir.

Fantastik (p157) A temple to kitsch, with kooky wonders from all around the world.

Teranyina (p159) The 'Spider's Web', so called for its intricate designs in intricate textiles.

For Souvenirs & Gifts

Born Centre de Cultura i Memòria (p84) The gift shop at this exhibition space stocks tasteful, well-made souvenirs and books about the city.

Les Topettes (p156) Creams, oils, perfumes and soaps that look every bit as tantalising as they smell.

Fantastik (p157) Offbeat gifts and curios sourced from around the globe.

Sabater Hermanos (p154) Divinely fragranced shop selling handmade soaps in pretty gift boxes.

For Food & Wine

Casa Gispert (p107) The speciality is roast nuts of every type, but you'll also find chocolate, conserves and olive oils, attractively labelled.

Vila Viniteca (p107) A jaw-dropping cathedral of wines from Catalonia and elsewhere in Spain, tucked away in a Born side street.

Barcelona Reykjavik (p157) The place to come for that organic spelt loaf or buttery croissant.

Caelum (p135) Deliciously wicked sweet treats made by nuns, with a little tea room downstairs.

★ Lonely Planet's Top Choices

Mercat de la Boqueria (p94) Stock up on budget delicacies amid one of Europe's most vibrant food markets.

Vila Viniteca (p107) Oenophiles unite at this wonderful wine shop.

Coquette (p160) Simple and beautiful designer clothes for women.

Loisaida (p159) Men's and women's fashion, antiques and retro vinyl.

🔒 La Rambla & Barri Gòtic

Torrons Vicens   Food
(Map p250; ☎93 304 37 36; www.vicens.com;
Carrer del Petritxol 15; ⏱10am-8.30pm Mon-Sat,
11am-8pm Sun; Ⓜ Liceu) You can find the
turrón (nougat) treat year-round at Torrons
Vicens, which has been selling its signature
sweets since 1775.

Sabater Hermanos   Cosmetics
(Map p250; ☎93 301 98 32; www.sabaterher
manos.es; Plaça de Sant Felip Neri 1; ⏱10.30am-
9pm; Ⓜ Jaume I) This fragrant little shop sells
handcrafted soaps of all sizes. Varieties
such as fig, cinnamon, grapefruit and
chocolate smell good enough to eat, while
sandalwood, magnolia, mint, cedar and
jasmine add spice to any sink or bathtub.

Escribà   Food & Drinks
(Map p250; ☎93 301 60 27; www.escriba.es; La
Rambla 83; ⏱9am-10pm; 📶; Ⓜ Liceu) Chocolates, dainty pastries and mouth-watering
cakes can be nibbled behind the Modernista mosaic facade here or taken away for
private, guilt-ridden consumption. This

Barcelona favourite is owned by the Escribà
family, a name synonymous with sinfully
good sweet things. More than that, it adds a
touch of authenticity to La Rambla.

Formatgeria La Seu   Food
(Map p250; ☎93 412 65 48; www.format
gerialaseu.com; Carrer de la Dagueria 16; ⏱10am-
2pm & 5-8pm Tue-Sat, closed Aug; Ⓜ Jaume I)
Dedicated to artisan cheeses from all
across Spain, this small shop is run by the
oh-so-knowledgeable Katherine McLaugh-
lin and is the antithesis of mass production – it sells only the best from small-scale
farmers and the stock changes regularly.
Wine and cheese tastings in the cosy room
at the back are fun.

L'Arca   Vintage, Clothing
(Map p250; ☎93 302 15 98; www.larca.es;
Carrer dels Banys Nous 20; ⏱11am-2pm &
4.30-8.30pm Mon-Sat; Ⓜ Liceu) Step inside
this enchanting shop for a glimpse of
beautifully crafted apparel from the past,
including 18th-century embroidered silk
vests, elaborate silk kimonos, and wedding
dresses and shawls from the 1920s. Thanks

Torrons Vicens

to its incredible collection, it has provided clothing for films including *Titanic, Talk to Her* and *Perfume: The Story of a Murderer*.

Herboristeria del Rei   Cosmetics
(Map p250; ☑93 318 05 12; www.herboristeri adelrei.com; Carrer del Vidre 1; ◷2.30-8.30pm Mon, 10am-8.30pm Tue-Sat; Ⓜ Liceu) Once patronised by Queen Isabel II, this timeless corner store flogs all sorts of weird and wonderful herbs, spices and medicinal plants. It's been doing so since 1823 and the decor has barely changed since the 1860s. However, some of the products have, and you'll find anything from fragrant soaps to massage oil nowadays.

Cereria Subirà   Homewares
(Map p250; ☑93 315 26 06; cereriasubira.net; Calle de la Llibreteria 7; ◷9.30am-1.30pm & 4-8pm Mon-Thu, 9.30am-8pm Fri, 10am-8pm Sat; Ⓜ Jaume I) Even if you're not interested in myriad mounds of colourful wax, pop in just so you've been to the oldest shop in Barcelona. Cereria Subirà has been churning out candles since 1761 and at this address since the 19th century; the interior has a beautifully baroque quality, with a picturesque *Gone With the Wind*–style staircase.

Artesania Catalunya   Arts & Crafts
(Map p250; ☑934 67 46 60; www.bcncrafts. com; Carrer dels Banys Nous 11; ◷10am-8pm Mon-Sat, to 2pm Sun; Ⓜ Liceu) A celebration of Catalan products, this nicely designed store is a great place to browse for unique gifts. You'll find jewellery with designs inspired by Roman iconography (as well as works that reference Gaudí and Barcelona's Gothic era), plus pottery, wooden toys, silk scarves, notebooks, housewares and more.

La Colmena   Food
(Map p250; ☑93 315 13 56; Plaça de l'Angel 12; ◷9am-9pm; Ⓜ Jaume I) A pastry shop selling many delicacies including pine-nut-encrusted *panellets* (sweet almond cakes), flavoured meringues and feather-light *ensaïmadas* (soft, sweet buns topped with powdered sugar) from Mallorca.

 Mercantic

Antique collectors could set aside a Sunday morning for a trip to **Mercantic** (☑93 674 49 50; www.mercantic. com; Av de Rius i Taulet 120; ◷9.30am-8pm Tue-Sat, 10am-3pm Sun; 🛜; 🚆 FGC line S2 to Volpelleres), a collection of gaily painted timber huts occupied by antique and bric-a-brac dealers selling records, books, vintage clothes, jewellery, artwork, home furnishings and much more. Ample food and drink vendors on hand add to the good cheer and there's even live music some days. The first Sunday of the month is delivery day, when the stallholders take delivery of a new wave of old stuff. The permanent market, with some 80 stallholders, is open during the week too. There's also an activities and play area for children.

Drap Art   Arts & Crafts
(Map p250; ☑93 268 48 89; www.drapart.org; Carrer Groc 1; ◷11am-2pm & 5-8pm Tue-Fri, 6-9pm Sat; Ⓜ Jaume I) A nonprofit arts organisation runs this small store and gallery space, which exhibits wild designs from artists near and far. Works change regularly, but you might find sculptures, jewellery, handbags and other accessories made from recycled products, as well as mixed-media installations.

La Manual Alpargatera   Shoes
(Map p250; ☑93 301 01 72; Carrer d'Avinyó 7; ◷9.30am-1.30pm & 4.30-8pm Mon-Fri, from 10am Sat; Ⓜ Liceu) All manner of clients, from Salvador Dalí to Jean Paul Gaultier, have ordered a pair of *espadrilles* (rope-soled canvas shoes) from this famous store. The shop was founded just after the Spanish Civil War, though the roots of the simple shoe design date back hundreds of years and originate in the Catalan Pyrenees.

Art & Crafts Market
Market

(Mostra d'Art; Map p250; Plaça de Sant Josep Oriol; ⏱11am-8.30pm Sat, 10am-3pm Sun; Ⓜ Liceu) The Barri Gòtic is enlivened by an art and crafts market on Saturdays and Sundays.

Coin & Stamp Market
Market

(Mercat de Numismàtica i Filatèlia; Map p250; Plaça Reial; ⏱9am-2.30pm Sun; Ⓜ Liceu) A relic of bygone Barcelona, in the shape of a dusty philatelic and coin market.

FC Botiga
Gifts & Souvenirs

(Map p250; ☏93 269 15 32; Carrer de Jaume I 18; ⏱10am-9pm Mon-Sat; Ⓜ Jaume I) Need a Lionel Messi football jersey, a blue and burgundy ball, or any other football paraphernalia pertaining to what many locals consider the greatest team in the world? This is a convenient spot to load up without traipsing to the stadium.

Papabubble
Food

(Map p250; ☏93 268 86 25; www.papabubble. com; Carrer Ample 28; ⏱10am-2pm & 4-8.30pm Mon-Fri, 10am-8.30pm Sat; Ⓜ Jaume I) It feels like a step into another era in this sweet shop, which makes up pots of rainbow-coloured boiled lollies, just like some of us remember from corner-store days as kids. Watch the sticky sweets being made before your eyes.

Petritxol Xocoa
Food

(Map p250; ☏93 301 82 91; www.xocoa-bcn.com; Carrer del Petritxol 11-13; ⏱9.30am-9pm; Ⓜ Liceu) Tucked along 'chocolate street' Carrer del Petritxol, this den of dental devilry displays ranks and ranks of original bars in stunning designs, chocolates stuffed with sweet stuff, gooey pastries and more. It has various other branches scattered about town.

🄐 El Raval

Les Topettes
Cosmetics

(Map p249; ☏93 500 55 64; www.lestopettes. com; Carrer de Joaquín Costa 33; ⏱11am-2pm & 4-9pm Tue-Sat, 4-9pm Mon; Ⓜ Universitat) It's a sign of the times that such a chic little temple to soap and perfume can exist in El Raval. The items in Les Topettes' collection have been picked for their designs as much as the products themselves, and you'll find

gorgeously packaged scents, candles and unguents from Diptyque, Cowshed and L'Artisan Parfumeur, among others.

Chök   Food
(Map p250; ☑93 304 23 60; www.chokbar celona.com; Carrer del Carme 3; ⊙8am-9pm; ⓂLiceu) Set inside an old chocolate-maker's, with original wooden shelving and stained glass, Chök now specialises in all things sweet, but especially doughnuts. These come in a huge array of colours and flavours, but there are also cookies, macarons, marshmallows and, of course, the ubiquitous cronut. There's also a tiny space where you can order and drink coffee.

Joan La Llar del Pernil   Food
(Map p250; ☑93 317 95 29; Stalls 667, 669, 670 & 671, Mercat de la Boqueria; ⊙8am-3pm Mon-Thu, to 8pm Fri & Sat; ⓂLiceu) This stall in the Mercat de la Boqueria sells some of the best ham in the city, which can be sliced and sold as a snack.

Barcelona Reykjavik   Food
(Map p249; ☑93 302 09 21; www.barcelona reykjavik.com; Carrer del Doctor Dou 12;

⊙10am-9pm Mon-Sat, 9.30am-8pm Sun; ⓂCatalunya) Bread lovers, rejoice! Good bread can be hard to find in Barcelona, but Reykjavik saves the day. All loaves are made using organic flour – spelt, wholemeal, mixed cereals and so on – and sourdough yeast, though this does make for fairly high prices. The bakery also produces excellent cakes. Three more shops can be found in the Born, Gràcia and L'Eixample.

Fantastik   Arts & Crafts
(Map p249; ☑93 301 30 68; www.fantastik. es; Carrer de Joaquín Costa 62; ⊙11am-2pm & 4-8.30pm Mon-Fri, 11am-3pm & 4-9pm Sat; ⓂUniversitat) Over 400 products, including a Mexican skull rattle, robot moon explorer from China and recycled plastic zebras from South Africa, are to be found in this colourful shop, which sources its items from Mexico, India, Bulgaria, Russia, Senegal and 20 other countries. It's a perfect place to buy all the things you don't need but can't live without.

Holala! Plaza   Fashion & Accessories
(Map p249; www.holala-ibiza.com; Plaça de Castella 2; ⊙11am-9pm Mon-Sat; ⓂUniversitat)

★ El Raval Shopping

El Raval boasts a handful of art galleries around MACBA, along with a burgeoning second-hand and vintage-clothes scene on Carrer de la Riera Baixa. Carrer dels Tallers is one of the city's main music strips.

From left: Chök; a branch of FC Botiga; espadrilles

ADAMSAV STUDIO/SHUTTERSTOCK ©

BILDERFINDER/SHUTTERSTOCK ©

5 Must-Buy Mementos

Cured Meat

Instead of *jamón* (cured ham), go for some local sausage such as *fuet* or *botifarra*. It's best bought in one of the market halls. They'll vacuum-pack it for you.

FC Barcelona Gear

Yes, everyone seems to have a Messi or Neymar shirt these days, but you can find harder-to-come-by Barça mementoes in their official shops.

Wine

Look for something you can't get back home – some small-producer Catalan red, or a hard-to-get *cava* (sparkling wine). Wine shops in La Ribera have an ample supply.

Fashion

Quality threads can be had all over town, but best seek out a small local design boutique to ensure you head back wearing something unique.

Build a Gaudí

We might not have the maestro's imagination, but by damn we can reconstruct his buildings in miniature. Available in most Gaudí buildings and museum shops.

Backing on to Carrer de Valldonzella, where it boasts an exhibition space for temporary art displays, this Ibiza import is inspired by that island's long-established (and somewhat commercialised) hippie tradition. Vintage clothes are the name of the game, along with an eclectic program of exhibitions and activities.

Teranyina · Arts & Crafts

(Map p249; www.textilteranyina.com; Carrer del Notariat 10; ◎11am-2pm & 5-8pm Mon-Fri; ⓂCatalunya) Artist Teresa Rosa Aguayo runs this textile workshop in the heart of the artsy bit of El Raval. You can join courses at the loom, admire some of the rugs and other works that Teresa has created and, of course, buy them.

La Portorriqueña · Coffee

(Map p249; Carrer d'en Xuclà 25; ◎9am-2pm & 5-8pm Mon-Fri, 9am-2pm Sat; ⓂCatalunya) Coffee beans from around the world, freshly ground before your eyes, have been the winning formula in this store since 1902. It also offers all sorts of chocolate goodies. The street it's on is good for little old-fashioned food boutiques.

🔒 La Ribera

See p104 for fabulous food-shopping choices in La Ribera.

El Rei de la Màgia · Magic

(Map p250; ☎93 319 39 20; www.elreydela magia.com; Carrer de la Princesa 11; ◎10.30am-2pm & 4-7.30pm Mon-Sat; ⓂJaume I) For more than 100 years, the people behind this box of tricks have been keeping locals both astounded and amused. Should you decide to stay in Barcelona and make a living as a magician, this is the place to buy levitation brooms, glasses of disappearing milk and decks of magic cards.

Marsalada · Gifts & Souvenirs

(Map p250; ☎93 116 20 76; www.marsaladade sign.com; Carrer de Sant Jacint 6; ◎10am-2pm, 4-8pm Mon-Sat; ⓂJaume I) For souvenirs with a difference, Marsalada has hand-printed tote bags in unbleached cotton, engravings

Designers

The heart of L'Eixample, bisected by Passeig de Gràcia, is known as the Quadrat d'Or (Golden Square) and is jammed with all sorts of glittering shops. Passeig de Gràcia is a bit of a who's who of international shopping – you'll find Spain's own high-end designers like Loewe, along with Armani, Chanel, Gucci, Stella McCartney and the rest.

In La Ribera, El Born, particularly Carrer del Rec, is big on cool designers like Isabel Marant, Marni, Chloé and Hoss Intropia, in small, clean-line boutiques. Some Barcelona-based designs are also sold here. This is a great area if you have money to spend and hours to browse.

and t-shirts. Each of these is emblazoned with a well-known Barcelona attraction, sketched in pen and ink and adorned with abstract colour mosaics.

Loisaida · Clothing, Antiques

(Map p250; ☎93 295 54 92; www.loisaidabcn. com; Carrer dels Flassaders 42; ◎11am-9pm Mon-Sat, 11am-2pm & 4-8pm Sun; ⓂJaume I) A sight in its own right, housed in what was once the coach house and stables for the Royal Mint, Loisaida (from the Spanglish for 'Lower East Side') is a deceptively large emporium of colourful, retro and somewhat preppy clothing for men and women, costume jewellery, music from the 1940s and '50s and some covetable antiques.

Arlequí Màscares · Arts & Crafts

(Map p250; ☎93 268 27 52; www.arlequimask. com; Carrer de la Princesa 7; ◎10.30am-8.30pm Mon-Sat, 10.30am-3pm & 4-7.30pm Sun; ⓂJaume I) A wonderful little oasis of originality, this shop specialises in masks for costume and decoration. Some of the pieces are superb, while stock also includes a beautiful range of decorative boxes in Catalan themes and some old-style marionettes.

Shopping Malls

Barcelona has no shortage of shopping malls. One of the first to arrive was **L'Illa Diagonal** (93 444 00 00; www.lilla.com; Avinguda Diagonal 549; 10am-9.30pm Mon-Sat; Maria Cristina), designed by star Spanish architect Rafael Moneo. The **Centre Comercial Diagonal Mar** (93 567 76 37; www.diagonalmar.com; Avinguda Diagonal 3; 10am-10pm Mon-Sat; El Maresme Fòrum), by the sea, is one of the latest additions.

The city's other emporia include **Centre Comercial de les Glòries** (93 486 04 04; www.lesglories.com; Gran Via de les Corts Catalanes 208; 10am-1am; Glòries), in the former Olivetti factory; **Heron City** (93 276 50 70; www.heroncitybarcelona.com; Avinguda de Rio de Janeiro 42; stores 10am-10pm Mon-Sat, cinema & restaurants 7am-1am daily; Fabra i Puig), just off Avinguda Meridiana, about 4km north of Plaça de les Glòries Catalanes; and the **Centre Comercial Gran Via 2** (902 301444; www.granvia2.com; Gran Via de les Corts Catalanes 75; shops 10am-8pm Mon-Sat, restaurants and cinema 10am-1am daily; FGC Ildefons Cerdà) in L'Hospitalet de Llobregat, which has 180 stores, a 15-screen cinema and two dozen eateries.

Centre Comercial Diagonal Mar
VENIAMIN KRASKOV/SHUTTERSTOCK ©

Coquette   Fashion & Accessories
(Map p250; 93 319 29 76; www.coquettebcn.com; Carrer del Rec 65; 11am-3pm & 5-9pm Mon-Fri, 11.30am-9pm Sat; Barceloneta) With its spare, cut-back and designer look, this

friendly fashion store is attractive in its own right. Women can browse through casual, feminine wear by such designers as Humanoid, Vanessa Bruno, UKE and Hoss Intropia and others, with a further collection nearby at **Carrer de Bonaire 5** (Map p250; 93 310 35 35; Carrer de Bonaire 5; 11am-3pm & 5-9pm Mon-Fri, 11.30am-9pm Sat; Barceloneta).

Nu Sabates   Shoes
(93 268 03 83; www.nusabates.com; Carrer dels Cotoners 14; 11am-9pm Mon-Sat; Jaume I) A couple of modern-day Catalan cobblers have put together some original handmade leather shoes for men and women (and a handful of bags and other leather items) in their friendly and stylish locale, which is enlivened by some inspired musical selections.

Custo Barcelona   Fashion & Accessories
(Map p250; 93 268 78 93; www.custo.com; Plaça de les Olles 7; 10am-9pm Mon-Sat, noon-8pm Sun; Barceloneta) The psychedelic decor and casual atmosphere lend this avant-garde Barcelona fashion store a youthful edge. Custo presents daring new women's and men's collections each year on the New York catwalks. The dazzling colours and cut of everything from dinner jackets to hot pants are for the uninhibited. It has three other stores around town.

Barceloneta & the Waterfront

Els Encants Vells   Market
(Fira de Bellcaire; 93 246 30 30; www.encantsbcn.com; Plaça de les Glòries Catalanes; 9am-8pm Mon, Wed, Fri & Sat; Glòries) In a gleaming open-sided complex near Plaça de les Glòries Catalanes, the 'Old Charms' flea market is the biggest of its kind in Barcelona. Over 500 vendors ply their wares beneath massive mirror-like panels. It's all here, from antique furniture through to second-hand clothes. A lot of it is junk, but occasionally you'll stumble across a *ganga* (bargain).

Els Encants Vells

System Action   Clothing

(📞93 225 79 90; www.systemaction.es; Carrer de Pere IV 122; ⏰10am-7pm Mon-Sat; Ⓜ Llacuna) If you like discovering local producers, then look no further than this outlet store on Pere IV. Though System Action has stores all across Catalonia (and in Madrid), its design headquarters are a few blocks south in a former Poblenou ice factory. Fashions are feminine but rugged and you'll find good basics here. Very wearable scarves, sweaters, skirts and even shoes.

La Bazart   Fashion & Accessories

(📞633 455378; www.labazart.com; Carrer de la Ciutat de Granada 44; ⏰10.30am-6pm Mon-Fri, to 2.30pm Sat; Ⓜ Llacuna) If you can't make it to the handicrafts market in South America, Bazart may be your next best option. This colourfully decorated shop stocks handcrafted goods from across the Andes. There are lots of great gift ideas, including silver jewellery from Ecuador, woven pillowcases from Bolivia and alpaca gloves, scarves and blankets from Chile (where the owner hails from).

Ultra-Local Records   Music

(📞661 017638; www.ultralocalrecords.com; Carrer de Pujades 113; ⏰4-8.30pm Mon-Fri, from 11am Sat; Ⓜ Llacuna) Tucked along a fairly empty stretch of Poblenou, this small, well-curated shop sells mostly used records (plus some re-releases and albums by current indie rock darlings) from Catalan, Spanish, French, American and British artists. Vinyl aside, you'll find a smaller CD selection, plus zines and a few other curiosities. There's a €1 bargain bin in front of the store.

Bestiari   Books, Handicrafts

(Map p250; www.bestiari.net; Plaça de Pau Vila 3; ⏰10am-7pm Tue-Sat, to 2.30pm Sun; Ⓜ Barceloneta) On the ground floor of the Museu d'Història de Catalunya, this nicely stocked shop sells books in English, Spanish and Catalan for all ages, plus you'll find lots of Catalan-themed gift ideas: CDs, T-shirts, umbrellas, messenger bags, chess sets, mugs and toys (along the lines of the build-your-own Gothic or Gaudí structures).

ⓐ La Sagrada Família & L'Eixample

See p124 for more shopping options in this area.

Norma Comics
Books

(☑93 244 81 25; www.normacomics.com; Passeig de Sant Joan 7-9; ☺10.30am-8.30pm Mon-Sat; Ⓜ Arc de Triomf) With a huge range of comics, both Spanish and international, this is Spain's biggest dealer – everything from Tintin to some of the weirdest sci-fi and sex comics can be found here. Also on show are armies of model superheroes and other characters produced by fevered imaginations. Kids from nine to 99 can be seen snapping up items to add to their collections.

Altaïr
Books

(Map p254; ☑93 342 71 71; www.altair.es; Gran Via de les Corts Catalanes 616; ☺10am-8.30pm Mon-Sat; ☜; Ⓜ Catalunya) Enter a wonderland of travel in this extensive bookshop, which is a mecca for guidebooks, maps, travel literature and all sorts of other books likely to induce a severe case of itchy feet. It has a travellers' noticeboard and, downstairs, a travel agent.

Antinous
Books

(Map p249; ☑93 301 90 70; www.antinouslibros. com; Carrer de Casanova 72; ☺11am-2pm & 5-8pm Mon-Sat; Ⓜ Universitat) Gay and lesbian travellers may want to browse in this spacious and relaxed bookshop, which has moved to the Gaixample from its long-held home in the Barri Gòtic. There are all kinds of titles, including kids books and comic books.

Flores Navarro
Flowers

(Map p254; ☑93 457 40 99; www.floristeri asnavarro.com; Carrer de València 320; ☺24hr; Ⓜ Diagonal) You never know when you might need flowers, and this florist never closes. It's a vast space (or couple of spaces, in fact) and worth a visit just for the bank of colour and wonderful fragrance.

Laie
Books

(Map p254; ☑93 318 17 39; www.laie.es; Carrer de Pau Claris 85; ☺9am-9pm Mon-Fri, 10am-9pm Sat; Ⓜ Catalunya, Urquinaona)

Altaïr

Laie has novels and books on architecture, art and film in English, French, Spanish and Catalan. It also has a great upstairs cafe where you can examine your latest purchases or browse through the newspapers provided for customers in true Central European style.

Mercat del Ninot   Market
(📞93 323 49 09; www.mercatdelninot.com; Carrer de Mallorca 157; ⊘9am-8pm Mon-Fri, 9am-2pm Sat; 🛜; Ⓜ Hospital Clínic) A gleaming, modern neighbourhood food market, selling mostly meat and fish, but there are also a couple of stalls where you can grab a bite to eat.

Cubiña   Homewares
(Map p254; 📞93 476 57 21; www.cubinya.es; Carrer de Mallorca 291; ⊘10am-2pm & 4.30-8.30pm Mon-Sat; Ⓜ Verdaguer) Even if interior design doesn't ring your bell, it's worth a visit here just to see the Domènech i Montaner building. Admire the enormous and whimsical wrought-iron decoration at street level before heading inside to marvel at the ceiling, timber work, brick columns and windows. It houses an extensive temple of furniture, lamps and just about any home accessory your heart might desire.

**El Bulevard
dels Antiquaris**   Antiques
(Map p254; 📞93 215 44 99; www.bulevard delsantiquaris.com; Passeig de Gràcia 55-57; ⊘10.30am-8.30pm Mon-Sat; Ⓜ Passeig de Gràcia) More than 70 stores (be warned most close for lunch) are gathered under one roof (on the floor above the more general Bulevard Rosa arcade) to offer the most varied selection of collector's pieces. These range from old porcelain dolls through to fine crystal, from Asian antique furniture to old French goods, and from African and other ethnic art to jewellery.

Joan Múrria   Food
(Map p254; 📞93 215 57 89; www.murria.cat; Carrer de Roger de Llúria 85; ⊘10am-8.30pm Tue-Fri, 10am-2pm & 5-8.30pm Sat; Ⓜ Passeig de Gràcia) Ramon Casas designed the

 Waterfront Markets

On weekends Port Vell springs to life with a handful of markets selling a mix of antiques and contemporary art and crafts at key points along the waterfront.

At the base of La Rambla, the small **Port Antic** (Plaça del Portal de la Pau; ⊘10am-8pm Sat & Sun; Ⓜ Drassanes) market is a requisite stop for strollers and antique hunters. Here you'll find old photographs, frames, oil paintings, records, shawls, cameras, vintage toys and other odds and ends.

Near the Palau de Mar, you'll find **Feria de Artesanía del Palau de Mar** (Map p250; Moll del Dipòsit; ⊘11am-8.30pm Sat & Sun; Ⓜ Barceloneta), with artisans selling a range of crafty items, including jewellery, graphic T-shirts, handwoven hats, fragrant candles and soaps, scarves and decorative items. In July and August the market runs daily.

Take a stroll along the pedestrian-only Rambla de Mar to reach the weekend art fair **Mercado de Pintores** (Passeig d'Ítaca; ⊘10am-8pm Sat & Sun; Ⓜ Drassanes), with a broad selection of paintings both collectable and rather forgettable.

Vintage market stall
ANASTASIA PETROVA/SHUTTERSTOCK ©

century-old Modernista shopfront advertisements featured at this culinary temple. For a century the gluttonous have trembled at this altar of speciality food goods from around Catalonia and beyond.

Regia Cosmetics

(Map p254; ☎93 216 01 21; www.regia.es; Passeig de Gràcia 39; ⊙9.30am-8.30pm Mon-Sat; ⓂPasseig de Gràcia) In business since 1928, Regia is reputed to be one of the best perfume stores in the city. It stocks all the name brands and also has a private museum out the back, the **Museu del Perfum** (Map p254; ☎93 216 01 21; www. museudelperfum.com; Passeig de Gràcia 39; adult/concession €5/3; ⊙10.30am-8pm Mon-Fri, 11am-2pm Sat; ⓂPasseig de Gràcia). The museum contains oddities from ancient Egyptian and Roman scent receptacles to classic eau de cologne bottles – all in all, some 5000 bottles of infinite shapes, sizes and histories. Aside from the range of perfumes, Regia sells all sorts of creams, lotions and colognes. It also has its own line of bath products.

⓪ Montjuïc, Poble Sec & Sant Antoni

Mercat de Sant Antoni Market

(Map p249; ☎93 426 35 21; www.mercat desantantoni.com; Carrer de Comte d'Urgell 1; ⊙7am-2.30pm & 5-8.30pm Mon-Thu, 7am-8.30pm Fri & Sat; ⓂSant Antoni) Just beyond the western edge of El Raval is Mercat de Sant Antoni, a glorious old iron and brick building that has been undergoing renovation since 2009. In the meantime, a huge marquee has been erected alongside to house a food market. The second-hand book market still takes place alongside on Sunday mornings. The latest estimates for the market's reopening is the end of 2017.

GI Joe Fashion

(☎93 329 96 52; www.gijoebcn.com; Ronda de Sant Antoni 49; ⊙10am-2pm & 4.30-8.30pm Mon-Sat; ⓂUniversitat) This is the best central army-surplus warehouse. Get your khakis here, along with urban army fashion T-shirts, and throw in a holster, gas mask or sky-blue UN helmet for a kinkier effect. You can also find vintage WWII items.

⓪ Gràcia & Park Güell

Amapola Vegan Shop Clothing

(Map p254; ☎93 010 62 73; www.amapola veganshop.com; Travessera de Gràcia 129; ⊙11am-2.30pm & 5-8.30pm Mon-Sat; ⓂFontana, Diagonal) A shop with a heart of gold, Amapola proves that you need not toss your ethics aside in the quest for stylish clothing and accessories. You'll find sleek leather alternatives for wallets, handbags and messenger bags by Matt & Nat, dainty ballerina-style flats by Victoria and elegant scarves by Barts.

Lady Loquita Clothing

(Map p254; ☎93 217 82 92; www.ladyloquita. com; Travessera de Gràcia 126; ⊙11am-2pm & 5-8.30pm Mon-Sat; ⓂFontana) Lady Loquita is a hip little shop, where you can browse through light summer dresses by Tirala-hilacha, evening wear by Japamala and handmade jewellery by local design label Klimbim. There are also whimsical odds and ends: dinner plates with dog people portraits and digital prints on wood by About Paola.

La Festival Wine

(Map p254; ☎93 023 22 81; Carrer de Verdi 67; ⊙5.30-9.30pm Mon, 10.30am-9.30pm Tue-Sat, 11am-2pm Sun; ⓂFontana) This handsomely designed shop earns high marks for its knowledgeable (and English-speaking) staff who can give you a wealth of information about the many excellent wines for sale here. Most bottles are from Spanish producers, though there are a few French options and some organic as well as bio-dynamic wines.

Magnesia Fashion & Accessories

(☎93 119 01 87; www.magnesiabcn.com; Carrer del Torrent de l'Olla 192; ⊙10.30am-2.30pm & 4.30-8pm Mon-Fri, 10.30am-2pm Sat; ⓂLesseps, Fontana) Tucked away on a quiet corner of Gràcia, Magnesia is a petite store so packed with intrigue that you might want to just gift-wrap the whole thing and slip it into your handbag. There are fairy-tale-esque greeting cards, bespoke stationery,

★ Where to Shop

For high fashion, design, jewellery and department stores, the principal shopping axis starts on Plaça de Catalunya, proceeds up Passeig de Gràcia and turns left into Avinguda Diagonal, along which it extends as far as Plaça de la Reina Maria Cristina. The densely packed section between Plaça de Francesc Macià and Plaça de la Reina Maria Cristina is an especially good hunting ground.

Top: Escribà (p154); Left: A branch of FC Botiga; Above: Shoe shopping in El Born

Mercat de Sant Antoni (p164)

one-of-a-kind framed illustrations, statement-piece jewellery and ceramics (tiny bowls, tea cups), herbal-infused candles and chunky puzzles (and other gift ideas) for kids.

Hibernian   Books
(📞93 217 47 96; www.hibernian-books.com; Carrer de Montseny 17; ⊙4-8.30pm Mon, 11am-8.30pm Tue-Sat; MFontana) The biggest second-hand English bookshop in Barcelona stocks thousands of titles covering all sorts of subjects, from cookery to children's classics. There is a smaller collection of new books in English too.

Surco   Music
(Map p254; 📞93 218 34 39; Travessera de Gràcia 144; ⊙10.30am-2pm & 5.30-9pm Mon-Sat; MFontana, FGC Gràcia) Surco is an obligatory stop for music lovers – especially for fans of vinyl. You'll find loads of new and used records and CDs here, with a mix of Tom Waits, Mishima (a Catalan band), Calexico and more.

Mushi Mushi   Fashion & Accessories
(Map p254; 📞93 292 29 74; www.mushimushi collection.com; Carrer de Bonavista 12; ⊙11am-3pm & 4.30-8.30pm Mon-Sat; MFontana) A gorgeous little fashion boutique in an area that's not short of them, Mushi Mushi specialises in quirky but elegant women's fashion and accessories. It stocks labels that include Des Petits Hauts, Sessùn, Orion London and small French labels such as Five. The collection changes frequently, with only a few of each item being stocked, so a return visit can pay off.

Bodega Bonavista   Wine
(Map p254; 📞93 218 81 99; Carrer de Bonavista 10; ⊙10am-2.30pm & 5-9pm Mon-Fri, noon-3pm Sat & Sun; MFontana) An excellent little neighbourhood wine shop that endeavours to seek out great wines at reasonable prices. The stock is mostly from Catalonia and elsewhere in Spain, but there's also a good selection from France. The Bonavista also acts as a deli and there are some especially good cheeses.

Mercat de l'Abaceria
Central
Market

(Map p254; Travessera de Gràcia 186; ⏱7am-2.30pm & 5.30-8pm Mon-Sat; Ⓜ️Fontana) This sprawling iron and brick market, which dates back to the 1890s, is a fine place to browse for fresh produce, cheeses, bakery items and snack foods. There's also a sushi stand and several food stalls where you can grab a quick bite on the cheap.

🄰 Camp Nou, Pedralbes & La Zona Alta

Labperfum
Cosmetics

(www.labperfum.com; Carrer de Santaló 45; ⏱10am-2.30pm & 5-8.30pm Mon-Sat; Ⓡ️FGC Muntaner) This tiny shop looks like an old apothecary, with its shelves lined with pretty glass bottles. What's for sale are extraordinary fragrances (for men and women) made in-house. Scents diverge from run-of-the-mill Obsession, with varieties like tobacco, black orchid and leather. You can also buy scented candles, soaps and creams. Beautiful packaging and fair prices (starting at €15 for 50mL).

Tomates
Fritos
Fashion & Accessories

(☑93 209 26 17; www.tomatesfritos.es; Carrer del Tenor Viñas 7; ⏱10.30am-8.30pm Mon-Fri, 10.30am-3pm & 5-8.30pm Sat; Ⓡ️FGC Muntaner) One of a growing number of boutiques along this street, Tomates Fritos is an obligatory stop for design-minded window shoppers and carries a trove of unique wares. The cache of global designers includes denim by IRO, handbags by Liebeskind, blouses and jackets by The Kooples and beautifully tailored tops by Scotch & Soda.

FC Botiga
Megastore
Gifts & Souvenirs

(☑93 409 02 71; www.fcbmegastore.com; Gate 9, off Avinguda Joan de XXIII; ⏱10am-7pm Mon-Sat, to 3.30pm Sun; Ⓜ️Palau Reial, Collblanc)

 An Outlet Outing

For the ultimate discount-fashion overdose, head out of town for some outlet shopping at **La Roca Village** (☑93 842 39 39; www.larocavillage.com; ⏱10am-9pm). Here, a village has been given over to consumer madness. At a long line of Spanish and international fashion boutiques you'll find clothes, shoes, accessories and designer homewares at (they claim) up to 60% off normal retail prices.

To get here, follow the AP-7 tollway north from Barcelona, take exit 12 (marked Cardedeu) and follow the signs for 'Centre Comercial'. The **Sagalés Bus Company** (☑902 130014; www.sagales.com) organises shuttles from Plaça de Catalunya (€9 return, if bought online 24 hours in advance, 40 minutes, 12 daily). Alternatively, take a slower bus from the same company from Fabra i Puig metro station (€4 one way online, four departures Monday to Friday, three in August), or a *rodalies* train to Granollers and pick up the shuttle (Monday to Friday only) or a taxi there.

La Roca Village
PERE RUBI/SHUTTERSTOCK ©

This sprawling three-storey shop in Camp Nou (p72) has footballs, shirts, scarves, socks, wallets, bags, sneakers, smartphone covers – pretty much anything you can think of – all featuring Barça's famous red-and-blue insignia.

BAR OPEN

Cocktails, *cava* and clubs galore

Bar Open

Barcelona is a nightlife-lovers' town, with an enticing spread of candlelit wine bars, old-school taverns, stylish lounges and kaleidoscopic nightclubs where the party continues until daybreak. The atmosphere varies tremendously – candlelit, mural-covered chambers in the medieval quarter, antique-filled converted storefronts and buzzing Modernista spaces are all part of the scene. Of course, where to go depends as much on the crowd as it does on ambience; you'll find a scene that suits in Barcelona.

In This Section

Opening Hours

Bars Typically open around 6pm and close at 2am (3am on weekends).

Clubs Open from midnight until 6am, Thursday to Saturday.

Beach bars 10am to around midnight (later on weekends) from April through October.

Gràcia & Park Güell
Young hipster crowd
(p187)

Camp Nou, Pedralbes
& La Zona Alta
High-end clubs
(p188)

La Sagrada Família
& L'Eixample
Student bars, tiny
lounges, LGBT venues
(p181)

La Ribera
Cava and wine
bars, lounges
(p177)

Port
Olimpic

El Raval
Bohemian bars,
small clubs
(p175)

La Rambla &
Barri Gòtic
Atmospheric bars, cafes,
outdoor spots, clubs
(p174)

Barceloneta &
the Waterfront
Neighbourhood taverns,
seaside bars,
touristy clubs
(p178)

Montjuïc, Poble Sec
& Sant Antoni
Art-minded bars, trendy cafes,
open-air spots
(p185)

Port
Vell

Mediterranean
Sea

Costs/Tipping

A coffee costs €1.20 to €1.70, a glass of wine will run €2 to €3.50 in most places and mixed drinks and cocktails will set you back €6 to €10.

Nightclubs charge anywhere from nothing to €20 for admission.

Tipping is not customary nor necessary.

Useful Words

Coffee

con leche – half coffee, half milk

solo – an espresso

cortado – an espresso with a dash of milk

Beer

cerveza – beer (bottle)

caña – small draught beer

tubo – large draught beer

quinto – a 200ml bottle

tercio – a 330ml bottle

clara – a shandy; a beer with a hefty dash of lemonade

The Best...

Experience Barcelona's
best drinking & nightlife spots

For Cocktails

Balius (p180) Beautifully mixed elixirs in Poblenou.

Elephanta (p187) The place to linger over a creative concoction.

Dry Martini (p181) Expertly made cocktails in a classy setting.

Juanra Falces (p178) White-jacketed waiters serve up artful elixirs.

Boadas (p176) An iconic drinking den that's been going strong since the 1930s.

The Mint (p179) Atmospheric drinkery with outstanding mojitos and infused gins.

Bohemian Hang-outs

Gran Bodega Saltó (p200) Poble Sec icon with psychedelic decor and an eclectic crowd.

Madame George (p180) Tiny, dramatically designed space with soulful DJs.

El Rouge (p185) Bordello-esque lounge with great people-watching.

Gipsy Lou (p196) For a night of surprises in El Raval.

For Wine Lovers

Viblioteca (p187) A small modern space famed for its wine (and cheese) selections.

Monvínic (p181) With a staggering 3000 varieties of wines, you won't lack for options.

La Vinya del Senyor (p178) Outdoor wine-sipping facing Basílica de Santa Maria del Mar.

For Beachfront

Santa Marta (p180) Sit at outdoor tables and watch the passing people parade.

Opium Mar (p180) Classic summer late-opening club with beachfront terrace.

Shôko (p180) Asia meets the Med at this elegant bar-club on the sand.

Lasal (p178) Worth the train ride for classic waterfront clubbing.

For Views

La Caseta del Migdia (p185) Great hillside spot for a sundowner.

Mirablau (p189) The whole city stretches out beneath you from the foot of Tibidabo.

Opium Mar (p180) Gaze over palms and beach from this club.

For Dancing

Marula Cafè (p174) Barri Gòtic favourite for its lively dance floor.

Moog (p175) A small Raval club that draws a fun, dance-loving crowd.

Antilla BCN (p182) The top name in town for salsa lovers.

City Hall (p182) A legendary Eixample dance club.

For Rock Lovers

Magic (p178) Basement club with rock and pop in heavy rotation.

Musical Maria (p187) Classic rock lives on in this neighbourhood favourite.

Manchester (p174) Hear the classic sounds of that city's legendary bands.

★ Top Choices for Craft Beer

BlackLab (p179) Innovative IPAs and APAs on the waterfront.

La Cervecita Nuestra de Cada Día (p179) Outstanding selection of rare brews.

Napar BCN (p181) The beautifully designed space makes a fine setting for sipping beers made on site.

El Drapaire (p176) Atmospheric tapas and creative microbrew joint in El Raval.

Garage Beer Co (p181) Subtle and tasty beers brewed on site.

🛇 La Rambla & Barri Gòtic

L'Ascensor   Cocktail Bar

(Map p250; 📞 93 318 53 47; Carrer de la Bellafila 3; ⏰ 6pm-2.30am Sun-Thu, to 3am Fri & Sat; 📶; Ⓜ Jaume I) Named after the lift (elevator) doors that serve as the front door, this elegant drinking den with its vaulted brick ceilings, vintage mirrors and marble-topped bar gathers a faithful crowd that comes for old-fashioned cocktails and lively conversation against a soundtrack of up-tempo jazz and funk.

Sor Rita   Bar

(Map p250; 📞 93 176 62 66; www.sorritabar.es; Carrer de la Mercè 27; ⏰ 7pm-3am Sun-Thu, to 3.30am Fri & Sat; 📶; Ⓜ Jaume I) A lover of all things kitsch, Sor Rita is pure eye candy, from its leopard-print wallpaper to its high-heel-festooned ceiling and deliciously irreverent decorations inspired by the films of Almodóvar. It's a fun and festive scene, with special-event nights including tarot readings on Mondays, €6 all-you-can-eat snack buffets on Tuesdays, cabaret on Wednesdays and karaoke on Thursdays.

Marula Café   Bar

(Map p250; 📞 93 318 76 90; www.marulacafe.com; Carrer dels Escudellers 49; ⏰ 11pm-6am Wed-Sun; Ⓜ Liceu) A fantastic find in the heart of the Barri Gòtic, Marula will transport you to the 1970s and the best in funk and soul. James Brown fans will think they've died and gone to heaven. It's not, however, a monothematic place and DJs slip in other tunes, from breakbeat to house. Samba and other Brazilian dance sounds also penetrate here.

Manchester   Bar

(Map p250; Carrer de Milans 5; ⏰ 6.30pm-2.30am Sun-Thu, to 3am Fri & Sat; 📶; Ⓜ Liceu) 🌐 A drinking den that has undergone several transformations over the years now treats you to the sounds of great Manchester bands, from Joy Division to Oasis, but probably not the Hollies. It has a pleasing rough-and-tumble feel, with tables jammed in every which way. There are DJs on Thursdays.

La Confiteria

Karma   Club

(Map p250; ☏93 302 56 80; www.karmadisco.
com; Plaça Reial 10; ☺6pm-5.30am Tue-Sun;
ⓂLiceu) During the week Karma plays good,
mainstream indie music, while on weekends the DJs spin anything from rock to
disco. A golden oldie in Barcelona, tunnel-
shaped Karma is small and becomes quite
tightly packed (claustrophobic for some)
with a good-natured crowd of locals and
out-of-towners. The bar and terrace on
the Plaça Reial open at 6pm and the club
opens at midnight.

El Raval

La Confitería   Bar

(Map p256; Carrer de Sant Pau 128; ☺7.30pm-
2.30am Mon-Thu, 6pm-3.30am Fri, 5pm-3.30am
Sat, 12.45pm-2.45am Sun; ⓂParal·lel) This is a
trip into the 19th century. Until the 1980s it
was a confectioner's shop and although the
original cabinets are now lined with booze,
the look of the place barely changed with
its conversion into a laid-back bar. A quiet
enough spot for a house *vermut* (€3; add
your own soda) in the early evening.

Casa Almirall   Bar

(Map p249; www.casaalmirall.com; Carrer de
Joaquín Costa 33; ☺6pm-2.30am Mon-Thu,
6.30pm-3am Fri, noon-3am Sat, noon-12.30am
Sun; ⓂUniversitat) In business since the
1860s, this unchanged corner bar is dark
and intriguing, with Modernista decor and
a mixed clientele. There are some great
original pieces in here, such as the marble
counter and the cast-iron statue of the
muse of the Universal Exposition, held in
Barcelona in 1888.

Moog   Club

(Map p250; www.masimas.com/moog; Carrer
de l'Arc del Teatre 3; admission €5-10; ☺mid-
night-5am Mon-Thu & Sun, to 6am Fri & Sat; 🚌14,
59, ⓂDrassanes) This fun and minuscule club
is a standing favourite with the downtown
crowd. In the main dance area, DJs dish out
house, techno and electro, while upstairs

 Wine & Cava Bars

A growing number of wine bars scattered around the city provide a showcase for the great produce from Spain
and beyond. Vine-minded spots such as
Monvínic (p181) serve a huge selection
of wines by the glass, with a particular
focus on stellar new vintages. A big part
of the experience is having a few bites
while you drink. Expect sharing plates,
platters of cheese and charcuterie and
plenty of tapas.

Cava bars tend to be more about
the festive ambience than the actual
drinking of *cava*, a sparkling white or
rosé, most of which is produced in
Catalonia's Penedès region. At the more
famous *cava* bars you'll have to nudge
your way through the garrulous crowds
and enjoy your bubbly standing up.
Two of the most famous *cava* bars are
El Xampanyet (p178) in La Ribera and
Can Paixano (p179) in Barceloneta.

you can groove to a nice blend of indie and
occasional classic-pop throwbacks.

Negroni   Cocktail Bar

(Map p249; www.negronicocktailbar.com; Carrer
de Joaquín Costa 46; ☺7pm-2.30am Mon-Thu,
7pm-3am Fri & Sat; ⓂUniversitat) Good things
come in small packages and this dark, teeny
cocktail bar confirms the rule. The mostly
black decor lures in a largely student set
to try out the cocktails; among them, of
course, is the celebrated Negroni, a Floren-
tine invention with one part Campari, one
part gin and one part sweet vermouth.

From left: Bar Pastís; Typical bodega in the Barri Gòtic; Restaurant terraces in Passeig del Born

Bar La Concha   Bar, Gay

(Map p250; www.laconchadelraval.com; Carrer de la Guàrdia 14; ⏱5pm-2.30am Sun-Thu, to 3.30am Fri & Sat; Ⓜ Drassanes) This place is dedicated to the worshipping of the actress Sara Montiel: the walls groan with more than 250 photos of the sultry star. La Concha used to be a largely LGBT+ haunt, but anyone is welcome and bound to have fun – especially when the drag queens come out to play. Moroccan ownership means you're also likely to see belly dancing.

Marmalade   Bar

(Map p249; www.marmaladebarcelona.com; Carrer de la Riera Alta 4-6; ⏱6.30pm-2.30am Mon-Wed, 10am-2.30am Thu-Sun; Ⓜ Sant Antoni) The golden hues of this backlit bar and restaurant beckon seductively through the glass facade. There are various distinct spaces, decorated in different but equally sumptuous styles, and there is a pool table next to the bar. Cocktails are big business here, and a selection of them are €5 all night.

Bar Marsella   Bar

(Map p250; ☎93 442 72 63; Carrer de Sant Pau 65; ⏱10pm-2.30am Mon-Thu, 10pm-3am Fri & Sat; Ⓜ Liceu) Bar Marsella has been in business since 1820 and has served the likes of Hemingway, who was known to slump here over an *absenta* (absinthe). The bar still specialises in absinthe, a drink to be treated with respect.

Boadas   Cocktail Bar

(Map p250; www.boadascocktails.com; Carrer dels Tallers 1; ⏱noon-2am Mon-Thu, noon-3am Fri & Sat; Ⓜ Catalunya) One of the city's oldest cocktail bars, Boadas is famed for its daiquiris. Bow-tied waiters have been serving up unique, drinkable creations since Miguel Boadas opened it in 1933 – in fact Miró and Hemingway both drank here. Miguel was born in Havana, where he was the first barman at the immortal La Floridita.

El Drapaire   Bar

(Map p249; ☎607 466446; Carrer de les Sitges 11; ⏱5pm-1am Sun-Thu, to 2am Fri & Sat; Ⓜ Catalunya) Part of the recent explosion in the craft-beer scene, this cosy, beamed tavern has been given a new lease of life

and now has 13 taps, featuring Spanish and international beers of all styles. There are tapas and platters of cheese and charcuterie to share.

Bar Pastís Bar

(Map p250; www.barpastis.es; Carrer de Santa Mònica 4; ☺7.30pm-2am; ⓂDrassanes) A French cabaret theme (with lots of Piaf in the background) dominates this tiny, cluttered classic. It's been going, on and off, since the end of WWII. You'll need to be in here before 9pm to have any hope of sitting, getting near the bar or anything much else. On some nights it features live acts, usually performing French *chansons*.

🅾 La Ribera

Guzzo Cocktail Bar

(Map p250; ☏93 667 00 36; www.guzzoclub. es; Plaça Comercial 10; ☺6pm-3am Mon-Thu, to 3.30am Fri & Sat, noon-3am Sun; ☏; ⓂBarceloneta) This swish but relaxed cocktail bar is run by much-loved Barcelona DJ Fred Guzzo, who is often to be found at the decks, spinning his delicious selection of

funk, soul and rare groove. You'll also find frequent live-music acts of consistently decent quality and a funky atmosphere at almost any time of day.

Rubí Bar

(Map p250; ☏647 773707; Carrer dels Banys Vells 6; ☺7.30pm-2.30am Sun-Thu, to 3am Fri & Sat; ⓂJaume I) With its boudoir lighting and cheap mojitos, Rubí is where the Born's *cognoscenti* head for a nightcap – or several. It's a narrow, cosy space – push through to the back where you might just get one of the coveted tables. The bar food is excellent, from Vietnamese rolls to more traditional selections of cheese and ham.

El Born Bar Bar

(Map p250; ☏93 319 53 33; www.elbornbar. neositios.com; Passeig del Born 26; ☺10am-2am Mon-Thu, to 3am Fri & Sat, noon-2.30am Sun; ☏; ⓂJaume I) El Born Bar effortlessly attracts everyone, from cool 30-somethings from all over town to locals who pass judgement on Passeig del Born's passing parade. Its staying power depends on a good selection of beers, spirits, and empanadas and other snacks.

Chiringuitos

During summer small wooden beach bars, affectionately known as *chiringuitos*, open up along the strand, from Barceloneta all the way up to Platja de la Nova Mar Bella. Here you can dip your toes in the sand and nurse a cocktail while watching the city at play against the backdrop of the deep-blue Mediterranean. Ambient grooves add to the laid-back environment. *Chiringuitos* are also great spots for a snack. The drink of choice is often a refreshing *cava sangria*.

One of the liveliest beachside bars lies northeast of the city on Cavaió beach in Arenys de Mar (accessible from Barcelona by train). Lasal (www.lasal.com) hosts top-notch DJs and has a tropical-themed party atmosphere. It opens daily from mid-May to September.

Sangria
ANJELIKAGR/SHUTTERSTOCK ©

La Vinya del Senyor   Wine Bar
(Map p250; 📞93 310 33 79; Plaça de Santa Maria del Mar 5; ⊙noon-1am Mon-Thu, noon-2am Fri & Sat, noon-midnight Sun; 🛜; Ⓜ Jaume I) Relax on the *terrassa*, which lies in the shadow of the Basílica de Santa Maria del Mar, or crowd inside at the tiny bar. The wine list is as long as *War and Peace* and there's a table upstairs for those who opt to sample by the bottle rather than the glass.

Juanra Falces   Cocktail Bar
(Map p250; 📞93 310 10 27; Carrer del Rec 24; ⊙10am-3pm Sun-Mon, 8pm-3am Tue-Thu, 7pm-

3am Fri & Sat; Ⓜ Jaume I) Transport yourself to a Humphrey Bogart movie in this narrow little bar, formerly (and still, at least among the locals) known as Gimlet. White-jacketed bar staff with all the appropriate aplomb will whip you up a gimlet or any other classic cocktail (around €10) that your heart desires.

El Xampanyet   Wine Bar
(Map p250; 📞93 319 70 03; Carrer de Montcada 22; ⊙noon-4pm & 7-11.15pm Tue-Sat, noon-4pm Sun; Ⓜ Jaume I) Nothing has changed for decades in this, one of the city's best-known *cava* (wine) bars. Plant yourself at the bar or seek out a table against the decoratively tiled walls for a glass or three of the cheap house *cava* and an assortment of tapas, such as the tangy *boquerones en vinagre* (fresh anchovies in vinegar).

Miramelindo   Bar
(Map p250; 📞93 310 37 27; www.barmiramelindobcn.com; Passeig del Born 15; ⊙8pm-2.30am Sun-Thu, to 3am Fri & Sat; 🛜; Ⓜ Jaume I) A spacious tavern in a Gothic building, this remains a classic on Passeig del Born for mixed drinks, while soft jazz and soul sounds float overhead. Try for a comfy seat at a table towards the back before it fills to bursting. A couple of similarly barn-sized places sit on this side of the *passeig*.

Magic   Club
(Map p250; 📞93 310 72 67; www.magic-club.net; Passeig de Picasso 40; ⊙11pm-6am Thu-Sat; Ⓜ Barceloneta) Although it sometimes hosts live acts in its sweaty, smoky basement, Magic is basically a straightforward, subterranean nightclub offering rock, mainstream dance faves and Spanish pop.

⊖ Barceloneta & the Waterfront

Absenta   Bar
(📞932 21 36 38; Carrer de Sant Carles 36; ⊙7pm-1am Tue & Wed, from 11am Thu-Mon; Ⓜ Barceloneta) Decorated with old paintings, vintage lamps and curious sculpture

(including a dangling butterfly woman and face-painted TVs), this whimsical and creative drinking den takes its liquor seriously. Stop in for the house-made vermouth or, for more bite, try one of the many absinthes on hand. Just go easy: with an alcohol content of 50% to 90%, these spirits have a kick!

Can Paixano   Wine Bar

(Map p250; ☑93 310 08 39; www.canpaixano. com; Carrer de la Reina Cristina 7; ⊗9am-10.30pm Mon-Sat; Ⓜ Barceloneta) This lofty old champagne bar (also called La Xampanyeria) has long been run on a winning formula. The standard poison is bubbly rosé in elegant little glasses, combined with bite-sized *bocadillos* (filled rolls) and tapas (€3 to €8). Note that this place is usually packed to the rafters and elbowing your way to the bar can be a titanic struggle.

BlackLab   Microbrewery

(Map p250; ☑93 221 83 60; www.blacklab.es; Plaça de Pau Vila 1; ⊗noon-1.30am; Ⓜ Barceloneta) Inside the historic Palau de Mar, BlackLab was Barcelona's first brewhouse

to open way back in 2014. With 20 taps (including 18 housemade brews, including saisons, double IPAs and dry stouts), it's an impressive operation, and the brewmasters are constantly experimenting with new flavours.

The Mint   Cocktail Bar

(Map p250; ☑647 737707; www.facebook. com/themintbarcelona; Passeig d'Isabel II, 4; ⊗7.30pm-3am; Ⓜ Barceloneta) Named after the prized cocktail ingredient, this mojito-loving drinkery has a little something for everyone. Linger upstairs with the grown-ups to peruse the first-rate house-infused gins (over 20 on hand, including creative blends like lemongrass and Jamaican pepper), or head downstairs with the young things to the brick-vaulted cellars, where red lights and driving beats create a more celebratory vibe.

La Cervecita Nuestra
de Cada Día   Bar

(Carrer de Llull 184; ⊗5.30-9.30pm Sun & Mon, 11.30am-2pm & 5.30-9.30pm Tue-Sat; Ⓜ Llacuna) Equal parts beer shop and craft brew bar,

Bars along Barceloneta Beach

La Cervecita has a changing selection of unique beers from around Europe and the USA. You might stumble across a Catalan sour-fruit beer, a rare English stout, a potent Belgian triple ale or half a dozen other draughts on hand – plus many more varieties by the bottle.

Madame George   Lounge
(www.madamegeorgebar.com; Carrer de Pujades 179; ⏱6pm-2am Mon-Thu, to 3am Fri & Sat, to 12.30am Sun; MPoblenou) A theatrical (veering towards campy) elegance marks the interior of this small, chandelier-lit lounge just off the Rambla del Poblenou. Deft bartenders stir up nicely balanced cocktails to a friendly, eclectic crowd, while off in the corner a DJ spins vintage soul and funk (bonus points for using vinyl).

Balius   Cocktail Bar
(☎93 315 86 50; www.baliusbar.com; Carrer de Pujades 196; ⏱5pm-1am Tue-Wed, to 3am Thu, 4pm-3am Fri & Sat, to midnight Sun; MPoblenou) There's an old-fashioned jauntiness to this vintage cocktail den in Poblenou. Friendly barkeeps pour a fair mix of classic libations as well as vermouths, and there's a small tapas menu. Stop by on Sundays to catch live jazz, starting around 7.30pm.

Santa Marta   Bar
(Carrer de Guitert 59; ⏱11am-11pm; 🚌45, 57, 59, 157, MBarceloneta) This chilled bar just back from the beach attracts a garrulous mix of locals and expats, who come for light meals, beers and prime people-watching at one of the outdoor tables near the boardwalk. It has some tempting food too: a mix of local and Italian items, with a range of satisfying sandwiches.

Espai Joliu   Cafe
(Carrer Badajoz 95; ⏱9am-7pm Mon-Fri; 📷; MLlacuna) Places like Espai Joliu are further proof that Poblenou is fast becoming the Brooklyn of Barcelona. This is a charming little space with art mags, handmade stationery and ceramics sold up front, and with a peaceful cafe (blonde wood tables, melodic indie rock) tucked up the steps at the back.

Ké?   Bar
(Carrer del Baluard 54; ⏱noon-2am; MBarceloneta) An eclectic and happy crowd hangs about this small bohemian bar run by a friendly Dutchman. Pull up a padded 'keg chair' or grab a seat on one of the worn lounges at the back and join in the animated conversation wafting out over the street. Outdoor seating in summer, just a few steps from Barceloneta's market.

Opium Mar   Club
(☎93 225 91 00; www.opiummar.com; Passeig Marítim de la Barceloneta 34; cover €10-20; ⏱club 11pm-5am, restaurant from noon; MCiutadella Vila Olímpica) This seaside dance place has a spacious dance floor that attracts a mostly North American crowd. It only begins to fill from about 3am and is best in summer, when you can spill onto a terrace overlooking the beach. The beachside outdoor section works as a chilled restaurant-cafe.

Shôko   Club
(www.shoko.biz; Passeig Marítim de la Barceloneta 36; ⏱club midnight-6am, restaurant from noon; MCiutadella Vila Olímpica) This stylish restaurant, club and beachfront bar brings in a touch of the Far East via potted bamboo, Japanese electro and Asian-Med fusion cuisine. As the food is cleared away, Shôko transforms into a deep-grooving nightspot with DJs spinning for the beautiful crowd. The open-sided beachfront lounge is a popular spot for a sundowner.

Bharma   Bar
(www.bharma.com; Carrer de Pere IV 93; ⏱8am-5pm Mon-Fri & 10.30pm-3am Fri & Sat; MLlacuna) Located in Barcelona's Poblenou district, Bharma is a wildly configured bar that pays homage to the famously addictive American TV series, *Lost*. Its stone-lined interior is reminiscent of the bunker-like 'hatch', save for the tail end of a plane wreck imbedded in one wall. The drink of choice is of course Bharma Initiative beer, an (almost) exact duplication of the Dharma logo.

La Sagrada Família & L'Eixample

Monvínic
Wine Bar

(Map p254; 93 272 61 87; www.monvinic.com; Carrer de la Diputació 249; 1-11pm Tue-Fri, 7-11pm Mon & Sat; Passeig de Gràcia) Apparently considered unmissable by El Bulli's sommelier, Monvínic is an ode, a rhapsody even, to wine loving. The interactive wine list sits on the bar for you to browse, on a digital tablet similar to an iPad, and boasts more than 3000 varieties.

Dry Martini
Bar

(93 217 50 80; www.drymartiniorg.com; Carrer d'Aribau 162-166; 1pm-2.30am Mon-Thu, 6pm-3am Fri & Sat, 7pm-2.30am Sun; Diagonal) Waiters with a discreetly knowing smile will attend to your cocktail needs and make uncannily good suggestions, but the house drink, taken at the bar or in one of the plush green leather banquettes, is a safe bet. The gin and tonic comes in an enormous mug-sized glass – drinking it will take you most of the night.

Garage Beer Co
Craft Beer

(Map p254; 93 528 59 89; garagebeer.co; Carrer del Consell de Cent 261; 5pm-midnight Sun-Thur, 5pm-3am Fri & Sat; Universitat) One of the first of the slew of craft beer bars to pop up in Barcelona in recent times, Garage brews its own in a space at the bar, and offers around 10 different beers at a time. The favourites are Garage (a delicate session IPA), and Slinger (a more robust IPA), which are always present on the board.

Napar BCN
Brewery

(Map p254; 606 546467; www.naparbcn.com; Carrer de la Diputació 223; noon-midnight Mon-Thu, to 2am Fri & Sat; Universitat) One of the bars that opened as part of Barcelona's burgeoning craft-beer scene, Napar has 14 beers on tap, six of which are beers brewed on site, including a mix of IPA, pale ale and stout. There's also an accomplished list of bottled beers. It's a stunning space, with a gleaming steampunk aesthetic, that serves some excellent food should hunger strike.

Catalan Wine

The bulk of denomination-of-origin (DO) wines in Catalonia are made from grapes produced in the Penedès area, which pumps out almost two million hectolitres a year. The other DO winemaking zones (spread as far apart as the Empordà area around Figueres in the north and the Terra Alta around Gandesa in the southwest) have a combined output of about half that produced in Penedès. The wines of the El Priorat area, which tend to be dark, heavy reds, have been promoted to DOC status, an honour shared only with those of the Rioja (categorised as such since 1926). Drops from the neighbouring Montsant area are frequently as good (or close) and considerably cheaper.

Most of the grapes grown in Catalonia are native to Spain and include the white varieties Garnacha, White Macabeo and Xarel·lo, and the reds Monastrell, Black Garnacha and Ull de Llebre (Hare's Eye). Foreign varieties (such as Chardonnay, Riesling, Chenin Blanc, Cabernet Sauvignon, Merlot and Pinot Noir) are also common.

There is plenty to look out for beyond Penedès. Raïmat, in the Costers del Segre DO area of Lleida province, produces fine reds and a couple of notable whites. Good fortified wines come from around Tarragona and some nice fresh wines are also produced in the Empordà area in the north.

City Hall — Club
(Map p254; ☎93 238 07 22; www.cityhall
barcelona.com; Rambla de Catalunya 2-4; cover
€10-15, incl 1 drink; ☺midnight-5am Wed &
Thu, midnight-6am Fri & Sat, 11pm-5am Sun;
ⓂCatalunya) A long corridor leads to the
dance floor of this venerable and popular
club, located in a former theatre. House
and other electric sounds dominate, with
occasional funk nights. Check the website
for details.

Milano — Cocktail Bar
(Map p254; ☎93 112 71 50; www.camparimilano.
com; Ronda de la Universitat 35; ☺noon-3am
Mon-Sat, 6pm-2.30am Sun; ⓂCatalunya) An
absolute gem of hidden Barcelona nightlife,
Milano is a subterranean old-school
cocktail bar with velvet banquettes and
glass-fronted cabinets, presided over by
white-jacketed waiters and completely in-
visible from street level. Check the website
for details on occasional live music.

Les Gens Que J'Aime — Bar
(Map p254; ☎93 215 68 79; www.lesgensque
jaime.com; Carrer de València 286; ☺6pm-
2.30am Sun-Thu, 7pm-3am Fri & Sat; ⓂPasseig
de Gràcia) This intimate basement relic of
the 1960s follows a deceptively simple formula: chilled jazz music in the background,
minimal lighting from an assortment of
flea-market lamps and a cosy, cramped
scattering of red-velvet-backed lounges
around tiny dark tables.

Antilla BCN — Club
(Map p249; ☎93 451 45 64; www.antillasalsa.
com; Carrer d'Aragó 141; Wed-Thu free, Fri &
Sat €10; ☺10pm-5am Wed, 11pm-5am Thu,
11pm-6am Fri & Sat, 7pm-dawn Sun; ⓂUrgell)
The salsateca in town, this is the place to
come for Cuban *son,* merengue, salsa and
a whole lot more. There are dance classes
from around 8pm or 9pm from Tuesday to
Friday. Check the website for details.

Aire — Lesbian
(Sala Diana; Map p254; ☎93 487 83 42; www.
grupoarena.com; Carrer de la Diputació 233; free
Thu, cover €5/6 Fri/Sat; ☺11pm-2.30am Thu-Sat;
ⓂPasseig de Gràcia) A popular locale for
lesbians; here the dance floor is spacious
and there is usually a DJ in command of
the tunes, which range from hits of the '80s
and '90s to Latin and techno. As a rule, only

STEFANO POLITI MARKOVINA/GETTY IMAGES ©

male friends of the girls are allowed entry, although in practice the crowd tends to be fairly mixed.

El Viti   Bar

(Map p254; ☎93 633 83 36; www.elvititaberna. com; Passeig de Sant Joan 62; ⊗noon-3.30pm & 7.30-11.30pm Tue-Fri, noon-4pm & 7.30pm-midnight Sat, 11am-4pm Sun; ☏; ⓂTetuan) Another of the hip bars to spring up along the Passeig de Sant Joan, El Viti checks all the boxes – high ceilings, brick walls both bare and glazed, black-clad staff and a barrel of artisanal vermouth on the bar. It also serves a good line in superior bar snacks, from a mini venison burger to a steamed pork bun.

Quilombo   Bar

(☎606 144272; Carrer d'Aribau 149; ⊗9.30pm-2.30am Wed-Sun; ⒭FGC Provença) Some formulas just work, and this place has been working since the 1970s. Set up a few guitars in the back room, which you pack with tables and chairs, add some cheapish pre-prepared mojitos and plastic tubs of nuts, and let the punters do the rest. They

pour in, creating plenty of *quilombo* (a mess-up).

Arena Madre   Gay

(Map p254; ☎93 487 83 42; www.grupoarena. com; Carrer de Balmes 32; cover Sun-Fri €6, Sat €12; ⊗12.30-5am Mon-Fri, to 6am Sat & Sun; ⓂPasseig de Gràcia) Popular with a hot young crowd, Arena Madre is one of the top clubs in town for boys seeking boys. Mainly electronic and house, with a striptease show on Monday, handbag on Thursday, and live shows throughout the week. Heteros are welcome but a minority.

Michael Collins Pub   Pub

(Map p254; ☎93 459 19 64; www.michael collinspubs.com; Plaça de la Sagrada Família 4; ⊗1pm-2.30am Sun-Thu, 1pm-3am Fri & Sat; ☏; ⓂSagrada Família) Locals and expats alike patronise this place, one of the city's best-loved Irish pubs. To be sure of a little Catalan-Irish *craic,* this barn-sized storming pub is just the ticket. It's ideal for football fans wanting big-screen action over their pints, too.

★ **Tapas & Tipples**
Planning a big night out? Wherever you end up, keep in mind that eating and drinking go hand in hand in Barcelona, and some of the liveliest bars serve up as many tapas as they do alcoholic tipples.

Barcelona in a Glass

Slices of lemon
& orange

Ice

Red vermouth

Goes well
with olives

Soda (optional)

La Hora del Vermut

ISAPHOTO2016/SHUTTERSTOCK ©

A Hipster Revival

Vermouth is a traditional pre-lunch
apéritif across Spain, but until recently
most under-60s would drink beer or
wine at la hora del vermut (vermouth
o'clock). A hipster revival has brought
this always-delicious drink bang back
into fashion and now vermuterías are
springing up everywhere. Seek out the
homemade (de la casa or de solera)
vermouths for an authentic experience.
Add soda for a lighter tipple.

★ Where to Drink *Vermut*

El Maravillas (p188) A glittering
hideaway that serves classic Spanish
drinks.

Absenta (p178) Whimsical and
creative bar with a house-made
vermouth.

La Confitería (p175) A laid-back
drinking hole that used to be a
confectioner's shop.

El Viti (p183) Look for the barrel of
artisanal vermouth on the bar.

Bormuth (p138) Serves old-school
tapas and all the favourite local
drinks.

Arena Classic   Club

(Map p254; ☎93 487 83 42; www.grupoarena.com; Carrer de la Diputació 233; cover €6/12 Fri/Sat; ⏰2.30-6am Fri & Sat; Ⓜ Passeig de Gràcia) Arena Classic attracts a mixed gay crowd that tends not to get too wild. The dominant sound is handbag and the vibe joyfully cheesy.

Bacon Bear   Gay

(Map p249; Carrer de Casanova 64; ⏰6pm-2.30am Mon-Thu, 6pm-3am Fri & Sat; Ⓜ Urgell) Every bear needs a cave to go to, and this is a rather friendly one. It's really just a big bar for burly gay folk. On weekends the music cranks up enough for a bit of bear-hugging twirl.

La Fira   Bar

(Map p254; ☎682 323714; Carrer de Provença 171; cover €5, incl 1 drink; ⏰11.30pm-5.30am Fri & Sat; ⒺFGC Provença) Wander in past crazy mirrors, penny slot machines and other ancient fairground attractions from Germany, with glowing cuboid stools and other futuristic furniture added more recently. The music swings wildly from whiffs of house through '90s hits to Spanish pop classics. You can spend the earlier part of the night trying some of the bar's shots – it claims to have 500 varieties.

❷ Montjuïc, Poble Sec & Sant Antoni

La Caseta del Migdia   Bar

(☎617 956572; www.lacaseta.org; Mirador del Migdia; ⏰8pm-1am Wed-Fri, noon-1am Sat & Sun Apr-Sep, noon-sunset Sat & Sun Oct-Mar; ☒150) The effort of getting to what is, for all intents and purposes, a simple *chiringuito* (makeshift cafe-bar) is worth it. Stare out to sea over a beer or coffee by day. As sunset approaches the atmosphere changes, as lounge music (from samba to funk) wafts out over the hillside. Drinks aside, you can also order barbecue, fired up on the outdoor grills.

👍 Guides for the Latest Nightlife

Barcelona Rocks (www.barcelonarocks.com)

Clubbing Spain (www.clubbingspain.com)

Barcelona Connect (www.barcelonaconnect.com)

Miniguide (www.miniguide.es)

Metropolitan (www.barcelona-metropolitan.com)

enBarcelona (www.enbarcelona.com)

Go Mag (www.go-mag.com)

Bar Calders   Bar

(Map p256; ☎93 329 93 49; Carrer del Parlament 25; ⏰5pm-2am Mon-Fri, 11am-2.30am Sat, 11am-midnight Sun; Ⓜ Sant Antoni) It bills itself as a wine bar, but actually the wine selection at Bar Calders is its weak point. As an all-day cafe and tapas bar, however, it's unbeatable, with a few tables outside on a tiny pedestrian lane. It has become the favoured meeting point for the neighbourhood's boho element.

El Rouge   Bar

(Map p256; ☎666 251556; Carrer del Poeta Cabanyes 21; ⏰11pm-2am Wed & Sun, to 2.30am Thu, to 3am Fri & Sat; ☎; Ⓜ Poble Sec) Decadence is the word that springs to mind in this bordello-red lounge-cocktail bar, with acid jazz, drum and bass and other sounds drifting along in the background. The walls are laden with heavy-framed paintings and mirrors, there are dim lamps, and no two chairs are alike. You can sometimes catch DJs, risqué poetry soirées, cabaret shows or even nights of tango dancing.

Pervert Club @ The One   Club

(Map p256; Avinguda Francesc Ferrer i Guàrdia 13, Poble Espanyol; cover €18; ⏰midnight-6am Sat; Ⓜ Espanya) This weekly fete takes place at The One club in Poble Espanyol. Electronic music dominates and, in spite

Out to the Discoteca

Barcelona's *discotecas* (clubs) are at their best from Thursday to Saturday. Indeed, many open only on these nights. A surprising variety of spots lurk in the old-town labyrinth, ranging from plush former dance halls to grungy subterranean venues that fill to capacity.

Along the waterfront it's another story. At Port Olímpic sun-scorched crowds of visiting yachties mix it up with tourists and a few locals at noisy, back-to-back dance bars right on the waterfront. The best spots are over on La Barceloneta side.

A sprinkling of well-known clubs is spread over the classy parts of town, in L'Eixample and La Zona Alta. They attract a beautiful crowd.

Barcelona by night
KAVALENKAVA/SHUTTERSTOCK ©

of the 6am finish, for many this is only the start of the 'evening'. Expect loads of tanned and buff gym bunnies – and plenty of topless eye candy.

Bar Olimpia   Bar
(Map p256; ☏606 200800; www.facebook. com/bar.olimpia.5; Carrer d'Aldana 11; ☉7pm-1am Wed & Thu, to 2.30am Fri & Sat, 6-11pm Sun; ⓂParal·lel) This great little neighbourhood bar is a little slice of Barcelona history. It was here (and on the surrounding block), where the popular Olimpia Theatre Circus once performed way back in the 1930s. Today the vaguely retro bar draws a diverse crowd, who come for house-made vermouth, snacks (like quesadillas,

cheese plates, tuna tartare) and satisfying gin and tonics.

Sala Plataforma   Club
(Map p256; ☏93 329 00 29; salaplataforma. com; Carrer Nou de la Rambla 145; cover €6-12; ☉10pm-6am Thu-Sat, 7pm-2am Sun; ⓂParal·lel) With two adjoining if smallish dance spaces, 'Platform' has the sense of a slightly clandestine location in an otherwise quiet residential street. Inside this friendly, straightforward dance dive, far from the glitzy Ibiza look, you'll find popular '80s grooves, timeless rock and occasional nights of live bands – plus drum and bass that attracts nostalgics in their 30s and younger partiers.

Redrum   Bar
(Map p256; Carrer de Margarit 36; ☉7pm-3am Tue-Sun; ⓂPoble Sec) A fine escape from the tapas circus down on Carrer de Blai, Redrum doles out craft brews, cocktails and Mexican street food (including excellent tacos and ceviche). It has a low-lit interior and the service is friendly – don't let the name deter you (a bone-chiller for anyone who's seen *The Shining*).

Tinta Roja   Bar
(Map p256; ☏93 443 32 43; www.tintaroja.cat; Carrer de la Creu dels Molers 17; ☉8.30pm-1am Wed, to 2am Thu, to 3am Fri & Sat; ⓂPoble Sec) A succession of nooks and crannies, dotted with flea-market finds and dimly lit in violets, reds and yellows, makes Tinta Roja an intimate spot for a drink and the occasional show in the back – with anything from actors to acrobats. This was once a *vaqueria* (small dairy farm), where they kept cows out the back and sold fresh milk at the front.

La Cambicha   Bar
(Map p256; ☏93 187 25 13; Carrer del Poeta Cabanyes 43; ☉6pm-2am Mon-Wed, 1pm-2am Thu-Sun; ⓂParal·lel) This shoebox-sized bar feels a bit like a lost cabin in the woods, what with the newspaper-covered walls, lantern-like lamps and old photos of sporting folk. Once you've wedged yourself alongside a tiny table, you can join the

young James Brown–loving crowd over inexpensive empanadas and glasses of vermouth. A bands plays every now and again.

🍸 Gràcia & Park Güell

Rabipelao   Cocktail Bar
(Map p254; 📞 93 182 50 35; www.elrabipelao. com; Carrer del Torrent d'En Vidalet 22; ⏰7pm-1.30am Sun-Thu, to 3am Fri & Sat, 1-4.30pm Sun; MJoanic, Fontana) An anchor of Gràcia's nightlife, Rabipelao is a celebratory space with a spinning disco ball and DJs spinning driving salsa beats. Patrons aside, there's much to look at here: a silent film plays in one corner beyond the red velvety wallpaper-covered walls and there's a richly hued mural above the bar – not to mention the tropical cocktails (mojitos and caipirinhas) and snacks (*arepas*, ceviche).

Elephanta   Bar
(Map p254; 📞 93 237 69 06; elephanta.cat; Carrer del Torrent d'en Vidalet 37; ⏰6pm-1.30am Mon-Wed, to 2.30am Thu, to 3am Fri & Sat, 5pm-10pm Sun; MJoanic, Fontana) This friendly and petite cocktail bar is a fine place to catch up with a friend. It has an old-fashioned vibe, with long plush green banquettes, art-lined walls and a five-seat bar topped with old vintage wooded stools.

Viblioteca   Wine Bar
(Map p254; 📞 93 284 42 02; www.viblioteca.com; Carrer de Vallfogona 12; ⏰6pm-1am Mon-Sat, 7pm-midnight Sun; MFontana) If the smell of ripe cheese doesn't float your boat, this is not the place for you – a glass cabinet piled high with the stuff assaults your olfactory nerves as you walk into this small, white, cleverly designed space. The real speciality at Viblioteca, however, is wine, and you can choose from 150 mostly local labels, many of them available by the glass.

Chatelet   Cocktail Bar
(Map p254; 📞 93 284 95 90; Carrer de Torrijos 54; ⏰6pm-2.30am Mon-Thu, to 3am Fri, noon-3am Sat, to 2.30am Sun; MJoanic, Fontana) A popular meeting point in the 'hood, Chatelet has big windows for watching the passing

people parade, and a buzzing art-filled interior that sees a wide cross-section of Gràcia society. Blues or old-school American soul plays in the background, while friends chatter over drinks and light fare (hummus, nachos, sandwiches).

La Cigale   Bar
(Map p254; 📞 93 457 58 23; www.facebook.com/ pages/La-Cigale-Barcelona; Carrer de Tordera 50; ⏰6pm-3am Tue-Sun; MJoanic) La Cigale is a very civilised place for a cocktail, with oil paintings on the walls, gilded mirrors and leatherbound volumes scattered about. Prop up the zinc bar, sink into a second-hand lounge chair around a teeny table or head upstairs.

El Sabor   Bar
(Map p254; 📞 674 993075; Carrer de Francisco Giner 32; ⏰9pm-3am Tue-Sun; MDiagonal) Ruled since 1992 by the charismatic Havana-born Angelito is this home of *ron y son* (rum and sound). A mixed crowd of Cubans and fans of the Caribbean island come to drink mojitos and shake their stuff in this diminutive, good-humoured hang-out. Stop by on Thursdays for a free two-hour salsa lesson (starting at 9.30pm).

Musical Maria   Bar
(Map p254; 📞 93 501 04 60; Carrer de Maria 5; ⏰9pm-3am; 📶; MDiagonal) Even the music hasn't changed since this place got going in the late 1970s. Those longing for rock 'n' roll crowd into this animated bar, listen to old hits and knock back beers. Out the back there's a pool table and the bar serves pretty much all the variants of the local Estrella Damm brew.

La Fourmi   Bar
(Map p254; 📞 93 213 30 52; Carrer de Milà i Fontanals 58; ⏰9am-1.30am Mon-Sat, from 10am Sun; MJoanic) Just off the beaten path, La Fourmi is a small, cosy spot for a cocktail or a bite no matter the time of day. It draws a mix of students, old-timers and hipsters to its weekday breakfast (and more of the latter for weekend brunch).

Traditional bar in the Barri Gòtic

Bar Canigó   Bar

(Map p254; ☎93 213 30 49; Carrer de Verdi 2; ⏰10am-2am Mon-Fri, 8pm-3am Sat; Ⓜ Fontana) Especially welcoming in winter, this corner bar overlooking Plaça de la Revolució de Setembre de 1868 is an animated spot to simply sip on an Estrella beer around rickety old marble-top tables, as people have done here since 1922. It's also a fine spot for coffee and a chat earlier in the day.

Raïm   Bar

(Map p254; Carrer del Progrés 48; ⏰9pm-2am Tue-Sat; Ⓜ Diagonal) The walls in Raïm are alive with black-and-white photos of Cubans and Cuba. Weathered old wooden chairs of another epoch huddle around marble tables, while grand old wood-framed mirrors hang from the walls. It draws a friendly, garrulous crowd who pile in for first-rate mojitos and an excellent selection of rum.

Le Journal   Bar

(Map p254; ☎93 368 41 37; Carrer de Francisco Giner 36; ⏰6pm-2am; Ⓜ Fontana) Students love the conspiratorial basement air of this narrow bar, whose walls and ceiling are plastered with newspapers (hence the name). Read the headlines of yesteryear while reclining in an old lounge. For a slightly more intimate feel, head upstairs to the rear gallery.

🔾 Camp Nou, Pedralbes & La Zona Alta

El Maravillas   Cocktail Bar

(☎93 360 73 78; www.elmaravillas.cat; Plaça de la Concòrdia 15; ⏰noon-12.30am Mon-Wed, to 3am Thu-Sun; Ⓜ Maria Cristina) Overlooking the peaceful Plaça de la Concòrdia, El Maravillas feels like a secret hideaway – especially if you've just arrived from the crowded lanes of the *ciutat vella* (old city). The glittering bar has just a few tables, with outdoor seating on the square when the weather warms. Creative cocktails, good Spanish red wines and easy-drinking vermouths are the drinks of choice.

Dō Bar
Bar

(🕿93 209 18 88; www.do-bcn.com; Carrer de Santaló 30, entrance on l'Avenir; ⊗7pm-midnight Tue-Thu, 8pm-1am Fri & Sat; 🕿; 🚇FGC Muntaner) This neighbourhood charmer has a warm and inviting interior, where friends gather over tall wooden tables to enjoy excellent gin and tonics, wines by the glass, craft beer and satisfying small plates (anchovies, mussels, tacos, charcuterie). On warm nights, arrive early for one of the terrace tables out the front.

Mirablau
Bar

(🕿93 418 58 79; www.mirablaubcn.com; Plaça del Doctor Andreu; ⊗11am-4.30am Mon-Thu, 10am-4.30am Fri-Sun; 🚇FGC Avinguda Tibidabo) Gaze out over the entire city from this privileged balcony restaurant on the way up to Tibidabo. Wander downstairs to join the folk in the tiny dance space. In summer you can step out on to the even smaller terrace for a breather.

Bikini
Club

(🕿93 322 08 00; www.bikinibcn.com; Avinguda Diagonal 547; cover €10-25; ⊗midnight-6am Thu-Sat; 🚌6, 7, 33, 34, 63, 67, 68, 🚇Entença) This old star of the Barcelona nightlife scene has been keeping the beat since the darkest days of Franco. Every possible kind of music gets a run, from Latin and Brazilian beats to 1980s disco, depending on the night and the space you choose.

Berlin
Bar

(🕿93 200 65 42; Carrer de Muntaner 240; ⊗10am-2am Mon-Thu, to 3am Fri & Sat; 🚇Diagonal, Hospital Clínic) This elegant corner bar offers views over Avinguda Diagonal. There is a cluster of tables outside on the ground floor and designer lounges downstairs. Service can be harried, but the location is excellent for starting an uptown night. All ages and creeds snuggle in and many kick on to nearby clubs afterwards.

Marcel
Bar

(🕿93 209 89 48; Carrer de Santaló 42; ⊗7.30am-1am Mon-Thu, to 3am Fri & Sat, 9.30am-midnight Sun; 🚇FGC Muntaner) A classic meeting place, Marcel has a homey,

👍 Streets & Plazas to Bar-Hop

Plaça Reial Barri Gòtic

Carrer dels Escudellers Barri Gòtic

Carrer de Joaquín Costa El Raval

Carrer Nou de la Rambla El Raval

Carrer del Parlament Sant Antoni

Platja de la Barceloneta La Barceloneta

Carrer d'Aribau L'Eixample

Plaça del Sol Gràcia

Passeig del Born La Ribera

Rambla del Raval El Raval

Plaça de la Vila de Gràcia Gràcia

Carrer Nou de la Rambla Poble Sec

Carrer de Margarit Poble Sec

Plaça Reial
JORDI SALAS/AGEFOTOSTOCK ©

old-world feel, with a wood bar, black-and-white floor tiles and high windows. It offers a few snacks and tapas as well. Space is somewhat limited and customers inevitably spill out onto the footpath, where there are also a few tables.

Otto Zutz
Club

(www.ottozutz.com; Carrer de Lincoln 15; cover €10-15; ⊗midnight-6am Thu-Sat; 🚇FGC Gràcia) Only beautiful people need apply for entry to this three-floor dance den. DJs come from the Ibiza rave mould.

Shake it all up to house on the ground floor, or head upstairs for funk and soul. The top floor is for VIPs (although at some ill-defined point in the evening the barriers all seem to come down).

SHOWTIME

See a flamenco performance,
catch a few bands or dance the night away

Showtime

From high culture to edgy backstreet performances, from opera to death metal, Barcelona teems with venues and stages hosting all manner of entertainment: underground cabaret, comic opera, contemplative drama. Dance companies are thick on the ground and popular local theatre companies, when not touring the rest of Spain, keep folks strapped to their seats. It's a cultural city par excellence.

In This Section

Tickets/Websites

The easiest way to get hold of tickets (*entradas*) for most venues throughout the city is through Ticketea (www.ticketea.com) or Ticketmaster (www.ticketmaster.es). Occasionally there are discounted tickets to be had on www.atrapalo.com.

For exhibitions and other free activities, check out www.forfree.cat.

KRASNEVSKY/GETTY IMAGES ©

Teatre Principal (p194)

The Best...

For Classical Music

Palau de la Música Catalana (p197) A Modernista fantasy, where the fabulous interior can distract from the finest musician.

Gran Teatre del Liceu (p194) One of Europe's most splendid opera houses, built to impress.

L'Auditori (p198) Fiercely modern concert venue, with a resident orchestra.

L'Ateneu (p194) This elegant old library is hard to enter if you're not a member – unless you catch one of its occasional concerts.

For Live Bands

Club City Hall (p199) The perfect mid-size venue for up-and-coming local and international acts.

Sala Apolo (p200) Cosy booths and a warm red glow give this hugely popular venue something special.

BARTS (p200) The latest contender on the live-music circuit, with superb sound and every mod con.

El Paraigua (p194) Head downstairs to the brick-and-stone basement bar area where live funk, soul, rock and blues bands hold court.

⊗ La Rambla & Barri Gòtic

Gran Teatre del Liceu   Theatre, Live Music

(Map p250; ☑93 485 99 00; www.liceubar celona.cat; La Rambla 51-59; ⊙box office 9.30am-8pm Mon-Fri, 9.30am-6pm Sat & Sun; MLiceu) Barcelona's grand old opera house, restored after a fire in 1994, is one of the most technologically advanced theatres in the world. To take a seat in the grand auditorium, returned to all its 19th-century glory but with the very latest in acoustics, is to be transported to another age.

L'Ateneu   Classical Music

(Map p250; ☑93 343 61 21; www.ateneubcn.org; Carrer de la Canuda 6; tickets free-€10; MCatalunya) This historic cultural centre (with roots dating back 150 years) hosts a range of highbrow fare, from classical recitals to film screenings and literary readings.

El Paraigua   Live Music

(Map p250; ☑93 302 11 31; www.elparaigua.com; Carrer del Pas de l'Ensenyança 2; ⊙noon-midnight Sun-Wed, to 2am Thu, to 3am Fri & Sat; MLiceu)

hA tiny chocolate box of dark tinted Modernisme, the 'Umbrella' has been serving up drinks since the 1960s. The turn-of-the-20th-century decor was transferred here from a shop knocked down elsewhere in the district and cobbled back together to create this cosy locale.

Sidecar Factory Club   Live Music

(Map p250; ☑93 302 15 86; www.sidecarfac toryclub.com; Plaça Reial 7; ticket prices vary; ⊙7pm-6am Mon-Sat; MLiceu) The entrance is on Plaça Reial and you can come here for a meal before midnight or a few drinks at ground level (which closes by 3am at the latest), or descend into the red-tinged, brick-vaulted bowels for live music most nights. Just about anything goes here, from UK indie through to country punk, but rock and pop lead the way.

Teatre Principal   Live Music

(Map p250; ☑662 018517; www.teatreprinci palbcn.com; La Rambla 27; concerts €25-50; ⊙9.30-11.30pm Mon-Sat Café Principal, 8pm & 10pm Sala B; MLiceu) Following a €6 million renovation, this historic theatre has been

Gran Teatre del Liceu

HOLBOX/SHUTTERSTOCK ©

transformed into a lavish concert space, though most of it is currently used for one-off events. There are flamenco shows in the atmospheric Sala B, all columns and wood and red velvet banquettes.

Jamboree
Live Music

(Map p250; 📞93 319 17 89; www.masimas.com/jamboree; Plaça Reial 17; tickets €10-20; ⏱8pm-6am; Ⓜ Liceu) For over half a century, Jamboree has been bringing joy to the jivers of Barcelona, with high-calibre acts featuring jazz trios, blues, Afrobeats, Latin sounds and big-band sounds. Two concerts are held most nights (at 8pm and 10pm), after which Jamboree morphs into a DJ-spinning club at midnight. WTF jam sessions are held Mondays (entrance a mere €5).

Harlem Jazz Club
Jazz

(Map p250; 📞93 310 07 55; www.harlemjazzclub.es; Carrer de la Comtessa de Sobradiel 8; tickets €6-15; ⏱10.30pm-3am Sun & Tue-Thu, to 5am Fri & Sat; Ⓜ Liceu) This narrow, old-city dive is one of the best spots in town for jazz, as well as funk, Latin, blues and gypsy jazz. It attracts a mixed crowd who maintains a respectful silence during the acts. Most concerts start around 10pm. Get in early if you want a seat in front of the stage.

Sala Tarantos
Flamenco

(Map p250; 📞93 304 12 10; www.masimas.com/tarantos; Plaça Reial 17; tickets €15; ⏱shows 8.30pm, 9.30pm & 10.30pm; Ⓜ Liceu) Since 1963, this basement locale has been the stage for up-and-coming flamenco groups performing in Barcelona. These days Tarantos has become a mostly tourist-centric affair, with half-hour shows held three times a night. Still, it's a good introduction to flamenco and not a bad setting for a drink.

Boulevard
DJ

(Map p250; 📞622 438423; www.boulevardcultureclub.es; La Rambla 27; entry free up to €15, depending on night; ⏱11.45pm-5am Sun-Thu, to 6am Fri & Sat; Ⓜ Drassanes) Boulevard (also known as Dome, depending on the night) is flanked by striptease bars (in the spirit of the lower Rambla's old days) and has undergone countless reincarnations. With

 La Fura dels Baus

Keep your eyes peeled for any of the eccentric (if not downright crazed) performances of Barcelona's La Fura dels Baus (www.lafura.com) theatre group. It has won worldwide acclaim for its brand of startling, often acrobatic, theatre in which the audience is frequently dragged into the chaos. The company grew out of Barcelona's street-theatre culture of the late 1970s and, although it has grown in technical prowess and received great international acclaim, it has not abandoned the rough-and-ready edge of street performances.

GERARD JULIEN/STAFF/GETTY IMAGES ©

three different dance spaces, one of them upstairs, it has a deliciously tacky feel, pumping out anything from 1980s hits to house music (especially on Saturdays in the main room). There's no particular dress code.

El Raval

Filmoteca de Catalunya
Cinema

(Map p250; 📞93 567 10 70; www.filmoteca.cat; Plaça de Salvador Seguí 1-9; adult/concession €4/3; ⏱screenings 5-10pm, ticket office 10am-3pm & 4-9.30pm Tue-Sun; Ⓜ Liceu) After almost a decade in the planning, the Filmoteca de Catalunya – Catalonia's national cinema – moved into this modern 6000-sq-metre building in 2012. It's a glass, metal and concrete beast that hulks in the midst of the most louche part of

El Raval, but the building's interior shouts revival, with light and space, wall-to-wall windows, skylights and glass panels that let the sun in.

Gipsy Lou   Live Music

(Map p249; www.gipsylou.com; Carrer de Ferlandina 55; ☺8pm-2.30am Sun-Thu, 8pm-3am Fri & Sat; ⓂSant Antoni) A louche little bar that packs 'em in for live music from rumba and pop to flamenco, along with occasional storytelling events and whatever else Felipe feels like putting on. There are decent bar snacks to keep you going on a long night of pisco sours, the house speciality.

23 Robadors   Live Music

(Map p250; Carrer d'en Robador 23; admission varies; ☺8pm-3am; ⓂLiceu) On what remains a sleazy Raval street, despite the slow-but-steady gentrification of the area, this narrow little bar has made a name for itself with its shows and live music. Jazz is the name of the game, but you'll also find live poetry, flamenco and plenty more.

Jazz Sí Club   Live Music

(Map p249; ☎93 329 00 20; www.tallerdemusics. com/en/jazzsi-club; Carrer de Requesens 2; admission incl drink €4-10; ☺8.30-11pm Tue-Sat, 6.30-10pm Sun; ☐20, 24, 64, ⓂSant Antoni) A cramped little bar run by the Taller de Músics (Musicians' Workshop) serves as the stage for a varied program of jazz jams through to some good flamenco (Friday and Saturday nights). Thursday night is Cuban night, Tuesday and Sunday are rock, and the rest are devoted to jazz and/or blues sessions. Concerts start around 9pm but the jam sessions can get going earlier.

Teatre Romea   Theatre

(Map p250; ☎93 309 70 04; www.teatreromea. com; Carrer de l'Hospital 51; ticket prices vary; ☺box office 5.30pm until start of show Tue-Fri, from 4.30pm Sat & Sun; ⓂLiceu) Just off La Rambla, this 19th-century theatre was resurrected at the end of the 1990s and is one of the city's key stages for quality drama. It usually fills up for a broad range of interesting plays, often classics with a contemporary flavour, in Catalan and Spanish.

Teatre Llantiol
Theatre

(Map p249; ☎93 329 90 09; www.llantiol.com; Carrer de la Riereta 7; ticket prices vary; MSant Antoni) This charming little cafe-theatre, which has a certain scuffed elegance, stages all sorts of odd stuff, from concerts and theatre to magic shows. The speciality, though, is stand-up comedy, which is occasionally in English. Check the website for details.

El Cangrejo
Gay

(Map p250; ☎93 301 29 78; www.facebook. com/elcangrejoeixample; Carrer de Montserrat 9; ☺11pm-3am Fri & Sat; MDrassanes) This altar to kitsch, a dingy dance hall that has transgressed since the 1920s, is run by the luminous underground cabaret figure of Carmen Mairena and exudes a gorgeously tacky feel, especially with the midnight drag shows on Friday and Saturday. Due to its popularity with tourists, getting in is all but impossible unless you turn up early.

✪ La Ribera

Palau de la Música Catalana
Classical Music

(Map p254; ☎93 295 72 00; www.palaumusica. cat; Carrer de Palau de la Música 4-6; tickets from €15; ☺box office 9.30am-9pm Mon-Sat, 10am-3pm Sun; MUrquinaona) A feast for the eyes, this Modernista confection is also the city's most traditional venue for classical and choral music, although it has a wide-ranging program, including flamenco, pop and – particularly – jazz. Just being here for a performance is an experience. In the foyer, its tiled pillars all a-glitter, sip a pre-concert tipple.

Tablao Nervión
Dance

(Map p250; ☎93 315 21 03; www.restaurant enervion.com; Carrer de la Princesa 2; show incl 1 drink €17, show & set dinner €28; ☺shows 8-10pm Wed-Sun; MJaume I) For admittedly tourist-oriented flamenco, this unassuming bar (shows take place in the basement) is cheaper than most and has good offerings. Check the website for further details.

★ Alfresco Cinema
Outdoor cinema screens are set up in summer in the moat of the Castell de Montjuïc, on the beach and in the Fòrum. Foreign films with subtitles and original soundtracks are marked 'VO' *(versió original)* in movie listings.

From left: Teatre Nacional de Catalunya (p198); Sculpture at the Palau de la Música Catalana; Eva Fernández Group perform at the Luz de Gas (p203)

PASCALE BEROUJON/GETTY IMAGES ©

CHRISTIAN BERTRAND/SHUTTERSTOCK ©

 Flamenco

Seeing good performances of this essentially Andalucian dance and music is not easy. The few *tablaos* are touristy and often tacky. You can catch flamenco on Friday and Saturday nights at the **Jazz Sí Club** (p196); also watch out for big-name performers at the **Palau de la Música Catalana** (p197).

The Festival de Flamenco de Ciutat Vella (ciutatflamenco.com) is held in May. A series of concerts can be seen from April to July as part of the Barcelona Guitar Festival (www.guitarbcn.com).

Los Vivancos dance company perform at the Teatre Grec (p200)
MAXISPORT/SHUTTERSTOCK ®

✪ Barceloneta & the Waterfront

Sala Beckett — Theatre
(☏93 284 53 12; www.salabeckett.cat; Carrer de Pere IV 228-232; ⓂPoblenou) One of the city's principal alternative theatres, the Sala Beckett does not shy away from challenging theatre and stages an eclectic mix of local productions and foreign drama. Formerly based in Gràcia, the theatre moved in 2016 to this lovely new space (in the building that formerly housed the Cooperativa Pau i Justícia Poblenou).

Sala Monasterio — Live Music
(☏616 287197; www.facebook.com/sala.monasterio; Moll de Mestral 30; ⓒ9pm-2.30am; ⓂCiutadella-Vila Olímpica) Overlooking the bobbing masts and slender palm trees

of Port Olímpic, this pocket-sized music spot stages an eclectic line-up of live bands, including jazz, *forró* (music from northeastern Brazil), blues jams and rock (usually on Fridays and Saturdays).

Razzmatazz — Live Music
(☏93 320 82 00; www.salarazzmatazz.com; Carrer de Pamplona 88; tickets from €17; ⓒ11pm-5am; ⓂMarina, Bogatell) Bands from far and wide occasionally create scenes of near hysteria in this, one of the city's classic live-music and clubbing venues. Bands can appear throughout the week (check the website), with different start times. On weekends the live music then gives way to club sounds.

L'Auditori — Classical Music
(☏93 247 93 00; www.auditori.org; Carrer de Lepant 150; tickets €6.50-58; ⓒbox office 5-9pm Tue-Fri, 10am-1pm & 5-9pm Sat; ⓂMonumental) Barcelona's modern home for serious music lovers, L'Auditori puts on plenty of orchestral, chamber, religious and other music. The ultramodern building (designed by Rafael Moneo) is home to the Orquestra Simfònica de Barcelona i Nacional de Catalunya.

Teatre Nacional de Catalunya — Performing Arts
(☏93 306 57 00; www.tnc.cat; Plaça de les Arts 1; tickets €12-28; ⓒbox office 5-8pm Wed-Fri, 3pm-8pm Sat, to 6pm Sun; ⓂGlòries, Monumental) Ricard Bofill's ultra-neoclassical theatre, with its bright, airy foyer, hosts a wide range of performances, including dramas, comedies, musicals and dance. Some shows are free.

Yelmo Cines Icària — Cinema
(☏902 220922; www.yelmocines.es; Carrer de Salvador Espriu 61; ⓂCiutadella Vila Olímpica) This vast cinema complex screens movies in the original language on 15 screens, making for plenty of choice. Aside from the screens, you'll find several cheerful eateries, bars and the like to keep you occupied before and after the movies.

✪ La Sagrada Família & L'Eixample

Club City Hall
Concert Venue

(Map p254; ☎ 93 238 07 22; www.cityhallbar celona.com; Rambla de Catalunya 2-4; ticket prices vary; ⏱ 11.45pm-6am; Ⓜ Catalunya)
The early-evening incarnation of City Hall, this former theatre is the perfect size and shape for live music, holding a crowd of around 500. The acoustics are also great and the layout means everyone gets a good view of the stage.

Mediterráneo
Live Music

(Map p254; ☎ 93 453 58 45; www.elmedi.net; Carrer de Balmes 129; ⏱ 11pm-3am; Ⓜ Diagonal) This jam joint is a great hang-out that attracts a mostly casual student set. Order a beer, enjoy the free nuts and chat at one of the tiny tables while waiting for the next act to tune up at the back. Sometimes the young performers are surprisingly good.

📅 Entertainment Listings

● The Palau de la Virreina (p47) cultural information office has oodles of information on theatre, opera, classical music and more.

● The Guía del Ocio (www.guiadelocio bcn.es) has ample listings for all forms of entertainment, as does Time Out (www.timeout.cat).

● Good coverage of classical music is to be found on www.classictic.com.

Teatre Tívoli
Theatre

(Map p254; ☎ 93 412 20 63; www.grupbalana. com; Carrer de Casp 8; ticket prices vary; ⏱ box office noon-8pm; Ⓜ Catalunya) A grand old theatre with three storeys of boxes and a generous stage, the Tívoli has a fairly rapid turnover of drama and musicals, with pieces often not staying on for more than a couple of weeks.

Sara Baras performs *Voces* at the Teatre Tívoli

Live Music

Almost every big international act has passed through Barcelona at some point, more often than not playing at **Razzmatazz** (p198), **Bikini** (p189), **Sala Apolo** (p200) or **BARTS** (p200), although there are a number of other decent midsize venues. There are also abundant local gigs in institutions as diverse as **CaixaForum** (Map p256; ☎93 476 86 00; www.fundacio.lacaixa.es; Avinguda de Francesc Ferrer i Guàrdia 6-8; adult/student & child €4/free, 1st Sun of month free; ⏰10am-8pm; P; MEspanya), **La Pedrera** (p74) and **L'Ateneu** (p194).

Nacho Blanco and Eli Ayala perform at the Teatre Grec
MIQUEL BENITEZ/CONTRIBUTOR/GETTY IMAGES ©

Méliès Cinemes Cinema
(Map p249; ☎93 451 00 51; www.meliescinemes.com; Carrer de Villarroel 102; tickets €4-7; MUrgell) A cosy cinema with two screens, the Méliès specialises in the best of recent releases from Hollywood and Europe.

Montjuïc, Poble Sec & Sant Antoni

Hiroshima Live Performance
(Map p256; ☎93 315 54 58; www.hiroshima.cat; Carrer de Vilà i Vilà 67; ⏰5pm-1am Tue-Thu, to 3am Fri & Sat, noon-1am Sun; MParal·lel) Hiroshima is a creative trailblazer in Poble Sec. In a former elevator factory, Hiroshima stages emerging and avant-garde musicians, dancers and performing artists. It has two stages (seating 130 and 250 people, respectively) and a lively ground-floor bar where you can grab a drink after the show. For unconventional fare, this is a good place to look.

BARTS Concert Venue
(Barcelona Arts on Stage; Map p256; ☎93 324 84 92; www.barts.cat; Avinguda del Paral·lel 62; tickets €12-40; ⏰5pm-midnight Mon-Thu & Sun, 5pm-2am Fri & Sat; MParal·lel) BARTS has earned a reputation for its innovative line-up of urban dance troupes, electro swing, psychedelic pop and other eclectic fare. The theatre has a smart design that combines a comfortable midsized auditorium with excellent acoustics.

Teatre Grec Theatre
(Map p256; lameva.barcelona.cat/grec; Passeig de Santa Madrona; MEspanya) This lovely amphitheatre on Montjuïc stages one of the city's best festivals, with theatre, dance and music events running throughout the summer. Aside from the Teatre Grec, performances are held all over the city.

Gran Bodega Saltó Live Music
(Map p256; ☎93 441 37 09; www.bodegasalto.net; Carrer de Blesa 36; ⏰7pm-2am Mon-Thu, noon-3am Fri & Sat, noon-midnight Sun; MParal·lel) The ranks of barrels give away the bar's history as a traditional bodega. Now, after a little homemade psychedelic redecoration with odd lamps, figurines and old Chinese beer ads, it's a magnet for an eclectic barfly crowd. The crowd is mixed and friendly, and gets pretty animated on nights when there is live music.

Sala Apolo Live Music
(Map p256; ☎93 441 40 01; www.sala-apolo.com; Carrer Nou de la Rambla 113; club €12-18, concerts vary; ⏰12.30am-5am Mon-Thu, 12.30am-6am Fri & Sat; MParal·lel) This is a fine old theatre, where red velvet dominates and you feel as though you're in a movie-set dancehall scene featuring Eliot Ness. 'Nasty Mondays' and 'Crappy Tuesdays' are aimed at a diehard, we-never-stop-dancing crowd. Earlier in the evening, concerts generally take place, here and in 'La 2', a smaller auditorium downstairs.

Mosaic on the facade of the Palau de la Música Catalana (p197)

★ Classical Venues

The two historic – and iconic – music venues are the **Gran Teatre del Liceu** (p194) and the **Palau de la Música Catalana** (p197), while **L'Auditori** (p198) is the modern concert hall par excellence and home to the city's orchestra, the OBC.

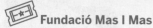
Fundació Mas I Mas

This **Fundació Mas I Mas** (📞93 319 17 89; www.masimas.com/fundacio; admission €12-15) promotes chamber and classical music, offering concerts in a couple of locations. Classical concerts, usually involving Catalan performers, are held regularly in the Sala Oriol Martorell of **l'Auditori** (p198), starting at around 8pm. For intense 30-minute sessions of chamber music, see its program of performances at **l'Ateneu** (p194), a hallowed academic institution-cum-club. These are typically held Fridays, Saturdays and Sundays at 6pm, 7pm and 8pm.

Sant Jordi Club — Live Music
(Map p256; 📞93 426 20 89; www.santjordiclub. cat; Passeig Olimpic 5-7; 🚇55, 150) With capacity for more than 4500 people, this concert hall, annexed to the Olympic stadium **Palau Sant Jordi** (www.palausantjordi.cat), is used for big gigs that do not reach the epic proportions of headlining international acts. Admission prices and opening times vary with the concerts.

Teatre Mercat De Les Flors — Dance
(Map p256; 📞93 256 26 00; www.mercatflors. cat; Carrer de Lleida 59; €10-22; ⊘box office 11am-2pm & 4-7pm Mon-Fri & 1hr before show; 🚇55) Next door to the Teatre Lliure, and together with it known as the Ciutat de Teatre (Theatre City), this is a key venue for top local and international contemporary dance acts. Dance companies perform all over Barcelona, but this spacious modern stage is number one.

Teatre Victòria — Theatre
(Map p256; 📞93 329 91 89; www.teatrevicto ria.com; Avinguda del Paral·lel 67; €12.50-45; ⊘box office 2hr before show; 🚇Paral·lel) This modern (and, on the street, rather nondescript-looking) theatre is on what used to be considered Barcelona's version of Broadway. It stages musicals (usually in Catalan), flamenco and contemporary dance.

Renoir Floridablanca — Cinema
(Map p249; 📞91 542 27 02; www.cinesrenoir. com; Carrer de Floridablanca 135; tickets €6-10; 🚇Sant Antoni) With seven screens, this is now the last standing in Barcelona of a small chain of art-house cinemas in Spain showing quality flicks. It is handily located just beyond El Raval, so you can be sure that there is no shortage of postfilm entertainment options nearby.

Teatre Lliure — Theatre
(Map p256; 📞93 289 27 70; www.teatrelliure. com; Plaça de Margarida Xirgu 1; €15-30; ⊘box office 9am-8pm Mon-Fri, 2hr before show Sat & Sun; 🚇Espanya) Housed in the magnificent former Palau de l'Agricultura building on Montjuïc (opposite the Museu d'Arqueologia) and consisting of two modern theatre spaces (Espai Lliure and Sala Fabià Puigserver), the 'Free Theatre' puts on a variety of quality drama (mostly in Catalan), contemporary dance and music.

✪ Gràcia & Park Güell

Soda Acústic — Live Music
(Map p254; 📞93 016 55 90; www.soda.cat; Carrer de les Guilleries 6; tickets from €4; ⊘8.30pm-2.30am Wed-Thu & Sun, 9pm-3am Fri & Sat; 🚇Fontana) This low-lit modern space stages an eclectic line-up of bands and performing artists. Jazz, Balkan swing, Latin rhythms and plenty of experimental, not easily classifiable musicians all receive their due. The acoustics are excellent. Check the website for upcoming shows.

CHRISTIAN BERTRAND/SHUTTERSTOCK ©

Beirut perform at the Primavera Sound festival (p11)

Teatreneu   Theatre
(Map p254; ☎93 285 37 12; www.teatreneu.
com; Carrer de Terol 26; ☺box office 1hr before
show; Ⓜ Fontana, Joanic) This lively theatre
(with a bustling, rambling downstairs bar
facing the street) dares to fool around with
all sorts of material, from monologues to
social comedy. Aside from the main theatre, two cafe-style spaces serve as more
intimate stage settings for small-scale
productions. Films are also shown.

Verdi   Cinema
(Map p254; ☎93 238 79 90; www.cines-verdi.
com; Carrer de Verdi 32; Ⓜ Fontana) A popular
original-language art-house cinema in the
heart of Gràcia, with five screens showing
a variety of independent international
movies. It is handy to lots of local eateries
and bars for pre- and post-film enjoyment.
The Verdi Park, one street over on Carrer de
Torrijos, is its four-screen annexe.

✪ Camp Nou, Pedralbes & La Zona Alta

Luz de Gas   Live Music
(☎93 209 77 11; www.luzdegas.com; Carrer de
Muntaner 246; tickets up to €20; ☺Thu-Sat;
🚌6, 7, 15, 27, 32, 33, 34, 58, 64, Ⓜ Diagonal)
Several nights a week this club, set in a
grand former theatre, stages concerts
ranging through rock, soul, salsa, jazz and
pop. From about 2am, the place turns into
a club that attracts a well-dressed crowd
with varying musical tastes, depending on
the night. Check the website for the latest
schedule. Concerts typically cost around
€12 and kick off around 10pm.

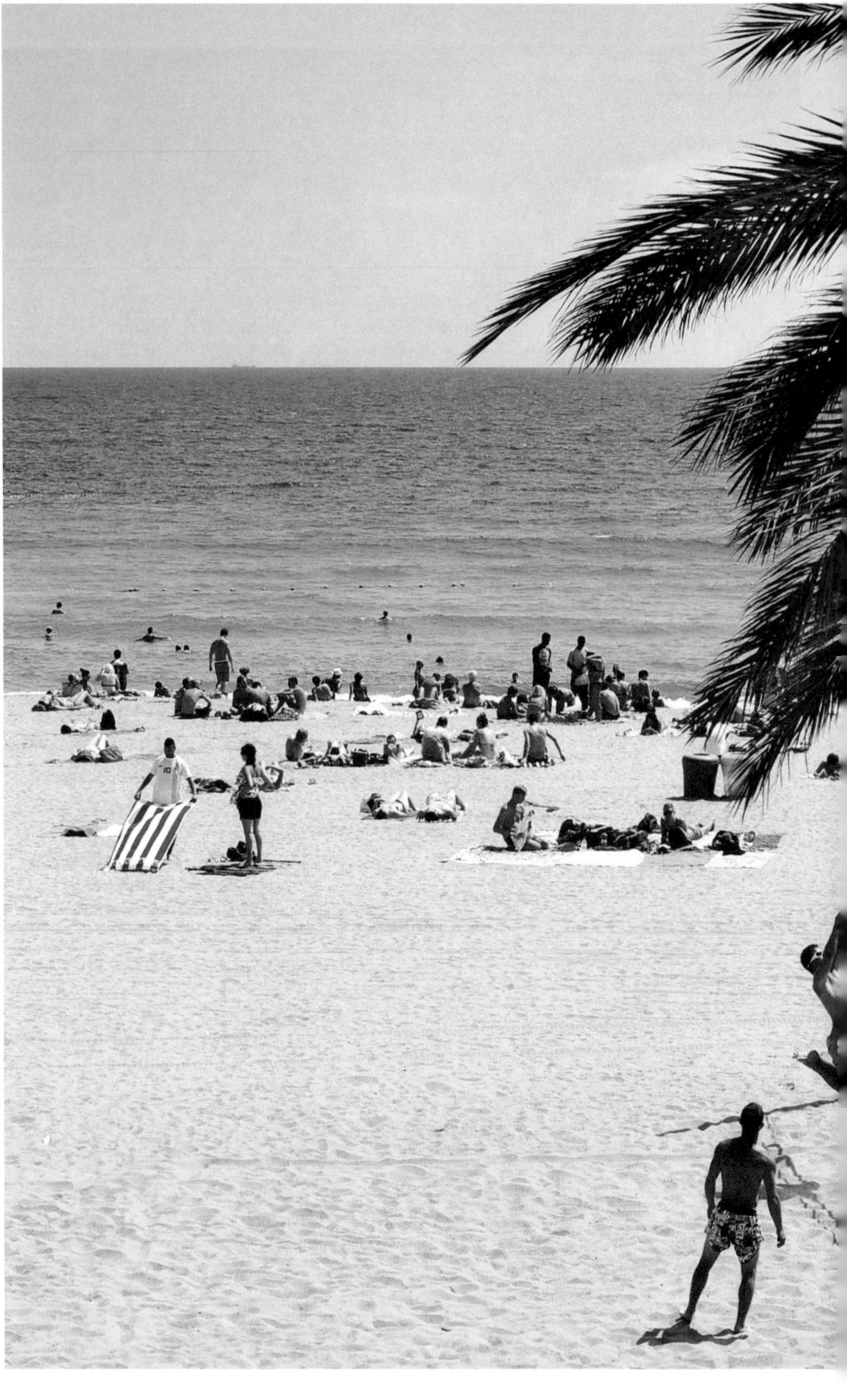

NITO/SHUTTERSTOCK ©

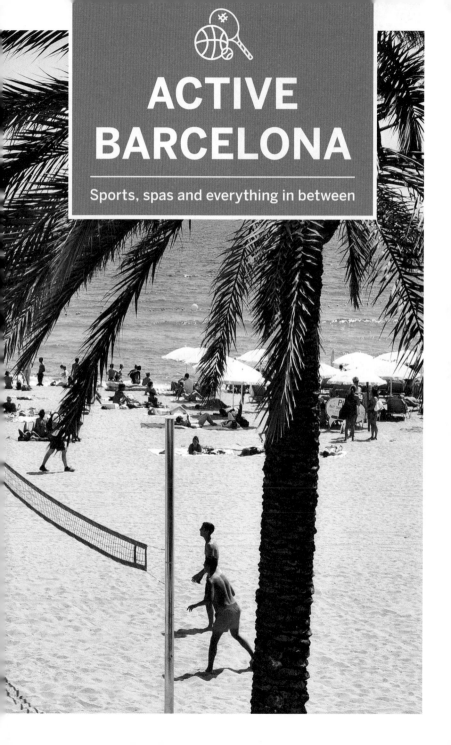

ACTIVE
BARCELONA

Sports, spas and everything in between

Active Barcelona

Mediterranean oceanfront and a rambling hilly park overlooking the city make fine settings for a bit of outdoor activity beneath the (generally) sunny skies of Barcelona. For a break from museum-hopping and overindulging at tapas bars, Barcelona has the antidote – running, swimming, cycling or simply pumping fists in the air at a never-dull FC Barcelona match. Football here has the aura of religion and for much of the city's population, support of the city's principal team is an article of faith. There's also a variety of ways to get a more active look at the city, whether on a specialised walking tour through the Old City or on a bicycle excursion around the city centre.

In This Section

Sports Seasons

The football season runs from late August to May.

The Spanish basketball season runs from October to June.

Asobal, the Spanish handball league, runs from September to May or early June.

The professional tennis season is in spring; the big event here is the Barcelona Open in April.

Camp Nou (p72)

The Best...

Activities

Castell de Montjuïc (p61) Barcelona's easily accessible mountain offers a scenic setting for running and biking.

Parc de Collserola (p101) The city's best mountain biking (and home to wild boar).

Camp Nou (p72) See FC Barcelona in action at their world-famous home stadium.

Rituels d'Orient (p210) A beautiful hamam in El Born.

Piscines Bernat Picornell (p210) A truly Olympian setting for a swim.

Waterfront Adventures

Molokai SUP Center (p210) Go for a gentle paddle out on the Mediterranean.

Platja de Sant Sebastià Further south than Platja de la Nova Icària (p122), this is the perfect starting point for a scenic run or cycle along the waterfront.

Orsom (p209) Watch the sunset on a peaceful sailing cruise.

🕙 Tours

Catalunya Bus Turístic   Bus
(🖉93 285 38 32; www.catalunyabusturistic.
com; Plaça de Catalunya; ⓂCatalunya) Routes
include a day in Colònia Güell and Montserrat (€70); Montserrat (€46); Girona and
Figueres (€76); and a Penedès wine and
cava jaunt with three winery tours and lunch
(€69). All tours leave at 8.30am or 10.30am
(Montserrat) from Plaça de Catalunya.

Devour Barcelona   Tours
(🖉mob 695 111 832; devourbarcelonafoodtours.
com; €75-99) Knowledgeable guides lead
food tours around Gràcia, the Old City and
Barceloneta that mix gastronomy with
history. The various tastings and spots
visited are especially focused on small,
local producers and family-run joints. Most
tours last three to four hours.

My Favourite Things   Tours
(🖉637 265 405; www.myft.net; tours from €26)
Offers tours (with no more than 10 partici-
pants) based on numerous themes: street
art, shopping, culinary tours, musical

journeys and forgotten neighbourhoods
are among the offerings. Other activities
include flamenco and salsa classes, cooking workshops and bicycle rides in and out
of Barcelona. Some of the more unusual
activities cost more and times vary.

Barcelona By Bike   Cycling
(🖉671 307 325; www.barcelonabybike.com; Carrer
de la Marina 13; tours from €24; ⓂCiutadella Vila
Olímpica) This outfit offers several tours by
bicycle, including 'The Original', a three-
hour pedal that takes in a bit of Gothic Barcelona, the Eixample (including Sagrada
Família) and the Barceloneta beachfront.

Barcelona Guide Bureau   Tours
(🖉93 315 22 61; www.barcelonaguidebureau.com;
Via Laietana 50) Barcelona Guide Bureau
places professional guides at the disposal
of groups for tailor-made tours of the city.
Several languages are catered for. It also
offers a series of daily tours, from a five-
hour 'highlights of Barcelona' tour (adult/
child €62/31, departing at 10am) to a trip
to Montserrat, leaving Barcelona at 3pm
and lasting about four hours (adult/child
€48/24).

Bike tours along the coastline

Orsom   Cruise
(93 441 05 37; www.barcelona-orsom.com;
Moll de les Drassanes; adult/child from €16/11;
May-Oct; Drassanes) Aboard a large
sailing catamaran, Orsom makes the
90-minute journey to Port Olímpic and
back. There are three departures per day
(four on weekends in July and August),
and the last is a jazz cruise, scheduled
around sunset.

Las Golondrinas   Cruise
(93 442 31 06; www.lasgolondrinas.com;
Moll de las Drassanes; 40min tour adult/child
€7.50/2.80; Drassanes) Golondrinas
offers several popular cruises from its
dock in front of Mirador de Colom. The
90-minute catamaran tour (€15) takes
you out past Barceloneta and the beaches
to the Fòrum and back. If you just want a
peak at the area around the port, you can
opt for the 40-minute excursion to the
breakwater and back. Both run frequently
throughout the day.

Runner Bean Tours   Walking
(636 108776; www.runnerbeantours.com;
Carrer del Carme 44; tours 11am year-round
& 4.30pm Apr-Sep, 3pm Mar; Liceu) Runner
Bean Tours offers several daily thematic
tours. It's a pay-what-you-wish tour, with
a collection taken at the end for the guide.
The **Old City tour** explores the Roman
and medieval history of Barcelona, visiting
highlights in the Ciutat Vella. The **Gaudí
tour** takes in the great works of Modernista Barcelona. It involves two hops on the
metro.

Barcelona Walking Tours   Walking
(93 285 38 34; www.barcelonaturisme.com;
Plaça de Catalunya 17; Catalunya) The Oficina
d'Informació de Turisme de Barcelona
organises guided walking tours. One
explores the Barri Gòtic (adult/child €16/
free; in English 9.30am daily); another
follows in Picasso's footsteps €22/7,
in English 3pm Tuesday, Thursday and
Saturday) and winds up at the Museu
Picasso. There is a 10% discount on all
tours if you book online.

Spas

A day at the spa can be a fantastic way
to recharge after a few days exploring,
or perhaps a few nights on the town.
The best spas come replete with candlelit ante rooms and sumptuous baths
and steam rooms. Most high-end hotels
have spas, though more charming
options are scattered around town.

Terra Diversions   Cycling
(93 416 08 05; www.terradiversions.com; Carrer de Santa Tecla 1bis; self-guided tour from €37,
one-day guided tour from €75; Diagonal) This
outfit offers a good range of cycling tours.
You can go mountain biking in the Parc
de Collserola or outside of Barcelona in
the Pyrenees; take a two-day trip around
the forests and lakes near Vic; or join a
road-biking tour on Barcelona's north
coast and beyond. Self-guided trips (with
GPS and gear) are also available.

BC Naval Tours   Boating
(93 443 60 50; www.barcelonanavaltours.
com; Moll de las Drassanes; cruise 40min/2hr
€7.50/20; Drassanes) BC Naval is one of
several companies running boat cruises
from the dock near Mirador de Colom.
The two-hour catamaran tour takes you
out past Barceloneta and the beaches
to Badalona and back (one way also
possible). If you just want a peek at the
area around the port, you can opt for the
40-minute excursion to the breakwater
and back.

Bus Turístic   Bus
(93 298 70 00; www.barcelonabusturistic.cat/
en; day ticket adult/child €29/16; 9am-8pm)
This hop-on, hop-off service covers three
circuits (44 stops) linking virtually all the
major tourist sights. Tourist offices, TMB
transport authority offices and many
hotels have leaflets explaining the system.
Each of the two main circuits takes ap-
proximately two hours.

FC Barcelona

One of the city's best-loved names is FC Barcelona (Barça). The team was long a rallying point for Catalans when other aspects of Catalan culture were suppressed. The club openly supported Catalonia's drive towards autonomy in 1918 and in 1921 the club's statutes were drafted in Catalan. The pro-Catalan leanings of the club and its siding with the republic during the Spanish Civil War earned reprisals from the government. Club president Josep Sunyol was killed by Franco's soldiers in 1936 and the club building was bombed in 1938.

In 1968 club president Narcís de Carreras uttered the now famous words, *El Barça: més que un club* ('more than a club'), which became the team's motto and emphasised its role as an anti-Franco symbol and catalyst for change in the province and beyond. Today FC Barça is one of the world's most admired teams; in 2014 FC Barcelona's social networks surpassed 100 million followers – the first team anywhere to reach this mark.

🚴 Activities

Molokai SUP Center Water Sports
(📞93 221 48 68; www.molokaisupcenter.com; Carrer de Meer 39; 2hr lesson €60, SUP rental per hr €15; Ⓜ Barceloneta) This respected outfit will give you a crash course in stand-up paddleboarding (SUP). In addition to the two-hour beginner class, Molokai can help you improve your technique (in intermediate and advanced lessons – all in two-hour blocks); gear and wetsuit are included. If you'd rather just hire a SUP board, they can get you out on the sea in no time.

Claror Marítim Swimming
(📞93 224 04 40; www.claror.cat/maritim; Passeig Marítim de la Barceloneta 33-35; Mon-Fri €17, Sat, Sun & holidays €20; ⏱7am-midnight Mon-Fri, 8am-9pm Sat, 8am-4pm Sun; Ⓜ Ciutadella Vila Olímpica) Water babies will squeal with delight in this thalassotherapeutic (seawater therapy) sports centre. In addition to the small pool for lap swimming, there is a labyrinth of hot, warm and freezing-cold spa pools, along with thundering waterfalls for massage relief.

Rituels d'Orient Spa
(📞93 419 14 72; www.rituelsdorient.com; Carrer de Loreto 50; baths €29; ⏱11am-9pm Sun, Tue & Wed, to 10pm Thu-Sat; Ⓜ Hospital Clínic) Rituels d'Orient offers a setting that resembles a Moroccan fantasy, with dark woods, window grills, candle lighting and ancient-looking stone walls. Luxuriate in the hammam or indulge in a massage, body scrub or other treatment.

Swing Maniacs Dancing
(📞93 187 69 85; www.swingmaniacs.com; Carrer l'Església 4; group/private 55min class from €12/40; ⏱hours vary, see website; Ⓜ Joanic, Fontana) In the last few years, swing dancing has arrived in full force in the Catalan capital with old-fashioned dance parties happening in far-flung corners of the city every night. To learn the moves, sign up for a class at Swing Maniacs. You can join a drop-in class and if you don't have a partner, one can be arranged for you.

Aire De Barcelona Hamam
(📞93 295 57 43; www.airedebarcelona.com; Passeig de Picasso 22; thermal baths & aromatherapy Mon-Thu €36, Fri-Sun €39; ⏱9am-10pm Sun-Tue, to 11pm Wed-Thu, to midnight Fri & Sat; Ⓜ Arc de Triomf) With low lighting and relaxing perfumes wafting around you, this basement hamam could be the perfect way to end a day. Hot, warm and cold baths, steam baths and options for various massages, including on a slab of hot marble, make for a delicious hour or so. Book ahead and bring a swimming costume.

Piscines Picornell Swimming
(📞93 423 40 41; www.picornell.cat; Avinguda de l'Estadi 30-38; adult/child €12/8, nudist hours €7/5; ⏱6.45am-midnight Mon-Fri, 7am-9pm Sat, 7.30am-4pm Sun; 🚌150) Barcelona's official

Stand-up paddleboarding, Barceloneta Beach

Olympic pool on Montjuïc. Admission also includes use of fitness room, sauna, Jacuzzi, steam bath and track. On Saturday nights, between 9pm and 11pm, the pool (with access to sauna and steam bath) is open only to nudists. On Sundays between October and May the indoor pool also opens for nudists only from 4.15pm to 6pm.

Courses

Espai Boisà   Cooking
(☎93 192 60 21; espaiboisa.com; Ptge Lluís Pellicer 8; cost varies; Ⓜ Hospital Clínic)✒ Run by a young, multilingual Venezuelan-Catalan couple, this first-rate outfit offers cooking courses on various themes and of various lengths. They emphasise organic, seasonal ingredients from local producers outside of Barcelona – put to good use in dishes including paella, a range of tapas dishes and *crema catalana* (a Catalan version of *crème brûlée*).

Antilla BCN
Escuela de Baile   Dancing
(☎610 900558, 93 451 45 64; www.antillaescueladesalsa.com; Carrer d'Aragó 141; per hour €35; ◷8-11pm Tue, 9-11pm Wed, 8pm-midnight Thu, 9pm-midnight Fri; Ⓜ Urgell) *The* salsateca in town, this is the place to come for Cuban *son*, merengue, salsa and a whole lot more. Classes in various forms of Latin and African dance, from salsa to kizomba.

Spectator Sports

See p72 for FC Barcelona's home ground, Camp Nou.

Estadi RCD Espanyol   Football
(☎93 292 77 00; www.rcdespanyol.com; Avinguda del Baix Llobrega; tickets from €30; ℝ FGC Cornellà Riera) Espanyol, based at the 40,500-seat Estadi RCD Espanyol, traditionally plays second fiddle to Barça, although it does so with considerable passion.

REST YOUR HEAD

Top tips for the best accommodation

Rest Your Head

Barcelona has an excellent range of accommodation, with high-end luxury hotels, sharp boutique lodgings and a varied spread of midrange and budget selections. There are also small-scale B&B-style apartment rentals scattered around the city, which are a good-value choice. Wherever you stay it's wise to book well ahead. If you plan to travel around holidays such as Easter, Christmas or New Year's Eve, or in summer, reserve a room three or four months ahead of time.

In This Section

Prices

A 'budget hotel' in Barcelona generally costs up to €75 for a double room during high season. For a modest midrange option, plan on spending €75 to €200. Luxury options run €200 and higher.

Virtually all accommodation is subject to IVA, a 10% value-added tax. There's also an additional tax of between €0.72 and €2.48 per person per night. These charges are usually included in the quoted rate.

Accommodation near La Rambla (p44)

Reservations & Check-in

Booking ahead is recommended, especially during peak periods, trade fairs and throughout much of summer.

If you arrive without prebooked lodging, the Plaça de Catalunya's tourist office (p238) can help.

Check-in is around 2pm or 3pm. If arriving earlier, you can usually leave your luggage at reception.

Check-out is generally noon.

Useful Websites

Oh-Barcelona (www.oh-barcelona.com) Good-value selection of hotels, hostels and apartment rentals.

Lonely Planet (www.lonelyplanet.com) Huge range of hotels, hostels, guesthouses, B&Bs and apartments.

Barcelona Bed and Breakfasts (www.barcelonabedandbreakfasts.com) Listings of low-key, oft-overlooked lodging options.

🛏 Accommodation Types

Hotels

Hotels cover a broad range. At the bottom end there is often little to distinguish them from better *pensiones* and *hostales,* and from there they run up the scale to five-star luxury. Some of the better features to look out for include rooftop pools and lounges, views (either of the sea or a cityscape – La Sagrada Família, Montjuïc, Barri Gòtic) and, of course, proximity to the important sights.

Pensiones & Hostales

If dorm living is not your thing, but you are still looking for a budget deal, check around the many *pensiones* (small private hotels) and *hostales* (budget hotels). These are family-run, small-scale hotels, often housed in sprawling apartments. Some are fleapits, others immaculately maintained gems.

You're looking at a minimum of around €35/55 for basic *individual/doble* (single/double) rooms, often without a private bathroom. (It is occasionally possible to find cheaper rooms, but they may be unappealing.)

Some places, especially at the lower end, offer triples and quads, which can be good value for groups. If you want a double bed (as opposed to two singles), ask for a *llit/cama matrimonial* (Catalan/Spanish). If your budget is especially tight, look at options outside the centre.

Hostels

Barcelona is chock-a-block with backpacker hostels, many of which offer state-of-the-art facilities that shame many midrange hotels. Depending on the season you can pay from €15 to €25 for a dorm bed in a youth hostel. Websites like Hostelworld (www.hostelworld.com) or Hostelbookers (www.hostelbookers.com) are useful resources.

Room & Apartment Rentals

A cosier (and sometimes more cost-effective) alternative to *hostales* and hotels is short-term apartment rental. A plethora of firms organise short lets across town. Typical prices are around €80 to €100 for two people per night.

One of the best options, with hundreds of listings, is Airbnb (www.airbnb.com). In addition to full apartments, the site also lists rooms available, which can be a good way to meet locals and/or other travellers if you don't mind sharing common areas. Prices for a room cost €30 to €60 on average.

Other apartment-rental services include the following:

○ **Oh-Barcelona** (www.oh-barcelona.com)

○ **Aparteasy** (www.aparteasy.com)

○ **Feel at Home Barcelona.com** (www.feelathomebarcelona.com)

○ **Friendly Rentals** (www.friendlyrentals.com)

○ **MH Apartments** (www.mhapartments.com)

Want to sleep on a local's couch? Try your luck at www.couchsurfing.com or www.hospitalityclub.org.

🛏 Travellers with Disabilities

Many hotels claim to be equipped for guests with disabilities, but reality frequently disappoints. The city runs a website aimed at disabled visitors at www.barcelona-access.cat.

Lonely Planet's free Accessible Travel guide can be downloaded here: shop.lonelyplanet.com/accessible-travel.

Where to Stay

There are good accommodation options in all of Barcelona's central districts, with pros and cons to each location. Choose from historic or seaside districts, or the charming neighbourhoods that are full of restaurants and nightlife.

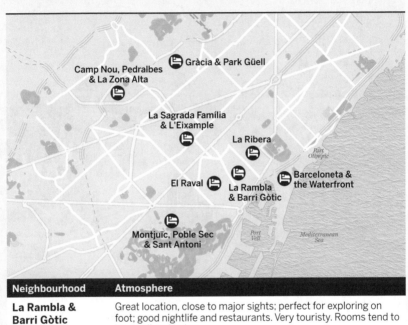

Neighbourhood	Atmosphere
La Rambla & Barri Gòtic	Great location, close to major sights; perfect for exploring on foot; good nightlife and restaurants. Very touristy. Rooms tend to be small and noisy.
El Raval	Central, with good nightlife and access to sights; bohemian vibe with few tourists. Some parts are seedy and a bit sketchy at night.
La Ribera	Central, with a great restaurant scene and neighbourhood exploring. Can be noisy and crowded, and is quite touristy.
Barceloneta & the Waterfront	Excellent seafood restaurants; handy for beaches. Not much accommodation. Barceloneta is central, the rest not very.
La Sagrada Família & L'Eixample	Wide range of options for all budgets; Modernista sights; good restaurants and nightlife; prime LGBT scene. Can be noisy with traffic. Not as strollable as the old city.
Montjuïc, Poble Sec & Sant Antoni	Near the museums, gardens and views of Montjuïc; great local exploring in Poble Sec. Area around Sants train station isn't great.
Gràcia & Park Güell	Youthful, local scene with lively restaurants and bars. It's quite far from the old town. Lots of rental rooms.
Camp Nou, Pedralbes & La Zona Alta	Good nightlife and restaurants in parts, but very far from the action, requiring frequent metro travel. More geared for business travellers.

Plaça d'Espanya at night

In Focus

National Day of Catalonia 2014

Barcelona Today

*Around Barcelona you'll likely see more than a few
esteladas, the flag with the lone star that symbolises
Catalonia's drive toward independence. A proposed
referendum on the issue in late 2017 might create more
questions than answers, given the strength of Spanish
government opposition. Of course, there's more brewing
in Barcelona than self-rule – innovation has led to improve-
ments in transport, communications and urban design.*

The Nation of Catalonia?

With its own language, unique traditions and proud history (at least prior to its conquest
by Spain in 1714), Catalonia has always thought of itself as distinct from other parts of
the country. But until recently, only a small fringe group sought a permanent and irrevo-
cable break from Madrid.

In the last few years, however, the number of separatists has sky-rocketed. Straitened
economic times have meant increasing bitterness about the fact that Catalonia contributes much more to the Spanish economy than it gets back. But perhaps the most
powerful force in favour of Catalan nationalism is the Spanish government's implacable
opposition to it and high-handed refusal to even discuss it.

belief systems
(% of population)

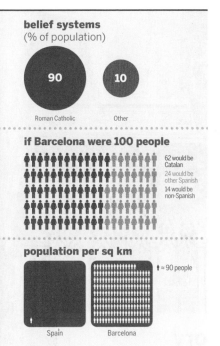

90 — Roman Catholic

10 — Other

if Barcelona were 100 people

62 would be Catalan
24 would be other Spanish
14 would be non-Spanish

population per sq km

♦ ≈ 90 people

Spain   Barcelona

Back in November 2014, Catalonia held a non-binding referendum; 80% of those who voted backed Catalan independence. Spain's Constitutional Court wasted little time in declaring the vote (and all future votes) on independence to be illegal and in March 2017 the former Catalan leader was convicted for having held it. In 2015, Catalan nationalists won a majority of the 135-seat regional assembly, which they viewed as an implicit endorsement of secession. A resolution was passed laying out the road map to independence.

The repercussions of Catalan secession would be wide-reaching. It could undermine the financial stability of Spain – and cause economic shock waves across the eurozone. All this is due to come to a head in September 2017, when the Catalan parliament has scheduled a referendum. The Spanish government and judiciary have said that it's illegal and won't go ahead. At time of writing it looked a deeply worrying impasse; it seemed that no scenario should be discounted in this high-stakes confrontation.

City of Innovation

The city that gave birth to Gaudí and the ingenious creations of Modernisme continues to break new ground in other realms. In particular, Barcelona has become a global model as a Smart City – a place where technology is harnessed to create a more sustainable, efficient and interconnected environment for both residents and visitors alike. Some 120 projects comprise the Smart City initiative, including wide-reaching innovations affecting transport, communications, public and social services, and even tourism.

Shrinking the city's carbon footprint is at the forefront of various new technologies. Self-powered lights installed along one stretch of beach use a combination of solar and wind energy, without needing to tap into the grid. Barcelona has the cleanest fleet of buses in Europe, with a large share of hybrids and natural-gas-powered vehicles (plus antipollution filters on its remaining diesel motors).

Speaking of buses, Barcelona has also launched new routes based on the flow of people using the system, creating a new, more intuitive grid that moves vertically, horizontally and diagonally across the city. It has also been expanding its network for electric cars, with 300 existing charging stations and more in the works. Another innovation: smart traffic lights that turn green when emergency vehicles are approaching so they can reach their destination faster.

Fuelling much of the innovation is the 220-hectare district known as 22@ (vint-i-dos arroba). This district in El Poblenou has seen enormous growth since its creation back in 2000. More than 90,000 jobs have been created under the 8000 firms at work, largely in the digital, creative and tech industries.

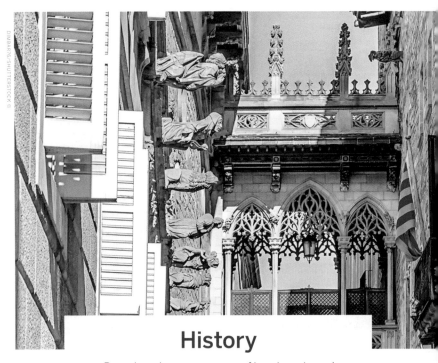

History

Barcelona has seen waves of immigrants and conquerors over its 2000-plus years. Fortunes have risen and fallen – from the golden era of 14th-century princely power to dark days of civil war and Franco's era. A fierce independent streak has always run through Barcelona, which continues today, with a desire for more autonomy (full independence, say some Catalans) from Spain.

15 BC	AD 415	718
Caesar Augustus grants the town of Barcino a city title.	Visigoths under Athaulf make Barcino their capital. It generally remains so until the 6th century.	Barcelona falls to Tariq's mostly Arab and Berber troops on their blitzkrieg march north into France.

Wilfred the Hairy & the Catalan Golden Age

It was the Romans who first etched Barcino onto Europe's map in the 3rd century BC, though the nascent settlement long played second fiddle to their provincial capital in Tarragona. The Visigoths came next, followed by the Moors, whose relatively brief occupation was usurped when the Franks put the city under the control of local counts in 801 as a buffer zone against the still Muslim-dominated caliphate to the south. Eccentrically named Wilfred the Hairy (Count Guifré el Pelós) moulded the entity we now know as Catalonia in the 9th century by wresting control over several neighbouring territories and establishing Barcelona as its key city. The hirsute one founded a dynasty that lasted nearly five centuries and developed almost independently from the Reconquista wars that were playing out in the rest of Iberia. The counts of Barcelona gradually expanded their territory south and, in 1137, Ramon Berenguer IV, the Count of Barcelona, married Petronilla, heir to the throne of neighbouring Aragón. Thus, the combined Crown of Aragón was created.

801	**1137**	**1348**
Future Frankish king Louis the Pious wrests Barcelona from Muslims and establishes the Spanish March under local counts.	Count Ramón Berenguer IV is betrothed to the daughter of the king of Aragón, creating a combined state, the kingdom of Aragón.	Plague devastates Barcelona. Over 25% of the city's population dies. More disasters soon deal further blows.

Shrapnel-scarred church in Plaça de Sant Felip Neri

★ **Best Civil War Echoes**

Bunkers del Carmel (p71)

Plaça de Sant Felip Neri (p86)

MUHBA Refugi 307 (p109)

Castell de Montjuïc (p61)

La Rambla (p44)

In the following centuries the kingdom became a flourishing merchant empire, seizing Valencia and the Balearic Islands from the Muslims and later taking territories as far flung as Sardinia, Sicily and parts of Greece.

The 14th century marked the golden age of Barcelona. Its trading wealth paid for great Gothic buildings: La Catedral, the Capella Reial de Santa Àgata (inside the Museu d'Història de Barcelona) and the churches of Santa Maria del Pi and Santa Maria del Mar. King Pere III (1336–87) later created the breathtaking Reials Drassanes (Royal Shipyards) and extended the city walls yet again to include El Raval.

Marginalisation & Decline

Overstretched, racked by civil disobedience and decimated by the Black Death, Catalonia began to wobble. When the last count of Wilfred the Hairy's dynasty expired without leaving an heir, the Crown of Aragón was passed to a noble of Castile. Soon these two Spanish kingdoms merged, with Catalonia left as a very junior partner. As business shifted from the Mediterranean to the Atlantic after the 'discovery' of the Americas in 1492, Catalans were increasingly marginalised from trade.

The region, which had retained some autonomy in the running of its own affairs, was dealt a crushing blow when it supported the wrong side in the War of the Spanish Succession (1702–14). Barcelona, under the auspices of British-backed archduke Charles of Austria, fell after a stubborn siege on 11 September 1714 (now celebrated as National Catalan Day) to the forces of Bourbon king Philip V, who established a unitary Castilian state. Barcelona faced a long backlash as the new king banned the writing and teaching of Catalan, swept away the remnants of local legal systems and tore down a whole district of medieval Barcelona in order to construct an immense fort (on the site of the present-day Parc de la Ciutadella), the sole purpose of which was to watch over Barcelona's troublemakers.

The Catalan Renaissance

Buoyed by the lifting of the ban on its trade with the Americas in 1778, Barcelona embarked on the road to industrial revolution, based initially on textiles but spreading to wine, cork and iron in the mid-19th century. It soon became Spain's leading city. As the

1469	1640–52	1888
Isabel, heir to the Castilian throne, marries Aragonese heir Fernando, effectively subjugating Catalonia to the Castilian state.	Catalan peasants declare their independence under French protection. Spain eventually crushes the rebellion.	Showcasing the grand Modernista touches of recent years, Barcelona hosts Spain's first International Exposition.

economy prospered, Barcelona outgrew its medieval walls, which were demolished in 1854–56. Work on the grid-plan L'Eixample (the Extension) district began soon after. The so-called Renaixença (Renaissance) brought a revival of Catalan culture, as well as political activism. It sowed the seeds of growing political tension in the early 20th century, as demands for autonomy from the central state became more insistent.

Masses & Classes

Adding to the fiery mix was growing discontent among the working class. The grand Catalan merchant-bourgeois families grew richer, displaying their wealth in a slew of whimsical private mansions built with verve and flair by Modernista architects such as Antoni Gaudí. At the same time, the industrial working class, housed in cramped quarters such as Barceloneta and El Raval and oppressed by poverty and disease, became organised and, occasionally, violent. Spain's neutrality during WWI had boosted Barcelona's economy and from 1900 to 1930 the population doubled to one million, but the postwar global slump hit the city hard. Waves of strikes, organised principally by the anarchists' Confederación Nacional del Trabajo (CNT), brought tough responses. Left- and right-wing gangs took their ideological conflict to the streets. Tit-for-tat assassinations became common currency and the death toll mounted. When the Second Spanish Republic was created under a left-wing government in 1931, Catalonia declared independence. Later, under pressure, its leaders settled for devolution, which it then lost in 1934, when a right-wing government won power in Madrid. The election of a left-wing popular front in 1936 again sparked Catalan autonomy claims, but also led to the generals' rising that launched the Spanish Civil War (1936–39), from which Franco emerged the victor.

Jewish Barcelona

The narrow Barri Gòtic lanes of El Call were once home to a thriving Jewish population. Catalan Jews worked as merchants, scholars, cartographers and teachers. By the 11th century, as many as 4000 Jews lived in El Call.

As in much of Europe, during the 13th century a wave of anti-Semitism swept through Catalonia. Pogroms followed on from repressive laws; anti-Semitism peaked in 1391 when a frenzied mob tore through El Call, looting and destroying private homes and murdering hundreds of Jews. Most of the remaining Jews fled the city.

The War Years

The acting capital of Spain for much of the civil war, Barcelona was run by anarchists and the Partido Obrero de Unificación Marxista (Marxist Unification Workers' Party) Trotskyist militia until mid-1937. Unions took over factories and public services, hotels and mansions became hospitals and schools, everyone wore workers' clothes, bars and cafes were collectivised, trams and taxis were painted red and black (the colours of the anarchists), and one-way streets were ignored as they were seen to be part of the old system.

1909	1936	1939
After the call-up of reservists to war in Morocco, *barcelonins* riot. Over 100 are killed in 'Setmana Tràgica' (Tragic Week).	A military rising begins the Spanish Civil War. General Goded is defeated in Barcelona by left-wing militia, workers and loyalist police.	Franco's troops march into Barcelona. Thousands flee the city toward the French border.

Anarchists & the Tragic Week

When the political philosophy of anarchism began spreading through Europe, it was embraced by many industrial workers in Barcelona, who embarked on a road to social revolution through violent means.

One anarchist bomb at the Liceu opera house on La Rambla in the 1890s killed 22 people. Anarchists were also blamed for the Setmana Tràgica (Tragic Week) in July 1909 when, following a military call-up for Spanish campaigns in Morocco, rampaging mobs wrecked 70 religious buildings, and workers were shot on the street in reprisal.

The more radical anarchists were behind the burning of most of the city's churches and the shooting of hundreds of priests, monks and nuns. The anarchists in turn were shunted aside by the communists (directed by Stalin from Moscow) after a bloody internecine battle in Barcelona that left 1500 dead in May 1937.

Later that year the Spanish Republican government fled Valencia and made Barcelona the official capital (the government had left besieged Madrid early in the war). The Republican defeat at the hands of the Nationalists in the Battle of the Ebro in southern Catalonia in the summer of 1938 left Barcelona undefended. It fell to the Nationalists on 25 January 1939, triggering a mass exodus of refugees to France, where most were long interned in makeshift camps. Purges and executions under Franco continued until well into the 1950s. Former Catalan president Lluís Companys was arrested in France by the Gestapo in August 1940, handed over to Franco, and shot on 15 October on Montjuïc, despite international outrage. He is reputed to have died with the words *'Visca Catalunya!'* ('Long live Catalonia!') on his lips.

Recent Times

When the death of Franco was announced in 1975, *barcelonins* took to the streets in celebration. The next five years saw the gradual return of democracy and in 1977 Catalonia was granted regional autonomy.

Politics aside, the big event in post-Franco Barcelona was the successful 1992 Olympic Games, planned under the guidance of the popular Socialist mayor, Pasqual Maragall. The games spurred a burst of public works and brought new life to areas such as Montjuïc, where the major events were held. The once-shabby waterfront was transformed with promenades, beaches, marinas, restaurants, leisure attractions and new housing. After the turn of the millennium, Barcelona continued to invest in urban renewal.

In recent years, soaring unemployment and painful austerity measures – not to mention Catalonia's heavy tax burden – have led to anger and resentment toward Madrid and have fuelled the drive toward independence. Recent polls indicate about half of Catalans support the region becoming a new European state.

1992	**2015**	**2017**
Barcelona takes centre stage as it hosts the summer Olympic Games.	Following an election, separatists take control of Catalonia's government. They vow to continue the move toward full secession.	Despite the courts declaring any independence referendum illegal, the Catalan parliament vows to hold one by October.

Enric Miralles' Edifici de Gas Natural in La Barceloneta

KARSOL/GETTY IMAGES ©

Architecture

Barcelona's first big building boom came at the height of the Middle Ages, when its imposing Gothic churches, mansions and shipyards were raised. The second wave of Catalan creativity, Modernisme, also carried on the wind of boom times, came around the turn of the 20th century. More recently, the Barcelona Olympics and the new millennium have brought a suite of striking buidings.

Catalan Gothic

Barcelona's first big building boom came at the height of the Middle Ages, when its imposing Gothic churches, mansions and shipyards were raised, together creating what survives to this day as one of the most extensive Gothic quarters in Europe.

Catalan Gothic did not follow the same course as the style typical of northern Europe. Decoration here tends to be more sparing and the most obvious defining characteristic is the triumph of breadth over height. While northern European cathedrals reach for the sky, Catalan Gothic has a tendency to push to the sides, stretching its vaulting design to the limit. Another notable departure from what you might have come to expect of Gothic north of the Pyrenees is the lack of spires and pinnacles.

Casa Batlló's Modernista roofline

★ Modernista Creations

The Modernistas

The second wave of Catalan creativity, also carried on the wind of boom times, came around the turn of the 20th century. The urban expansion program known as L'Eixample (the Extension), designed to free the choking population from the city's bursting medieval confines, coincided with this blossoming of unfettered thinking in architecture that arrived in the back-draft of the 1888 International Exposition of Barcelona.

A key uniting element of the Modernistas was the sensuous curve, implying movement, lightness and vitality. But as well as modernity, architects often looked to the past for inspiration. Gothic, Islamic and Renaissance design all had something to offer. At its most playful, Modernisme was able to intelligently flout the rule books of these styles and create exciting new cocktails.

Gaudí

Born in Reus to a long line of coppersmiths, Antoni Gaudí was initially trained in metalwork. In childhood he suffered from poor health, including rheumatism, and became an early adopter of a vegetarian diet. He was not a promising student. In 1878, when he obtained his architecture degree, the school's headmaster is reputed to have said: 'Who knows if we have given a diploma to a nutcase or a genius. Time will tell.'

As a young man, what most delighted Gaudí was being outdoors. Throughout his work, he sought to emulate the harmony he observed in the natural world, eschewing the straight line and favouring curvaceous forms and more organic shapes.

Gaudí's masterpiece was La Sagrada Família (begun in 1882); in it you can see the culminating vision of many ideas developed over the years. Its massive scale evokes the grandeur of Catalonia's Gothic cathedrals, while organic elements foreground its harmony with nature. The church is rife with symbols that tangibly express Gaudí's Catholic faith through architecture. As well as being a devout Catholic he was a Catalan nationalist. He lived a simple life and was not averse to knocking on doors, literally begging for money to help fund construction on the basilica.

Gaudí died in 1926, struck down by a streetcar while taking his daily walk to the Sant Felip Neri church. Wearing ragged clothes, Gaudí was initially taken for a beggar and driven to a nearby hospital where he was left in a pauper's ward. He died two days later. Thousands attended his funeral procession to La Sagrada Família, where he was buried in the crypt.

Domènech i Montaner

Although overshadowed by Gaudí, Lluís Domènech i Montaner (1849–1923) was one of the great masters of Modernisme. He was a widely travelled man of prodigious intellect, with knowledge in everything from mineralogy to medieval heraldry; he was also an architectural professor, a prolific writer and a nationalist politician. The question of Catalan identity and how to create a national architecture consumed Domènech i Montaner, who designed over a dozen large-scale works in his lifetime.

The exuberant, steel-framed Palau de la Música Catalana is one of his masterpieces.

Gothic Masterpieces

La Catedral (p64)

Basílica de Santa Maria del Mar (p116)

Església de Santa Maria del Pi (p48)

Saló del Tinell in the **Museu d'Història de Barcelona** (p108)

The Drassanes – now the site of the **Museu Marítim** (p88)

The former monastery that houses the **Museu-Monestir de Pedralbes** (p98)

Puig i Cadafalch

Like Domènech i Montaner, Josep Puig i Cadafalch (1867–1956) was a polymath; he was an archaeologist, an expert in Romanesque art and one of Catalonia's most prolific architects. As a politician – and later president of the Mancomunitat de Catalunya (Commonwealth of Catalonia) – he was instrumental in shaping the Catalan nationalist movement.

One of his many Modernista gems is the Casa Amatller, a rather dramatic contrast to Gaudí's Casa Batlló next door; it is a house of startling beauty and invention blended with playful Gothic-style sculpture.

The New Millennium

Barcelona's latest architectural revolution began in the 1980s when, in the run up to the 1992 Olympics, the city set about its biggest phase of renewal since the heady days of L'Eixample.

In the new millennium, the Diagonal Mar district is characterised by striking modern architecture, including the hovering blue, triangular Edifici Fòrum by Swiss architects Herzog & de Meuron and a 24-storey whitewashed trapezoidal prism that serves as the headquarters for the national telephone company, Telefónica.

Another prominent addition to the city skyline came in 2005. The shimmering, cucumber-shaped Torre Agbar is a product of French architect Jean Nouvel.

Southwest, on the way to the airport, the new Fira M2 trade fair is now marked by red twisting twin landmark towers designed by Japanese star architect and confessed Gaudí fan Toyo Ito.

The heart of La Ribera got a fresh look with its brand-new Mercat de Santa Caterina. The market is quite a sight, with its wavy ceramic roof and tubular skeleton, designed by Enric Miralles, one of the most promising names in Catalan architecture until his premature death. Miralles' Edifici de Gas Natural, a 100m glass tower near the waterfront in La Barceloneta, is also extraordinary.

MACBA (Museu d'Art Contemporani de Barcelona; p96)

Modern Art

Barcelona is to modern art what Greece is to ruined temples. Three of the figures at the vanguard of 20th-century avant-gardism – Picasso, Miró and Dalí – were either born or spent their formative years here. The trilogy's powerful legacy is stamped all over Barcelona in museums and public installations. In the contemporary art world, Catalonia continues to be an incubator for innovative works.

The Crucial Three

Picasso

It wasn't until the late 19th century that truly great artists began to emerge in Barcelona and its hinterland, led by dandy portraitist Ramón Casas (1866–1932). Casas, an early Modernista, founded a Barcelona bar known as Els Quatre Gats, which became the nucleus for the city's growing art movement, holding numerous shows and expositions. An early host was a young, then unknown, *malagueño* named Pablo Picasso (1881–1973).

Picasso lived sporadically in Barcelona between the innocence-losing ages of 16 and 24, and the city heavily influenced his early painting. This was the period in which he amassed the raw materials for his Blue Period. In 1904, the then-mature Picasso moved to Paris where he found fame, fortune and Cubism, and went on to become one of the greatest artists of the 20th century.

★ **Best Places to See Modern Art**

Museu Picasso (p80)

Fundació Joan Miró (p58)

Fundació Antoni Tàpies (p53)

MACBA (p96)

Museu Nacional d'Art de Catalunya (p54)

Miró

At the time the 13-year-old Picasso arrived in Barcelona, his near-contemporary Joan Miró (1893–1983) was still learning to crawl in the Barri Gòtic, where he was born. Miró spent a third of his life in Barcelona but later divided his time between France, the Tarragona countryside and the island of Mallorca, where he ended his days.

Like Picasso, Miró attended the Escola de Belles Artes de la Llotja. In Paris from 1920, he mixed with Picasso, Hemingway, Joyce and friends, and made his own mark, after several years of struggle, with an exhibition in 1925. The masterpiece from this, his so-called realist period, was *La Masia* (*The Farmhouse*). It was during WWII that Miró's definitive leitmotifs emerged – arrangements of lines and symbolic figures in primary colours, with shapes reduced to their essence. Declaring he was going to 'assassinate art', Miró wanted nothing to do with the constricting labels of the era, although he has often been called a pioneering surrealist, Dadaist and automatist.

Dalí

The great Catalan artist Salvador Dalí i Domènech (1904–89) was born and died in Figueres, where he left his single greatest artistic legacy, the Teatre-Museu Dalí. Although few of his famed works are in Barcelona, the city provided a stimulating atmosphere, and places like Park Güell, with its surrealist-like aspects, had a powerful effect on Dalí.

Prolific painter, showman, shameless self-promoter or just plain weirdo, Dalí was nothing if not a character – probably a little too much for the conservative small-town folk of Figueres. Every now and then a key moment arrives that can change the course of one's life. Dalí's came in 1929, when the French poet Paul Éluard visited Cadaqués with his Russian wife, Gala. The rest, as they say, is histrionics. Dalí shot off to Paris to be with Gala and plunged into the world of surrealism.

In the 1930s Salvador and Gala returned to live at Port Lligat on the north Catalan coast, where they played host to a long list of fashionable and art-world guests until the war years – the parties were by all accounts memorable. They started again in Port Lligat in the 1950s. The stories of sexual romps and Gala's appetite for local young men are legendary. The 1960s saw Dalí painting pictures on a grand scale, including his 1962 reinterpretation of Marià Fortuny's *Batalla de Tetuán*. On his death in 1989, he was buried (according to his own wishes) in the Teatre-Museu he had created on the site of the old theatre in central Figueres, which also houses an awe-inspiring Dalí collection.

Art Goes Informal

Picasso, Miró and Dalí were hard acts to follow. Few envied the task of Catalan Antoni Tàpies in reviving the red hot Modernista flame. An early admirer of Miró, Tàpies soon began pursuing his own esoteric path embracing 'art informal' (a Jackson Pollock–like use of spontaneity) and inventing painting that utilised clay, string and even bits of rubbish. He was arguably Spain's greatest living painter before his death in 2012.

Sardana dancers

Catalan Culture

*The fortunes of Catalunya have risen and fallen
over the years, as Barcelona has gone from wealthy
mercantile capital to a city of repression under the
Franco regime, followed by the boom and bust of more
recent years. Despite today's economic challenges,
Catalan culture continues to flourish, with a vigorous
program of events, traditional music and dance, and
abundant civic pride.*

Language

In Barcelona, born and bred locals proudly speak Catalan, a Romance language related
to French, Spanish (Castilian) and Italian. It was only relatively recently, however, that
Catalan was deemed 'legitimate'. Ever since Barcelona was crushed in the War of the
Spanish Succession in 1714, the use of Catalan has been repeatedly banned or at least
frowned upon. Franco was the last of Spain's rulers to clamp down on its public use. All
that changed in 1980, when the first autonomous regional parliament was assembled
and adopted new laws towards *normalització lingüística* (linguistic normalisation).

Today Catalonia's school system is based on bilingual education, with graduates
showing equal skill in using both Catalan and Spanish. Around town, Catalan is the
lingua franca: advertising and road signs tend to be in Catalan, while newspapers,

magazines and other publications can be found in both languages (though you'll find about twice as many options in Catalan than in Spanish). You'll also find a mix of Catalan and Spanish programming on radio and TV stations.

Music & Dance

Barcelona's vibrant music and dance scene has been shaped by artists both traditional and cutting edge. From Nova Cançó, composed during the dark years of the dictatorship, to the hybridised Catalan rumba, to hands-in-the air rock ballads of the 1970s and '80s, Barcelona's music evolves constantly. Today's groups continue to push musical boundaries, blending rhythms from all corners of the globe. In the realm of dance, flamenco has a small loyal following, while the old-fashioned folk dance *sardana* continues to attract growing numbers.

Sardana

The Catalan dance par excellence is the *sardana*, the roots of which lie in the far northern Empordà region of Catalonia. Compared with flamenco, it is sober indeed, but not unlike a lot of other Mediterranean folk dances.

The dancers hold hands in a circle and wait for the 10 or so musicians to begin. The performance starts with the piping of the *flabiol*, a little wooden flute. When the other musicians join in, the dancers start – a series of steps to the right, one back and then the same to the left. As the music 'heats up' the steps become more complex, the leaps are higher and the dancers lift their arms. Then they return to the initial steps and continue. If newcomers wish to join in, space is made for them as the dance continues and the whole thing proceeds in a more or less seamless fashion.

On weekends year-round devotees of the folk dance gather in front of La Catedral (p64) at noon on Sunday or 6pm on Saturday, while a 10-piece band puts everyone in motion. Catalans of all ages come out for the dance; all are welcome to join in, though you'll have to watch a few rounds to get the hang of it.

For upcoming details of *sardana* dancing, visit the website of the **Agrupació Cultural Folklòrica de Barcelona** (☏93 315 14 96; www.acfbarcelona.cat).

Nova Cançó

Curiously, it was probably the Franco repression that most helped foster a vigorous local music scene in Catalan. In the dark 1950s the Nova Cançó (New Song) movement was born to resist linguistic oppression with music in Catalan (getting air time on the radio was long close to impossible), throwing up stars that in some cases won huge popularity throughout Spain, such as the Valencia-born Raimon.

Essential Reading

o *Barcelona* (Robert Hughes, 1992) Witty and passionate study of 2000 years of history.

o *The Shadow of the Wind* (Carlos Ruiz Zafón, 2001) Page-turning mystery set in post-civil-war Barcelona.

o *Homage to Catalonia* (George Orwell, 1938) Orwell's classic account of the early days of the Spanish Civil War.

Essential Listening

o *Techari*, Ojos de Brujo

o *Anells d'Aigua*, Maria del Mar Bonet

o *Verges 50*, Lluís Llach

o *Wild Animals*, Pinker Tones

o *Set Tota la Vida*, Mishima

o *Voràgine*, 08001

o *Rey de la Rumba*, Peret

o *X Anniversarium*, Estopa

Pau Casals

Born in Catalonia, Pau Casals (1876–1973) was one of the greatest cellists of the 20th century. Living in exile in southern France, he declared he would not play in public as long as the Western democracies continued to tolerate Franco's regime. In 1958 he was a candidate for the Nobel Peace Prize.

More specifically loved in Catalonia as a Bob Dylan–style 1960s protest singer-songwriter is Lluís Llach, whose 1968 song *L'Estaca* has become an anthem of the Catalan independence movement. Much of his music is more or less antiregime, and he stood for election in 2015 as part of a pro-independence alliance. Joan Manuel Serrat is another legendary figure. His appeal stretches from Barcelona to Buenos Aires. Born in the Poble Sec district, this poet-singer is equally at ease in Catalan and Spanish. He has repeatedly shown that record sales are not everything to him. In 1968 he refused to represent Spain at the Eurovision song contest if he were not allowed to sing in Catalan. Accused of being anti-Spanish, he was long banned from performing in Spain.

Born in Mallorca, the talented singer Maria del Mar Bonet arrived in Barcelona in 1967 and embarked on a long and celebrated singing career. She sang in Catalan and many of her searing and powerful songs were banned by the dictatorship.

Havaneres

The oldest musical tradition to have survived to some degree in Catalonia is that of the *havaneres* (from Havana) – nostalgic songs and melancholy sea shanties brought back from Cuba by Catalans who lived, sailed and traded there in the 19th century. Even after Spain lost Cuba in 1898, the *havanera* tradition (a mix of European and Cuban rhythms) continued. A magical opportunity to enjoy these songs is the Cantada d'Havaneres (www.havanerescalella.cat), an evening concert held on the Costa Brava in early July. Otherwise, you may stumble across performances elsewhere along the coast or even in Barcelona, but there is no set program.

La Rumba

Back in the 1950s, a new sound mixing flamenco with salsa and other Latin sounds emerged in *gitano* (Roma people) circles in the bars of Gràcia and the Barri Gòtic. One of the founders of rumba Catalana was Antonio González, known as El Pescaílla (married to the flamenco star Lola Flores). Although El Pescaílla was well-known in town, the Mataró-born *gitano* Peret later took this eminently Barcelona style to a wider (eventually international) audience.

By the end of the 1970s, however, rumba Catalana was running out of steam. Peret had turned to religion and El Pescaílla lived in Flores' shadow in Madrid. But Buenos Aires–born Javier Patricio 'Gato' Pérez discovered rumba in 1977 and gave it his own personal spin, bringing out several popular records, such as *Atalaya,* until the early 1980s.

After Pérez, it seemed that rumba was dead. But not so fast! New rumba bands, often highly eclectic, have emerged in recent years. Ai Ai Ai, Barrio Negro, El Tío Carlos and La Pegatina are names to look out for. Others mix rumba with styles as diverse as reggae or ragga.

Survival Guide

Directory A–Z

Discount Cards

Articket (www.articketbcn.org) Gives admission to six sites for €30 and is valid for six months. You can pick up the ticket at the tourist offices at Plaça de Catalunya, Plaça de Sant Jaume and Estació Sants.

Barcelona Card (www.barcelona card.com) Handy if you want to see lots in a limited time; costs €20/45/55/60 for two/three/four/five days (about 50% less for children aged four to 12). Includes free transport and discounted admission prices (up to 30% off) or free entry to many museums and other sights, as well as minor discounts on purchases at a small number of shops, restaurants and bars. Pick up the card at tourist offices or online (buying online saves you 10%).

Ruta del Modernisme (www. rutadelmodernisme.com) This guidebook and discount pack costs €12 and is well worth looking into for visiting Modernista sights at discounted rates.

Emergency

The general emergency number is 112.

Electricity

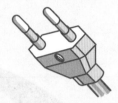

Type C 220V/230V/50Hz

Insurance

○ A travel-insurance policy to cover theft, loss, medical problems and cancellation or delays of your travel arrangements is a good idea.

○ European Union residents can access free Spanish healthcare with an EHIC card (ehic.europa.eu).

○ Paying for your ticket with a credit card can often provide limited travel-accident insurance and you may be able to reclaim the payment if the operator doesn't deliver.

○ Worldwide travel insurance is available at lonely-planet.com/travel_services. You can buy, extend and claim online any time – even if you're on the road.

Internet Access

Wi-fi is widespread. Data packages with a local pay-as-you-go SIM card are very reasonable, so take an unlocked smartphone and connect.

LGBT+ Travellers

Barcelona has a vibrant gay and lesbian scene. Despite fierce opposition from the Catholic Church, Spain legalised same-sex marriage in 2005, becoming the fourth country in the world to do so.

As a rule, Barcelona is pretty tolerant, and the sight of gay or lesbian couples arm in arm is generally unlikely to raise eyebrows. Transgenderism, too, is increasingly accepted.

Note that Spain's LGBT capital is the saucily hedonistic Sitges, 35km southwest of Barcelona.

Useful Websites

60by80 (www.60by80.com/barcelona) An excellent website for gay travellers.

Gay Barcelona (www.gaybarce lona.com) A handy listings site for visitors to Barcelona.

Tillate (www.tillate.es) Discover upcoming parties in this nightlife guide to regions around Spain, including Catalonia.

GaySitges (www.gaysitges.com) A specific site dedicated to this LGBT-friendly coastal town.

Money

ATMs

○ Barcelona abounds with banks; many have ATMs.

○ ATMs are also in plentiful supply around Plaça de Catalunya, Plaça de Sant Jaume (in the Barri Gòtic) and La Rambla.

○ Most ATMs allow you to use international debit or credit cards to withdraw money in euros.

○ There is usually a charge (around 1.5% to 2%) on ATM cash withdrawals when abroad.

Credit & Debit Cards

Cards can be used in many hotels, restaurants and shops, although there may be a minimum purchase requirement of €5 or €10.

When paying with a credit card, photo ID is often required, even for chip cards where you're required to enter your PIN (for travellers without chip cards, just indicate that you'll give a signature).

Tipping

Bars It's rare to leave a tip in bars, though a bit of small change is always appreciated.

Restaurants Catalans typically leave 5% or less at restaurants. Leave more for exceptionally good service.

Taxis Optional, but most locals round up to the nearest euro.

Opening Hours

Standard opening hours:

Banks 8.30am to 2pm Monday to Friday; some also 4pm to 7pm Thursday or 9am to 1pm Saturday

Bars 6pm to 2am (to 3am weekends)

Clubs Midnight to 6am Thursday to Saturday

Department stores 10am to 10pm Monday to Saturday

Museums & art galleries Vary considerably; generally 10am to 8pm (some shut for lunch around 2pm to 4pm). Many close all day Monday and from 2pm Sunday.

Restaurants 1pm to 4pm & 8.30pm to midnight

Shops 9am or 10am to 1.30pm or 2pm and 4pm or 4.30pm to 8pm or 8.30pm Monday to Saturday

Public Holidays

New Year's Day (Any Nou/Año Nuevo) 1 January

Epiphany/Three Kings' Day (Epifanía or El Dia dels Reis/Día de los Reyes Magos) 6 January

Good Friday (Divendres Sant/ Viernes Santo) March/April

Easter Monday (Dilluns de Pasqua Florida) March/April

Labour Day (Dia del Treball/ Fiesta del Trabajo) 1 May

Day after Pentecost Sunday (Dilluns de Pasqua Granda) May/June

Feast of St John the Baptist (Dia de Sant Joan/Día de San Juan Bautista) 24 June

Feast of the Assumption (L'Assumpció/La Asunción) 15 August

Catalonia's National Day (Diada Nacional de Catalunya) 11 September

Festes de la Mercè 24 September

Spanish National Day (Festa de la Hispanitat/Día de la Hispani- dad) 12 October

All Saints Day (Dia de Tots Sants/Día de Todos los Santos) 1 November

Constitution Day (Día de la Constitución) 6 December

Feast of the Immaculate Conception (La Immaculada Concepció/La Inmaculada Concepción) 8 December

Christmas (Nadal/Navidad) 25 December

Boxing Day/St Stephen's Day (El Dia de Sant Esteve) 26 December

Practicalities

○ **Currency** Euro (€)

○ **Smoking** Banned in restaurants and bars

○ **Major Barcelona newspapers** *La Vanguardia* and *El Periódico* are available in Spanish and Catalan. *El País* publishes an online English supplement (elpais.com/ inenglish.html).

Taxes & Refunds

Value-added tax (VAT) is also known as IVA (*impuesto sobre el valor añadido;* pronounced 'EE-ba'). IVA is 10% on accommodation and restaurant prices and is usually – but not always – included in quoted prices. On most retail goods the IVA is 21%.

Non-EU residents are entitled to a refund of the 21% IVA on purchases costing more than €90 from any shop, if the goods are taken out of the EU within three months. Ask the shop for a Cashback (or similar) refund form showing the price and IVA paid for each item and identifying the vendor and purchaser, then present the form at the customs booth for IVA refunds when you depart from Spain (or elsewhere in the EU). You will need your passport and a boarding card that shows you are leaving the EU, and your luggage (so do this before checking in bags). The officer will stamp the invoice and you hand it in at a bank at the departure point to receive a reimbursement.

Telephone

Local SIM cards Can be used in unlocked phones. Data packages are the best-value way to stay in touch and make international calls. You'll likely need a passport to register a local SIM.

Making calls To call Barcelona from outside Spain, dial the international access code, followed by the code for Spain (34) and the full number (including Barcelona's area code, 93). To make an international call from Barcelona, dial the international access code (00), country code, area code and number.

Time

Spain is one hour ahead of GMT/UTC during winter, and two hours ahead during daylight savings (the last Sunday in March to the last Sunday in October).

Tourist Information

Several tourist offices operate in Barcelona (barcelonaturisme.com). A couple of general information telephone numbers worth bearing in mind are 010 and 012. The first is for Barcelona and the other is for all Catalonia (run by the Generalitat). You sometimes strike English speakers, though for the most part operators are Catalan/Spanish bilingual. In addition to tourist offices, information booths operate at Estació del Nord and at Portal de la Pau, at the foot of the Mirador de Colom at the port end of La Rambla.

Others set up at various points in the city centre in summer.

Plaça de Catalunya (🖉932 853 834; Plaça de Catalunya 17; ⊙9.30am-9.30pm; Ⓜ Catalunya)

Plaça Sant Jaume (🖉932 853 832; Carrer de la Ciutat 2, Plaça Sant Jaume; ⊙8.30am-8.30pm Mon-Fri, 9am-7pm Sat, 9am-2pm Sun & holidays; Ⓜ Jaume I)

Estació Sants (⊙8am-8pm; Ⓡ Estació Sants)

El Prat Airport (⊙8.30am-8.30pm)

Palau Robert Regional Tourist Office (🖉932 388 091; www.palaurobert.gencat.cat; Passeig de Gràcia 107; ⊙10am-8pm Mon-Sat, to 2.30pm Sun; Ⓜ Diagonal) Offers a host of material on Catalonia, audiovisual resources, a bookshop and a branch of Turisme Juvenil de Catalunya (for youth travel).

Travellers with Disabilities

❂ Some hotels and public institutions have wheelchair access.

❂ All buses in Barcelona are wheelchair accessible and a growing number of metro stations are theoretically wheelchair accessible (generally by lift, although there have been complaints that they are only good for people with prams). Lines 2, 9, 10 and 11 are completely adapted, as are the majority of stops on Line 1. In all, about 80% of stops have been adapted (you can check which ones by looking at a network map at www.tmb.cat/en/transport-accessible).

○ Ticket vending machines in metro stations are adapted for disabled travellers, and have Braille options for those with a visual impairment.

○ Several taxi companies have adapted vehicles, including **Taxi Amic** (📞934 208 088; www.taxi-amic-adaptat.com) and **Green Taxi** (📞900 827 900; www.green taxi.es).

○ Most street crossings in central Barcelona are wheelchair-friendly.

○ Lonely Planet's free Accessible Travel guide can be downloaded here: lptravel.to/AccessibleTravel

Transport

Arriving in Barcelona

After Madrid, Barcelona is Spain's busiest international transport hub. A host of airlines, including many budget carriers, fly directly to Barcelona from around Europe. Most travellers enter Barcelona through El Prat Airport. Some budget

airlines, including Ryanair, use Girona-Costa Brava Airport or Reus Airport.

Travelling by train is a pricier but perhaps more romantic way of reaching Barcelona from other European cities. The new TGV takes around seven hours from Paris to Barcelona. Eighteen high-speed Tren de Alta Velocidad Española (AVE) trains between Madrid and Barcelona run daily in each direction, nine of them in under three hours.

Barcelona is well-connected by bus to other parts of Spain, as well as to major European cities.

El Prat Airport

Barcelona's **El Prat Airport** (📞 902 404 704; www.aena.es) lies 17km southwest of Plaça de Catalunya at El Prat de Llobregat. The airport has two main terminal buildings: the new T1 terminal and the older T2, itself divided into three terminal areas (A, B and C).

Bus

Frequent aerobúses operated by **A1** (📞 902 100 104; www.aerobusbcn.com; one way/return €5.90/10.20; ⏱ 5am-1am) make the 35-minute run from Terminal 1 to Plaça de Catalunya every five/ten minutes from 5.35am to 1am, with a few stops along the way. The A2 Aerobús from Terminal 2 works to the same hours and follows the same route, with departures every ten minutes all day.

Return departures from Plaça de Catalunya are from 5am to 12.30am. Buy tickets on the bus or from agents at the bus stop.

Taxi

A taxi from the airport will cost around €25 and take around 35 minutes.

Estació Sants

Long-distance trains arrive in **Estació Sants** (www.adif.es; Plaça dels Països Catalans; 🅼Estació Sants), about 2.5km west of La Rambla. The train station is linked by metro to other parts of the city.

Estació del Nord

Barcelona's long-haul **bus station** (📞902 260 606; www.barcelonanord.cat; Carrer d'Ali Bei 80; 🅼Arc de Triomf) is located in L'Eixample, about 1.5km northeast of Plaça de Catalunya, and is a short walk from several metro stations.

Girona-Costa Brava Airport

Girona-Costa Brava Airport (www.girona-airport.net) is 12km south of Girona and 92km northeast of Barcelona. The **Sagalés Airport Line** (📞902 130 014; sagale-sairportline.com) is timed with Ryanair flights and goes direct to Barcelona's Estació del Nord (one way/return €16/25, 75 minutes) or to other destinations on the Costa de Barcelona or the Costa Brava.

Reus Airport

Reus Airport (☎902 404 704; www.aena.es) is 13km west of Tarragona and 108km southwest of Barcelona. Buses operated by **Hispano-Igualadina** (☎902 292 900; www.igualadina.com; Carrer de Viriat; Ⓜ Estació Sants) are timed with Ryan-air flights and go direct to Barcelona's Estació Sants (one way/return €16/25, 90 minutes).

Getting Around

Barcelona has abundant options for getting around town. The excellent metro can get you most places, with buses and trams filling in the gaps. Taxis are the best option late at night.

Metro & Train

The easy-to-use **Transports Metropolitans de Barcelona** (TMB; ☎932 987 000; www. tmb.net) metro system has 11 numbered and colour-coded lines. It runs from 5am to midnight Sunday to Thursday and holidays, from 5am to 2am on Friday and days immediately preceding holidays, and 24 hours on Saturday.

Ongoing work to expand the metro continues on several lines. Lines 9 and 10 will eventually connect with the airport (2016 at the earliest).

Suburban trains run by the **Ferrocarrils de la Generalitat de Catalunya** (FGC; ☎900 901 515; www. fgc.net) include a couple of useful city lines. All lines heading north from Plaça de Catalunya stop at Carrer de Provença and Gràcia. One of these lines (L7) goes to Tibidabo and another (L6 to Reina Elisenda) has a stop near the Monestir de Pedralbes. Most trains from Plaça de Catalunya continue beyond Barcelona to Sant Cugat, Sabadell and Terrassa. Other FGC lines head west from Plaça d'Espanya, including one for Manresa that is handy for the trip to Montserrat.

Depending on the line, these trains run from about 5am (with only one or two services before 6am) to 11pm or midnight Sunday to Thursday, and from 5am to about 1am on Friday and Saturday.

Bus

Transports Metropolitans de Barcelona buses run along most city routes every few minutes from around 5am or 6.30am to around 10pm or 11pm. Many routes pass through Plaça de Catalunya and/or Plaça de la Universitat. After 11pm a reduced network of yellow *nitbuses* (night buses) runs until 3am or 5am. All *nitbus* routes pass through Plaça de Catalunya and most run every 30 to 45 minutes.

Public Transport Tickets

The metro, FGC trains, *rodalies/cercanías* (Renfe-run local trains) and buses come under one zoned-fare regime. Single-ride tickets on all standard transport within Zone 1 cost €2.15.

Targetes are multitrip transport tickets. They are sold at all city-centre metro stations. The prices given here are for travel in Zone 1. Children under four years of age travel free. Options include the following:

⊙ Targeta T-10 (€10.30) – 10 rides (each valid for 1¼ hours) on the metro, buses, FGC trains and *rodalies*. You can change between each transport type.

⊙ Targeta T-DIA (€8.40) – unlimited travel on all transport for one day.

⊙ Two-/three-/four-/five-day tickets (€14/21/27/32) – unlimited travel on all transport except the Aerobús; buy them at metro stations and tourist offices.

⊙ T-Mes (€53) – 30 days unlimited use of all public transport.

⊙ Targeta T-50/30 (€43) – 50 trips within 30 days, valid on all transport.

⊙ T-Trimestre (€142) – 90 days unlimited use of all public transport.

Climate Change & Travel

Every form of transport that relies on carbon-based fuel generates CO_2, the main cause of human-induced climate change. Modern travel is dependent on aeroplanes, which might use less fuel per kilometre per person than most cars but travel much greater distances. The altitude at which aircraft emit gases (including CO_2) and particles also contributes to their climate change impact. Many websites offer 'carbon calculators' that allow people to estimate the carbon emissions generated by their journey and, for those who wish to do so, to offset the impact of the greenhouse gases emitted with contributions to portfolios of climate-friendly initiatives throughout the world. Lonely Planet offsets the carbon footprint of all staff and author travel.

Taxi

Taxis charge €2.10 flag fall plus meter charges of €1.10 per kilometre (€1.30 from 8pm to 8am and all day on weekends). A further €3.10 is added for all trips to/from the airport, and €1 for luggage bigger than 55cm × 35cm × 35cm. The trip from Estació Sants to Plaça de Catalunya, about 3km, costs about €11. You can flag a taxi down in the street or call one. Try **Fonotaxi** (⏺933 001 100; www.fonotaxi.net) or **Ràdio Taxi 033** (⏺933 033 033; radiotaxi033.com).

The call-out charge is €3.40 (€4.20 at night and on weekends). In many taxis it is possible to pay with a credit card and, if you have a local telephone number, you can join the T033 Ràdio taxi service for booking taxis online (www.radiotaxi033.com). You can also book online at www.catalunyataxi.com.

There is a special taxi service for people with disabilities or difficult situations (such as transport of big objects). **Taxi Amic** (⏺934 208 088; www.taxi-amic-adaptat.com) should be booked at least 24 hours in advance if possible.

Bicycle

Over 180km of bike lanes have been laid out across the city, so it's possible to commute on two environmentally friendly wheels. A waterfront path runs northeast from Port Olímpic towards Riu Besòs. Scenic itineraries are mapped for cyclists in the Collserola parkland, and the *ronda verda* is an incomplete 75km cycling path that extends around the city's outskirts. You can cycle a well-signed 22km loop path (part of the *ronda verda*) by following the seaside bike path northeast of Barceloneta.

Cable Car

Several aerial cable cars operate in Barcelona and provide excellent views over the city.

Teleférico del Puerto (www.telefericodebarcelona.com; Passeig Escullera; one way/return €11/16.50; ⏱11am-7pm Mar-Oct, to 5.30pm Nov-Feb; 🚌17, 39, 64, Ⓜ Barceloneta) travels between the waterfront southwest of Barceloneta and Montjuïc.

Teleféric de Montjuïc (www.telefericdemontjuic.cat; return adult/child €12.50/9; ⏱10am-9pm Jun-Sep, shorter hours rest of the year) runs between Estació Parc Montjuïc and the Castell de Montjuïc.

Tram

There are a handful of tram lines in the city. All standard transport passes are valid. A scenic option is the *tramvia blau* (blue tram), which runs up to the foot of Tibidabo.

Language

Catalan and Spanish both have official-language status in Catalonia. In Barcelona, you'll hear as much Spanish as Catalan, so we've provided some Spanish to get you started. Spanish pronunciation is not difficult as most of its sounds are also found in English. You can read our pronunciation guides below as if they were English and you'll be understood just fine. And if you pronounce 'th' in our guides with a lisp and 'kh' as a throaty sound, you'll even sound like a real Spanish person.

To enhance your trip with a phrasebook, visit **lonelyplanet.com**. Lonely Planet iPhone phrasebooks are available through the Apple App store.

Basics

Hello.
Hola.   o·la
How are you?
¿Qué tal?   ke tal
I'm fine, thanks.
Bien, gracias.   byen *gra*·thyas
Excuse me. (to get attention)
Disculpe.   dees·*kool*·pe
Yes./No.
Sí./No.   see/no
Thank you.
Gracias.   *gra*·thyas
You're welcome./That's fine.
De nada.   de *na*·da
Goodbye. /See you later.
Adiós./Hasta luego.   a·*dyos/as*·ta *lwe*·go
Do you speak English?
¿Habla inglés?   a·bla een·*gles*
I don't understand.
No entiendo.   no en·*tyen*·do
How much is this?
¿Cuánto cuesta?   *kwan*·to *kwes*·ta
Can you reduce the price a little?
¿Podría bajar un   po·*dree*·a ba·*khar* oon
poco el precio?   *po*·ko el *pre*·thyo

Accommodation

I'd like to make a booking.
Quisiera reservar   kee·*sye*·ra re·ser·*var*
una habitación.   *oo*·na a·bee·ta·*thyon*

How much is it per night?
¿Cuánto cuesta por noche? *kwan*·to *kwes*·ta por *no*·che

Eating & Drinking

I'd like ..., please.
Quisiera ..., por favor.   kee·*sye*·ra ... por fa·*vor*
That was delicious!
¡Estaba buenísimo!   es·*ta*·ba bwe·*nee*·see·mo
Bring the bill/check, please.
La cuenta, por favor.   la *kwen*·ta por fa·*vor*

I'm allergic to ...
Soy alérgico/a al ... (m/f) soy a·*ler*·khee·ko/a al ...
I don't eat ...
No como ...   no *ko*·mo ...
   chicken   *pollo*   *po*·lyo
   fish   *pescado*   pes·*ka*·do
   meat   *carne*   *kar*·ne

Emergencies

I'm ill.
Estoy enfermo/a. (m/f)   es·toy en·*fer*·mo/a
Help!
¡Socorro!   so·*ko*·ro
Call a doctor!
¡Llame a un médico!   *lya*·me a oon *me*·dee·ko
Call the police!
¡Llame a la policía!   *lya*·me a la po·lee·*thee*·a

Directions

I'm looking for a/an/the ...
Estoy buscando ...   es·*toy* boos·*kan*·do ...
   ATM
   un cajero   oon ka·*khe*·ro
   automático   ow·to·*ma*·tee·ko
   bank
   el banco   el *ban*·ko
   ... embassy
   la embajada de ... la em·ba·*kha*·da de ...
   market
   el mercado   el mer·*ka*·do
   museum
   el museo   el moo·*se*·o
   restaurant
   un restaurante   oon res·tow·*ran*·te
   toilet
   los servicios   los ser·*vee*·thyos
   tourist office
   la oficina de   la o·fee·*thee*·na de
   turismo   too·*rees*·mo

Behind the Scenes

Acknowledgements

Climate map data adapted from Peel MC, Finlayson BL & McMahon TA (2007) 'Updated World Map of the Köppen-Geiger Climate Classification', Hydrology and Earth System Sciences, 11, 163344.

Illustrations pp42–3, pp62–3 by Javier Zarracina.

Special thanks to CASA BATLLÓ S.L.U. for use of images.

This Book

This guidebook was curated by Andy Symington and researched by Andy and Josephine Quintero. The previous edition was researched by Andy, Sally Davies and Regis St Louis. This guidebook was commissioned in Lonely Planet's Melbourne office, and produced by the following:

Destination Editor Tom Stainer

Product Editor Hannah Cartmel

Senior Cartographer Anthony Phelan

Book Designer Virginia Moreno

Assisting Editors Katie Connolly, Kathryn Rowan, Maja Vatrić, Amanda Williamson

Cover Researcher Wibowo Rusli

Thanks to Ania Bartoszek, Michelle Bennett, Bridget Blair, Meri Blazevski, Melanie Dankel, Liz Heynes, Indra Kilfoyle, Catherine Naghten, Lauren O'Connell, Vicky Smith, Lyahna Spencer, Tony Wheeler, Tracy Whitmey

Send Us Your Feedback

We love to hear from travellers – your comments keep us on our toes and help make our books better. Our well-travelled team reads every word on what you loved or loathed about this book. Although we cannot reply individually to postal submissions, we always guarantee that your feedback goes straight to the appropriate authors, in time for the next edition. Each person who sends us information is thanked in the next edition, the most useful submissions are rewarded with a selection of digital PDF chapters.

Visit lonelyplanet.com/contact to submit your updates and suggestions or to ask for help. Our award-winning website also features inspirational travel stories, news and discussions.

Note: We may edit, reproduce and incorporate your comments in Lonely Planet products such as guidebooks, websites and digital products, so let us know if you don't want your comments reproduced or your name acknowledged. For a copy of our privacy policy visit lonelyplanet.com/privacy.

244

Index

22@ district 221

A

accommodation 19, 213-17
  internet resources 19, 215
  useful language 242
activities 205-11, see also individual activities
air travel 239-40
airports 239-40
aquariums 91
archaeological sites
  Espai Santa Caterina 84
  Roman Walls 67
  Temple Romà d'August 67
  Via Sepulcral Romana 48-9
architects
  Domènech i Montaner, Lluís 25, 40, 53, 66, 102-3, 118, 163, 229
  Gaudí, Antoni 36, 228, see also Gaudí buildings
  Puig i Cadafalch, Josep 53, 62, 76, 118-19, 229
architecture 26-7, 227-9, see also Gaudí buildings, Modernista architecture, notable buildings
area codes 238
art 230-1
art galleries, see museums
arts, see individual arts
arts centres, see cultural centres
ATMs 237

B

Barcelona Marathon 8
Barcelona Open 9

000 Map pages

Barceloneta & the Waterfront
  drinking & nightlife 178-80
  entertainment 198
  food 141-2
  shopping 160-2
Barceloneta Beach 22
Barri Gòtic 21, **250-1**
  drinking & nightlife 174-5
  entertainment 194-5
  food 132-5
  itineraries 86-7, **86-7**
  shopping 154-6
Basílica de Santa Maria del Mar 25, 116-17
basketball 206
beach bars 178
beaches 22, 122-3
beer 8, 171, 173
bicycle travel, see cycling
books 15, 233
budgeting, see costs
bus stations 239
bus travel 240
business hours 151, 170, 237

C

cable cars 241
  Telefèric de Montjuïc 61
  Teleférico del Puerto 23, 61
caganer 16, 17
Camp Nou 16, 72-3
  drinking & nightlife 188-9
  entertainment 203
  food 147
  shopping 167
Carnaval 7
Casa Amatller 53
Casa Batlló 50-3
Casa Lleó Morera 53
Casals, Pau 234
Castell de Montjuïc 61
Catalan cuisine 139
Catalonia 220-1
cathedrals, see churches

cava 14, 175
cell phones 18, 238
children, travel with 32-3
chiringuitos 178
churches
  Basílica de Santa Maria del Mar 25, 116-17
  Església de Betlem 46
  Església de la Puríssima Concepció i Assumpció de Nostra Senyora 77
  Església de les Saleses 40
  Església de Santa Maria del Pi 48
  La Catedral 64-7
  La Sagrada Família 21, 36-43, **42-3**
cinemas 197
Ciutat Vella **250-1**
classical music 193, 201, 202
climate 6-17, 19
clubs 170-82
Colònia Güell 120-1
cooking courses 211
costs 18
  accommodation 214
  drinking & nightlife 171
  food 128
courses 211
credit cards 237
cruises 209
cultural centres
  Agrupació Cultural Folklòrica de Barcelona 233
  Centre d'Art Santa Mònica 49
  Centre de Cultura Contemporània de Barcelona 97
  Poble Espanyol 57
culture 232-4
currency 18
cycling 208-9, 241

D

Dalí, Salvador 231
dance 233-4, see also flamenco

Barcelona Maps

El Raval & Sant Antoni

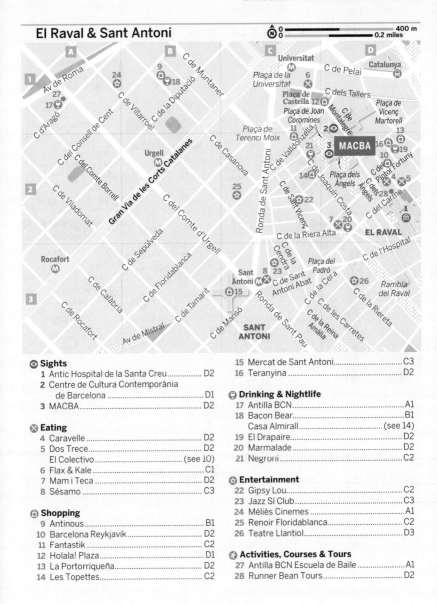

⊙ Sights
1 Antic Hospital de la Santa Creu D2
2 Centre de Cultura Contemporània
   de Barcelona D1
3 MACBA D2

⊗ Eating
4 Caravelle D2
5 Dos Trece D2
  El Colectivo .... (see 10)
6 Flax & Kale C1
7 Mam i Teca D2
8 Sésamo C3

⊕ Shopping
9 Antinous B1
10 Barcelona Reykjavik D2
11 Fantastik C2
12 Holala! Plaza D1
13 La Portorriqueña D2
14 Les Topettes C2

15 Mercat de Sant Antoni C3
16 Teranyina D2

⊙ Drinking & Nightlife
17 Antilla BCN A1
18 Bacon Bear B1
  Casa Almirall .... (see 14)
19 El Drapaire D2
20 Marmalade D2
21 Negroni C2

⊕ Entertainment
22 Gipsy Lou C2
23 Jazz Sí Club C3
24 Méliès Cinemes A1
25 Renoir Floridablanca C2
26 Teatre Llantiol D3

⊕ Activities, Courses & Tours
27 Antilla BCN Escuela de Baile A1
28 Runner Bean Tours D2

Barri Gòtic, Ciutat Vella & La Ribera

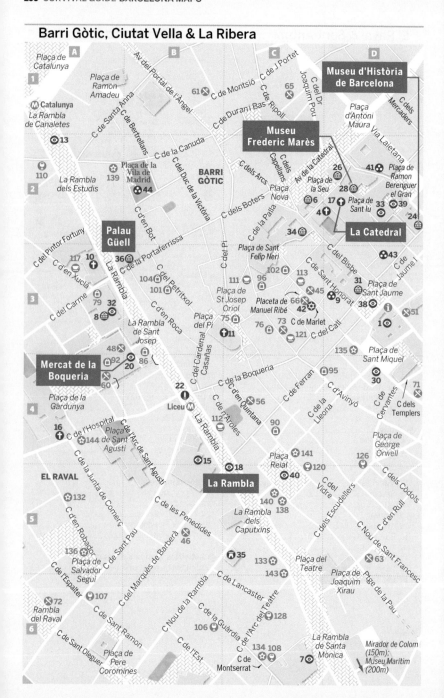

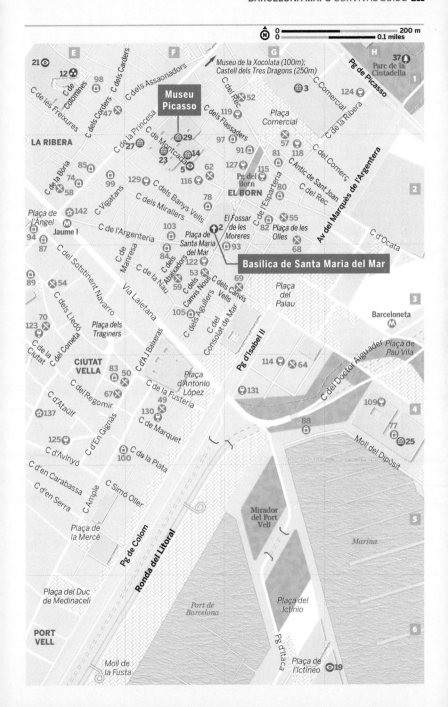

N

0   200 m
0   0.1 miles

21

12

98

C de les Freixures

C de les Cotonines

C dels Corders

C dels Carders

C dels Assaonadors

C del Rec

52

119

Museu Picasso

97

Museu de la Xocolata (100m);
Castell dels Tres Dragons (250m)

Plaça Comercial

3

124

Pg de Picadero

37

Parc de la Ciutadella

1

C de la Ribera

C Comercial

LA RIBERA

C de la Bòria

85

74

58

47

C dels Corders

C de la Princesa

27

C de Montcada

29

23

14

5

62

116

91

81

57

118

C del Comerç

C Antic de Sant Joan

C del Rec

80

115

C de l'Esparteria

Av del Marquès de l'Argentera

2

99

129

C dels Banys Vells

C dels Mirallers

127

Pg del Born

EL BORN

78

142

Plaça de l'Àngel

Jaume I

94

87

C de l'Argentera

C de Manresa

103

84

C dels Abaixadors

122

C de la Nau

53

59

Plaça de Santa Maria del Mar

El Fossar de les Moreres

2

93

82

55

Plaça de les Olles

68

Basílica de Santa Maria del Mar

C d'Ocata

C del Sotstinent Navarro

89

54

70

123

Via Laietana

C dels Lledó

C de la Ciutat

C del Cometa

105

C dels Agullers

C dels Canvis Nous

C dels Canvis Vells

69

C del Consolat de Mar

Plaça del Palau

3

Barceloneta

Plaça dels Traginers

CIUTAT VELLA

83

50

67

49

137

C del Regomir

C d'Ataülf

130

C de Marquet

C d'En Gignàs

C de la Fusteria

Plaça d'Antonio López

C d'A J Baixeras

Pg d'Isabell II

114

64

131

C del Doctor Aiguader

Plaça de Pau Vila

109

88

77

25

4

Moll del Dipòsit

125

100

C d'Avinyó

C de la Plata

C d'en Carabassa

C d'en Serra

C Ample

C Simó Oller

Plaça de la Mercè

Pg de Colom

Ronda del Litoral

Plaça del Duc de Medinaceli

PORT VELL

Moll de la Fusta

Port de Barcelona

Mirador del Port Vell

Marina

5

Plaça del Ictínio

Pg d'Itaca

Plaça de l'Ictíneo

19

6

Barri Gòtic, Ciutat Vella & La Ribera

L'Eixample & Gràcia

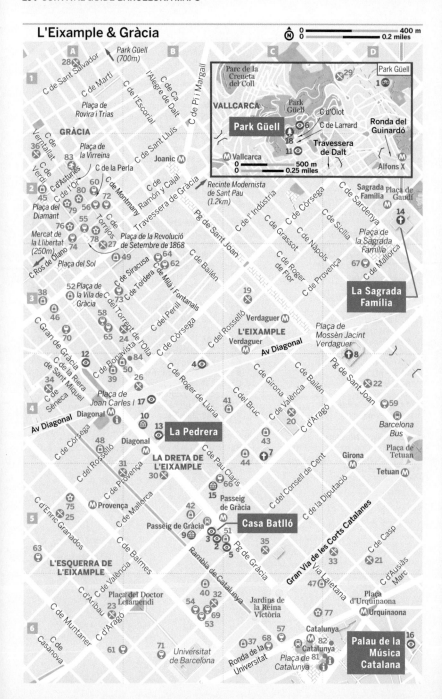

L'Eixample & Gràcia

Montjuïc

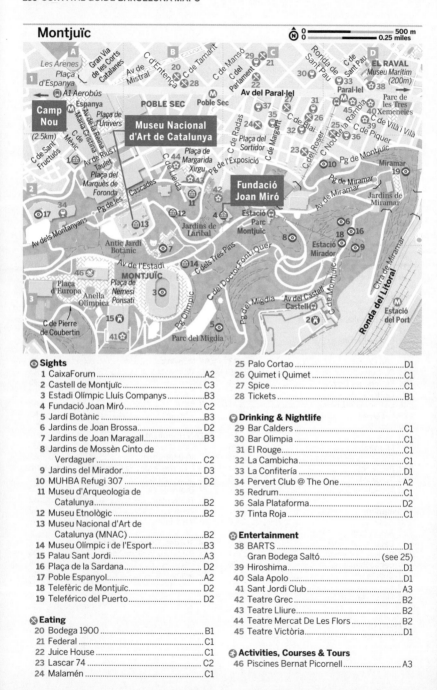

◉ Sights
1 CaixaForum A2
2 Castell de Montjuïc C3
3 Estadi Olímpic Lluís Companys B3
4 Fundació Joan Miró C2
5 Jardí Botànic B3
6 Jardins de Joan Brossa.................. D2
7 Jardins de Joan Maragall B3
8 Jardins de Mossèn Cinto de
   Verdaguer C2
9 Jardins del Mirador D3
10 MUHBA Refugi 307 .... D2
11 Museu d'Arqueologia de
   Catalunya B2
12 Museu Etnològic B2
13 Museu Nacional d'Art de
   Catalunya (MNAC) B2
14 Museu Olímpic i de l'Esport...........A3
15 Palau Sant Jordi A3
16 Plaça de la Sardana D2
17 Poble Espanyol A2
18 Telefèric de Montjuïc...................... D2
19 Teleférico del Puerto D2

◉ Eating
20 Bodega 1900 .... B1
21 Federal C1
22 Juice House C1
23 Lascar 74 .... C2
24 Malamén C1

25 Palo Cortao D1
26 Quimet i Quimet C1
27 Spice C1
28 Tickets B1

◉ Drinking & Nightlife
29 Bar Calders C1
30 Bar Olimpia C1
31 El Rouge C1
32 La Cambicha C1
33 La Confitería D1
34 Pervert Club @ The One A2
35 Redrum C1
36 Sala Plataforma D2
37 Tinta Roja C1

◉ Entertainment
38 BARTS D1
   Gran Bodega Saltó......................... (see 25)
39 Hiroshima D1
40 Sala Apolo D1
41 Sant Jordi Club A3
42 Teatre Grec B2
43 Teatre Lliure B2
44 Teatre Mercat De Les Flors B2
45 Teatre Victòria D1

◉ Activities, Courses & Tours
46 Piscines Bernat Picornell A3

Symbols & Map Key

Look for these symbols to quickly identify listings:

◉ Sights
✪ Activities
✪ Courses
✪ Tours
✪ Festivals & Events

✪ Eating
✪ Drinking
✪ Entertainment
✪ Shopping
ℹ Information & Transport

These symbols and abbreviations give vital information for each listing:

🍃 Sustainable or green recommendation
FREE No payment required

☎ Telephone number
☉ Opening hours
P Parking
☺ Nonsmoking
❄ Air-conditioning
@ Internet access
📶 Wi-fi access
🏊 Swimming pool

🚌 Bus
⛴ Ferry
🚊 Tram
🚆 Train
📋 English-language menu
🌿 Vegetarian selection
👫 Family-friendly

Find your best experiences with these Great For... icons.

🖼 Art & Culture
🏖 Beaches
👛 Budget
☕ Cafe/Coffee
🚲 Cycling
↱ Detour
🍷 Drinking
🎭 Entertainment
🎆 Events
👨‍👩‍👧 Family Travel
🍽 Food & Drink

📔 History
💬 Local Life
🐦 Nature & Wildlife
📷 Photo Op
🔭 Scenery

🛍 Shopping

✈ Short Trip
🏀 Sport
🚶 Walking
❄ Winter Travel

Sights

🏖 Beach
🐦 Bird Sanctuary
🏯 Buddhist
🏰 Castle/Palace
✝ Christian
☯ Confucian
🕉 Hindu
☪ Islamic
卍 Jain
✡ Jewish
🗿 Monument
🏛 Museum/Gallery/Historic Building
🏚 Ruin
⛩ Shinto
☬ Sikh
☯ Taoist
🍇 Winery/Vineyard
🦁 Zoo/Wildlife Sanctuary
◉ Other Sight

Points of Interest

🏄 Bodysurfing
⛺ Camping
☕ Cafe
🛶 Canoeing/Kayaking
• Course/Tour
🤿 Diving
🍸 Drinking & Nightlife
🍴 Eating
🎭 Entertainment
♨ Sento Hot Baths/Onsen
🛍 Shopping
⛷ Skiing
🛏 Sleeping
🤿 Snorkelling
🏄 Surfing
🏊 Swimming/Pool
🚶 Walking
🏄 Windsurfing
✪ Other Activity

Information

💲 Bank
🏛 Embassy/Consulate
➕ Hospital/Medical
@ Internet
👮 Police
✉ Post Office
☎ Telephone
🚻 Toilet
ℹ Tourist Information
• Other Information

Geographic

🏖 Beach
⊢ Gate
🏠 Hut/Shelter
🗼 Lighthouse
👁 Lookout
▲ Mountain/Volcano
🌴 Oasis
🌳 Park
)(Pass
🧺 Picnic Area
💧 Waterfall

Transport

✈ Airport
Ⓑ BART station
✖ Border crossing
Ⓣ Boston T station
🚌 Bus
🚠 Cable car/Funicular
🚲 Cycling
⛴ Ferry
Ⓜ Metro/MRT station
🚝 Monorail
P Parking
⛽ Petrol station
Ⓢ Subway/S-Bahn/Skytrain station
🚕 Taxi
🚉 Train station/Railway
🚋 Tram
Ⓣ Tube Station
Ⓤ Underground/U-Bahn station
• Other Transport

Our Story

A beat-up old car, a few dollars in the pocket and a sense of adventure. In 1972 that's all Tony and Maureen Wheeler needed for the trip of a lifetime – across Europe and Asia overland to Australia. It took several months, and at the end – broke but inspired – they sat at their kitchen table writing and stapling together their first travel guide, *Across Asia on the Cheap*. Within a week they'd sold 1500 copies. Lonely Planet was born.

Today, Lonely Planet has offices in Franklin, London, Melbourne, Oakland, Dublin, Beijing and Delhi, with more than 600 staff and writers. We share Tony's belief that 'a great guidebook should do three things: inform, educate and amuse'.

Our Writers

Andy Symington

Andy has worked on over a hundred books and other updates for Lonely Planet and other publishers, and has written for a variety of newspapers, magazines and websites. He part-owns and operates a rock bar, and is currently working on several fiction and non-fiction writing projects. Andy, from Australia, moved to northern Spain many years ago. When he's not off with a backpack in some far-flung corner of the world, he can probably be found watching the tragically poor local football side or tasting local wines after a long walk in the nearby mountains.

Josephine Quintero

Josephine launched her journalism degree at a wine magazine in the Napa Valley in the mid '70s. This was followed, ironically, with a move to 'dry' Kuwait where she worked until 1 August 1990 – the day Iraq invaded. After spending six weeks as a hostage and surviving a hairy convoy escape route, Josephine moved to the relaxed shores of Andalucía in southern Spain where she initially earned a crust as a ghostwriter. She has also written for in-flight magazines, and has had some minor publishing success with her short stories.

STAY IN TOUCH LONELYPLANET.COM/CONTACT

AUSTRALIA The Malt Store, Level 3, 551 Swanston St, Carlton, Victoria 3053 ☎ 03 8379 8000, fax 03 8379 8111

IRELAND Unit E, Digital Court. The Digital Hub, Rainsford St, Dublin 8, Ireland

USA 124 Linden Street, Oakland, CA 94607 ☎ 510 250 6400, toll free 800 275 8555, fax 510 893 8572

UK 240 Blackfriars Road, London SE1 8NW ☎ 020 3771 5100, fax 020 3771 5101

 twitter.com/ lonelyplanet

 facebook.com/ lonelyplanet

 instagram.com/ lonelyplanet

 youtube.com/ lonelyplanet

 lonelyplanet.com/ newsletter